THE INDIAN NATIONAL CONGRESS
AND THE *RAJ*, 1929–1942

CAMBRIDGE COMMONWEALTH SERIES

Published in association with the Managers of the Cambridge
University Smuts Memorial Fund for the Advancement of
Commonwealth Studies

General Editor: E. T. STOKES, Smuts Professor of the History
of the British Commonwealth, University of Cambridge

Titles published by the Cambridge University Press

John S. Galbraith: *Mackinnon and East Africa, 1878–1895*
G. Andrew Maguire: *Toward 'Uhuru' in Tanzania*
Ged Martin: *The Durham Report and British Policy*
Ronald Robinson (editor): *Developing the Third World*

Titles published by Macmillan

Roger Anstey: *The Atlantic Slave Trade and British Abolition,
  1760–1810*
Partha Sarathi Gupta: *Imperialism and the British Labour
  Movement, 1914–1964*
Ronald Hyam and Ged Martin: *Reappraisals in British
  Imperial History*
B. R. Tomlinson: *The Indian National Congress
  and the Raj, 1929–1942*
John Manning Ward: *Colonial Self-Government: The British Experience,
  1759–1856*

The Indian National Congress and the *Raj*, 1929–1942

The Penultimate Phase

B. R. TOMLINSON

M

First published 1976 by
THE MACMILLAN PRESS LTD
London and Basingstoke
Associated companies in New York
Dublin Melbourne Johannesburg and Madras

SBN 333 19369 5

Printed in Great Britain by
EYRE & SPOTTISWOODE LTD
GROSVENOR PRESS
Portsmouth

Contents

Acknowledgements

This book is based in part on my doctoral thesis *Nationalism and Indian Politics: the Indian National Congress 1934–1942* (Cambridge, 1974). In the course of my postgraduate and post-doctoral research work I have incurred many obligations.

I am grateful to the Department of Education and Science for a Hayter Research Studentship that enabled me to work in India and Britain; to the Managers of the Smuts Memorial Fund, Cambridge, who have made a contribution towards the cost of this publication and to the Master and Fellows of Trinity College, Cambridge, who granted me Studentships in 1969 and 1973, assisted with the cost of this publication and made generous extra contributions towards the expenses incurred during my researches.

I wish to record the kind assistance of the librarians and staffs of the India Office Library, the British Museum, the Public Record Office, the National Archives of India, the Nehru Memorial Museum and Library, the State Central Record Office, Patna, the Sinha Memorial Library, Patna, the A. N. Sinha Institute for the Social Sciences, Patna, and the Cambridge University Library. I am also indebted to the Editors of the *Indian Nation* and *Searchlight* newspapers for allowing me to use their archives; and to the Foreign and Commonwealth Office for allowing me to base the map on p. 161 on one which appeared in the 1940 *India Office List*.

I should like to thank my many friends and teachers who have contributed so much to this book, in particular Chris Baker, Chris Bayly, John Gallagher, Gil MacDonald, Rajat Ray, Peter Reeves, Francis Robinson and David Washbrook. My greatest debts are to Anil Seal, who has provided constant help and encouragement at every stage of my research; Eric Stokes, who has greatly assisted the transformation of a thesis into a book; and Caroline, my wife, who has been helpmate, research assistant, copy-editor and breadwinner for the last six years.

Trinity College, Cambridge   B. R. TOMLINSON
July 1975

Abbreviations

A.I.C.C.	All India Congress Committee
AICC	All India Congress Committee Office Papers
A.I.V.I.A.	All India Village Industries Association
CAB	Cabinet Office Papers
C.C.C.	City Congress Committee
C.L.A.	Central Legislative Assembly
C.P.	Central Provinces and Berar
C.P.B.	Congress Parliamentary Board
C.S.P.	Congress Socialist Party
D.C.C.	District Congress Committee
G.o.I.	Government of India
I.N.C.	Indian National Congress
I.O.L.	India Office Library
M.L.A.	Member Legislative Assembly
N.A.I.	National Archives of India
N.M.M.	Nehru Memorial Museum and Library
P.C.C.	Provincial Congress Committee
P.L.A.	Provincial Legislative Assembly
P.L.C.	Provincial Legislative Council
P&J	Public and Judicial Department
PREM	Premier's Office Papers
Pt.	Pandit (see Glossary)
S.C.R.O.	State Central Record Office
T.C.C.	Town or Taluka Congress Committee
U.P.	United Provinces

Introduction

This book is a study of the collapse of British power in India and of the rise of the Indian National Congress, which has dominated the government and politics of independent India since 1947. The winding up of the British empire is one of the most significant events of modern history. India was once the jewel in Britain's imperial crown and the ending of the *Raj* removed the coping-stone of the largest empire that the world has known. The primary aim of this book is to provide a documented and analytical account both of imperial policy and of nationalist politics during the penultimate phase of British rule in India. This account will also investigate the reasons that dictated the timing and manner of the collapse of British control and of the rise of the forces that successfully challenged and replaced it. In this process, several different strands of policy-making and political action were at work. The three major participants were imperial planners in London, the Government of India in New Delhi and the central leaders of the Indian National Congress. All three did have certain concepts and problems in common, and at times the paths of their activities crossed, but each was pursuing separate aims along separate roads and each was affected by different constraints. Taken together, their tripartite meanderings comprise a major part of the political history of British India.

The work concentrates on the years 1929 to 1942, a short but vital period in the history of modern India. In this period the British devised a new strategy for rule in India. While handing over some power in the provinces, they aimed to retain some of the vital attributes of sovereignty, keeping control over crucial departments of central government (defence and foreign affairs) and substituting influence for control over others (setting up a semi-independent Reserve Bank to manage the currency and national debt). At the same time they hoped to enlist collaborators at the all-India level by giving them responsibility over some areas of central government. These plans were embodied in the 1935 Government of India Act. The next seven years revealed their shortcomings. By March 1942 London had been forced to recognise that the constitutional structure of the *Raj* would have to be reshaped yet again, and that the extent of British formal rule in India would have to be limited still further.

From first to last, the activities of the all-India political associations were closely connected with the constitutional arrangements of the *Raj*. Whether they wanted to press for further concessions, or to work reforms once they had been conceded, Indian politicians, particularly on the national stage, could not ignore the framework of rule which the British imposed. Thus a period which saw important changes in the structure of British rule is bound to be a vital one in the history of Indian political development. The Indian National Congress was the most important and powerful political association in the sub-continent and the history of its activities falls into this pattern of stimulus and response. But the Congress was also capable of imposing upon itself periods of exile from constitutional politics, periods in which it resorted to full-scale agitation against the *Raj*. Between 1930 and 1934 the Congress had been following a programme of civil disobedience and in 1942 it again took up the non-violent cudgels of revolt in an attempt to force the British to quit India. But, in perspective, it is constitutional politics rather than agitation which characterises the history of the Congress, and by 1934 Congressmen were preparing themselves to work within the scheme of the new reforms. In 1936–7 the Congress contested the elections for provincial government and between 1937 and 1939 it supplied the ministries in six of the eleven provinces of British India. These events led to a considerable rise in the membership and the power of the Congress in the provinces and, by 1939, in the control of the central leaders over their subordinates. The greatest fear of the British administrators who were trying to make the 1935 Act work was that the internal structure of the Congress, and its support in the country at large, would prove strong enough to enable the all-India Congress leaders to secure a stranglehold on the working of responsible government in the provinces and at the centre. This is what happened in 1939. Although the contemporary view of the dictatorial powers of the Congress Working Committee was false, by 1939 the central Congress leaders had managed to impose their dominance on their followers in the localities and provinces, as was symbolised by their success in securing the resignation of all the Congress ministries on the outbreak of war. For the next year and a half, the Congress leaders used both constitutional and agitational techniques to further their struggle against the British. The years from 1934 to 1942 established the Congress as the most important of the opponents of British rule and as the best-equipped of the heirs apparent to the *Raj*. Between 1929 and 1934 the British had been able to construct a new Government of India Act while virtually ignoring the voice of the Congress; by 1942 it was clear that Congress consent would be one of the essential preconditions of any further scheme of constitutional advance.

This account deals with high policy, with the metropolitan institutions and interests that decided and controlled the main lines of constitutional development in India, and with the Government of India which had the task of putting flesh on the bare bones of London's schemes and of dealing with the residual problems of keeping the Indian empire solvent and secure. Similarly, this is a study of high politics, dealing with the all-India stage and with the activities of the three national Congress institutions, the All India Working Committee, the All India Congress Committee and the annual General Session of delegates. However, although at first sight this national institutional life appears to have been complete and self-contained, it can only properly be understood by looking at events in the localities, districts and provinces. Many of the issues which dominated the all-India stage during this period – the question of contesting elections and accepting office, the role of agitation, the problem of the relationship of the Congress to other political associations – were in fact thrown up from the subordinate levels of the organisation. Again, the strength and efficacy of the hierarchy of control within the Congress can only be judged by looking in detail both at those who were trying to lead and at those who were supposed to follow. The high politics of the Congress organisation between 1929 and 1942 are most important to understanding the movement's development in this period, but only a detailed investigation of the relationship between the all-India leaders and their subordinates and of the context of internal constraints and imperatives that determined the actions and plans of the men participating in those politics can explain them fully.

A study of all-India politics such as this might seem to be going against the current trends of historiography. Most recent studies of Indian politics have concentrated on particular provinces or on smaller areas. By focusing on localities these studies have brought an important new dimension into the subject. The traditional framework of reference, of a centralised and all-powerful British administration, formulating and executing consistent and universal policy in India and evoking a similarly homogeneous and united Indian response, has been shown to be inadequate. The study of the localities and provinces has revealed the particularism of the individual administrative units and has stressed the diversity and parochial nature of the political development within them. If one reads a number of these studies, one is left with the impression that the sub-continent was so vast, and was made up of so many individual and exceptional parts, that there is no hope of writing a single useful line about India as a whole. Does this, then, mean that any attempt to deal with the larger themes of imperial policy and national politics is doomed to failure?

As those who are engaged on research on the localities and provinces are the first to admit, the all-India level of politics did exist and was important. Complete histories of the eleven provinces or the two-hundred-and-fifty-odd districts of British India would not, in sum, constitute a complete history of modern India. There was a central government in India, with increasingly distinct functions and roles. There were all-India political organisations, with matching structures of centralised authority, which became increasingly powerful. There were matters which were all-India in scope, and not just an amalgam of provincial interests. There were politicians – Gandhi, Jawaharlal Nehru, and Jinnah for example – who operated solely at the all-India level. There was, then, an all-India level of policy and politics; the real problem is how to study it. Although there was a clearly defined all-India level of activity, this was not a self-contained whole fully insulated from events in the provinces and localities. What is needed is a framework of analysis in which the interrelationship between the various levels of the body politic can be isolated and understood. Studies of the minutiae of politics in the provinces and localities have shown how the hierarchy of executive and local self-government institutions set up by the British acted as linkages between the various levels of politics. In the nineteenth century these represented the only interlocking institutional structure within the Indian polity, but by the 1920s and 1930s another, parallel, system had grown up, composed of the local, district, provincial and all-India Congress Committees. These twin networks represented not only the most important channels through which local and particular pressures and interests were forced upwards to higher levels, but were also the main agencies through which the fiats of the central authorities were imposed on, or perverted by, their subordinates in the provinces and localities.

This book concentrates on the all-India level because it is impossible to understand the collapse of the *Raj* or the rise of the Congress from any other standpoint. But it should by now be clear to the reader that going back to the themes of national politics and imperial policy at the all-India level does not mean compounding the old errors about the nature of imperialism and nationalism in India. The analysis developed here is based on a study of the men who sat at the top of the twin institutional structures, of government and of the Congress, that provided the most important sets of vertical linkages within the Indian polity. But it avoids the assumption that, because the British policymakers in London and New Delhi and the national Congress leaders were at the pinnacles of their respective pyramids, their power was correspondingly absolute. The ability of the British Government and of the Government of India to control events was limited, while the Congress was not, as Gandhi wished it to be, a well-disciplined army unquestioningly obeying the orders of a central command. The influence of both imperial policy-makers and national Congress leaders depended on a delicate balance of many different factors; only by keeping this in mind can one hope to understand the true nature of events at the national level.

It will already be apparent that this work does not pretend to be a comprehensive history of British policy in India or of Indian political development between 1929 and 1942. Nor does it even attempt a complete account of the internal history of the Indian National Congress. Although the activities of Congressmen in various provinces and localities, as well as at the all-India level, are touched on, only six of the twenty Congress provinces – Bihar, United Provinces, Utkal (Orissa), Mahakoshal (the Hindi-speaking areas of the Central Provinces), Nagpur (the Marathi-speaking areas of the Central provinces) and Vidarbha (Berar) – are dealt with in any detail. These provinces were important ones, and they illustrate many general points about the subordinate levels of the movement as a whole. But they were all areas in which the Congress was successful in this period, areas in which, along with Madras and Bombay, Congress ministries were formed in 1937. This makes them especially useful for a study which concentrates on the increasing strengths of the Congress position, but work on the areas in which the Congress failed, the Punjab or Bengal for example, might reveal rather different aspects of provincial politics. At the all-India level, this study concentrates more on matters which relate to the transfer of power than to those which explain Partition. The rise of the Muslim League, the growth of Muslim separatism and the negotiations between the British, the Congress and the Muslim leaders have not been considered in great detail. This omission might seem to be a vital one, and in defence of it one can only say that, certainly before 1939 and to a large extent before 1942, the documents reveal that the Congress leaders were not greatly concerned with these matters. It is that omission that is really important. The account of British policy is not complete either. Many of the problems that exercised the minds of the British administrators – of minorities, of the Princes, of economic development and social justice – have only briefly been sketched in. The more metaphysical and intangible aspects of the British position in India, notions of empire in British public opinion at home and abroad, and the 'will to rule' are also largely beyond our scope here.

This Introduction has attempted to set out the main lines of the historiographical and conceptual framework within which the book should be read. Chapter 1 gives an overall perspective of the objectives of and constraints on British rule in India from the late nineteenth century to 1935 by examining the changing role that India was assigned within the imperial system, describes the British attempt to use the constitutional reforms of the 1935 Government of India Act to put their position in India on a more secure footing and suggests why this attempt failed. In Chapter 2 we turn away from the British policy-makers to their opponents in the Indian National Congress. The chapter summarises briefly the problems of leadership faced by the Congress centre in the 1920s and early 1930s and describes the slow

and tortuous search for a policy for the Congress from 1933 to 1937.
Chapter 3 investigates developments within the local and provincial
Congress organisations from the end of civil disobedience to 1939. It
shows how internal Congress politics worked in practice and how the
strengths and weaknesses of the system can be used to explain the
events of the provincial legislature elections of 1936–7 and of the Congress ministries of 1937–9. Chapter 4 returns to the all-India stage for
the years 1937–9 and describes the new relationship which evolved
between the established central leadership, their opponents at the
centre and their subordinates in the provinces and localities as a result
of the strains brought about by the Congress ministries. Chapter 5
examines the British attitude to India after 1939 and considers the
policy of the British and the Congress leaders in the first two years of
war in the light of the internal tensions within the position of both. The
chapter ends with an account of the purposes of the Cripps Mission –
the first serious attempt by the British to find a new political solution to
the Indian problem. Finally, a brief epilogue attempts to place the
events of 1929–42 in a wider historical context.

English was still the language of politics at the top level of the Congress in this period. There are, therefore, few problems of translation or
transliteration. Place and personal names have been spelt in the form in
which they most commonly occur in the sources; vernacular terms have
been kept to a minimum and are explained in a glossary at the end of
the text. The only serious editorial problem has resulted from the poor
standard of the typists employed by Congress leaders. Almost every
typed letter from one Congress leader to another contains several errors
of spelling, typing or punctuation. To help the flow of the text these
minor errors have been corrected in passages quoted directly, except
where there is an ambiguity of sense.

1 British Policy and the Indian Problem 1919–35

The political and constitutional history of British rule in India is a story of the changing, modifying and rethinking of systems of control. To rule India successfully the British had to devise, and constantly to adjust, a structure of bureaucratic and political institutions which would allow them to control the vital areas of government while ensuring the co-operation or acquiescence of the bulk of their subjects. From the middle of the nineteenth century onwards the British *Raj* in India was the exception to every rule about the nature of the British empire. In the high Victorian period of informal expansion India had been held under formal, bureaucratic rule: in the later nineteenth century, when Britain's formal empire was expanding in Africa and elsewhere, the control of India was being secured by increasingly informal techniques. Between 1919 and 1935 British policy makers were faced by the problem of how to create an institutional structure of government which would enable the central government to rule India effectively in a changing political climate. As this chapter will show, they failed to find a solution.

The Indian *Raj* was one of Britain's major assets. From the late eighteenth century onwards it had lain at the heart of the imperial system of world power and profit. British rule in India was not maintained for the benefit of India, nor for the sake of direct British interests in India; the *Raj* existed to provide the foundations on which much of the structure of formal and informal empire rested. In their heyday, the half-century before 1914, British interests in India were considerable. India was an important market for British manufactures and exports to India made good about two-fifths of Britain's balance of payments deficit with Europe and North America.[1] India was a fertile field for expatriate commercial activity and for British investment; the Indian Army, one quarter of it British troops, provided half the British world force at no expense to Britain. The Government of India had an imperial commitment to maintain these interests; but that did not mean that the British Government slavishly counted every item of British manufacture sold in India, or that the Cabinet or the India Office listened attentively to the grievances of every Calcutta merchant. It is by no means clear that the British consciously realised India's role in the

international pattern of settlements. Even within the formal empire
London did not control every aspect of colonial economies. India's
imperial commitment meant three things in practice: that the Government of India should not impose any artificial barriers, especially any
tariffs, to impede the flow of British exports to India; that the Indian
administration should ensure the repayment of interest on guaranteed
railway stock and debt bonds and should pay its annual Home Charges
(for the upkeep of the India Office, pensions of retired civilian and
military personnel etc.); that the Indian Army should be kept available
for the imperial cause.

Each prong of this tripartite commitment cost the Government of
India money. The requirements of British exporters obstructed
attempts to impose a revenue tariff and to create a protected market to
encourage the growth of Indian industry. The Home Charges, between
£25 and £30 million a year, were always a strain on governmental
resources and could be crippling when the rupee exchange was weak.
The army, with its high percentage of British troops whose training
costs, pay and pensions had to be provided for, was another expense,
especially when it was overseas playing an imperial role. For London
the twin imperatives of India policy were that the Indian empire should
pay for itself and that Indian resources should be available in the
imperial cause. But the Government of India's revenues were limited
and the secret of successful government in India was thought to be low
taxation; thus imperial demands for Indian resources had to be balanced against internal pressures. To keep itself solvent and secure the
Government of India had to weigh imperial commitments against the
demands of its subjects – maintaining this balance lay at the heart of
the problems of the governance of the *Raj*.

The first solution devised to meet this problem was the decentralisation of government and the widening of its political base. When the
Government of India Act of 1858 brought the East India Company's
control over India to an end the administrative structure had been
rigidly centralised and bureaucratic. Yet although the centralised
empire of 1858 was a magnificent structure, it was also a hollow one,
being unable to raise enough revenue to support itself and containing
no administrative machinery by which, short of rebellion, its subjects
could attract its attention. To meet the financial crises after the Mutiny
new forms of taxation were required, but the central government did
not know enough about its subjects to be able to devise and administer
effective and safe new taxes. Devolution was the only answer.

This devolution took two forms. Firstly, provincial and local
administrations (in the form of the provincial governments and district
and municipal councils) were encouraged to find new revenue
resources and were given some autonomy of administration. Secondly,
representative Indians, nominated at first and then elected, were

associated with these local and provincial administrations. During the 1870s, 1880s and 1890s the provincial governments were allowed to retain a larger and larger share of the revenues they collected, only the money from 'imperial' sources – customs, salt, land revenue and posts and telegraphs – being passed on to the Government of India. At the same time, the power of Indian representatives in local government was increased. It was thought that Indian members of municipalities and district boards would be more efficient in raising, and more careful in spending, local taxes if they were responsible to an electorate. Thus in the United Provinces each successive financial crisis after 1860 resulted in municipal government being made more representative, while Baring and Colvin, the Finance Members of the Government of India in the early 1880s, were the main supporters of Lord Ripon's attempts to make the structure of local government democratic.[2]

Once begun, the devolutionary process carried on under its own steam. Granting administrative responsibility encouraged greater, not less, expenditure; Indians could not be given doles of political power only as it suited the fiscal needs of the *Raj*. The political assumptions which had underlain the granting of administrative responsibility to Indians in the late nineteenth and early twentieth centuries had been that, by so doing, the British would draw into active politics the natural leaders of Indian society – landowners and yeoman farmers, and the spokesmen of important caste, communal and class interests – and thus widen the basis of their support while exposing the pretensions of the western educated professional men who, as nationalists, claimed to spajfor a subject India. But these assumptions revealed a fundamental ignorance of the process of political development and mobilisation in India. British acts of constitutional reform only created unfulfilled expectations in larger and larger sections of Indian society and the early leaders of the nationalist movement were able, spasmodically and haltingly it is true, to draw on wider and wider ripples of frustration and discontent to launch appeals and agitations for further advance. As Evelyn Baring had pointed out in 1883, 'when once the ball of political reform is set rolling, it is apt to gather speed as it goes on'.[3]

By 1919 the Government of India had already been drawn into a complex pattern of stimulus and response with its subjects. The demands made by Britain during the First World War placed enormous new strains on government and people alike. In 1914 Indian revenues had supported 80,000 British troops and 230,000 Indian ones (including non-combatants). During the war India recruited over 800,000 combatants and over 400,000 non-combatant military personnel. These new troops had to be paid for, and although the British Government did reimburse India for a good deal of her expenditure in the imperial cause the money was paid in London and could not easily be remitted to India. The Government of India raised its revenue demand by 16 per cent in 1916–17, by a further 14 per cent in 1917–18 and by an additional 10 per cent .in 1918–19. The war also had a dramatic effect on the pattern and level of Indian trade and, although international demand for Indian exports of raw produce soared, government controls, shortages of finance and the disruption of railways and internal communications generally obstructed the export boom. These strains on the economy affected everyday life. The problems of transport and remittance led to a price inflation in staple imports such as piece-goods, sugar, salt and kerosene, and disrupted the established patterns of internal production and distribution. In 1917 only exceptional harvests kept the price of agricultural produce down, but in 1918 extensive military activity and large new recruitment increased the army's demand for food and cloth at the same time as a failure in the monsoon occurred. Famine and epidemic disease broke out for the first time in ten years and only the rundown of the military establishment following the armistice kept the situation under control.

The major effect of the war on Indian politics was the acceleration of various schemes of constitutional reform, culminating in the Government of India Act of 1919. The new cry from India for a statement of long-term British aims was met by the declaration of 1917 that 'the progressive realisation of responsible government in India'[4] was the goal of British policy. But the main plank of the reforms scheme devised by the Secretary of State, Edwin Montagu, and the Viceroy, Lord Chelmsford, in 1918 and embodied in the 1919 Act was a simple extension of the principle of decentralisation. The new reforms established eight fully autonomous provincial governments in which Indian ministers responsible to elected legislatures were to have control over half the functions of government in dyarchic administrations. The provinces were now to be financially autonomous and all revenue collected in each province, including the land revenue, was to be spent there. In 1924 the Muddiman Committee, appointed by the Government of India to review the working of the new constitution, suggested the abolition of dyarchy as the next step of political development.[5]

The avowed purpose of the 1919 Government of India Act was to create machinery by which the principles of the 1917 declaration could be implemented. Yet for all its liberal veneer the Act simply embodied a medium-term political calculation. It attempted to solve, for a decade (the Act contained a clause for its own revision within ten years), the problem of how an influential section of Indian opinion was to be brought forward to support the *Raj*. While writing their *Report on Indian Constitutional Reforms* of 1918, Montagu and Chelmsford had conceived of political responsibility 'such as comes from the prospect of having to assume office in turn'[6] as the key device to moderate Indian critics of government and to speed up the process of constructive political education in India. The provinces were the only suitable arenas; as Montagu later admitted, 'the Government of India . . . was concerned with the supreme interests of the country and was not the right sphere in which to initiate constitutional changes.'[7] However, the principle of devolution had always been a double-edged weapon for central government. Now, by establishing a vociferous but subordinate Central Legislative Assembly and by throwing the Government of India back onto the purely central revenue resources of tariffs, income tax, salt duty and opium and other excise, the 1919 Act materially increased the problems of the central administrators and seriously impaired their ability to meet imperial commitments.

Before the provinces received financial autonomy in 1919 a complicated system of settlements and grants had governed the division of revenue resources between central and provincial administrations. Broadly speaking, the provinces had enjoyed all revenue collected in the localities, with the exception of the staple land revenue, while the Government of India appropriated central taxation. The land revenue was collected by the provincial governments and then sent up to the Government of India, which repaid some of it in grants reviewed quinquennially. In times of crisis, the Government of India was also able to take up provincial revenue surpluses to meet imperial commitments. When the 1919 Act ended this system the Government of India lost Rs 10 lakhs (one million rupees: about £100,000) a year. To compensate for this, a system of provincial grants to the centre was instituted in 1920. However these were never popular with the provinces and were allowed to lapse in 1927–8 after only six years. In any case the 1920 settlement only restored what the Government of India had lost in 1919, while the major problem facing the central government in the early 1920s was the need to raise vast amounts of new revenue.

From 1918–19 to 1922–3 the central budget was in deficit. Monsoon failures, trade and agrarian depression, wild fluctuations in the rupee exchange rate and hostilities on the North-West Frontier and with Afghanistan resulted in an excess of expenditure over revenue of almost Rs 100 crores (one thousand million rupees) in five years. Increasing revenue and reducing expenditure was now the only answer; but both halves of this formula affected India's imperial commitment, for more revenue meant a tariff on British imports and less expenditure meant cuts in the army budget.

In the winter of 1916–17 the Government of India had won the right to tax Lancashire cotton without a countervailing excise on Indian cloth by insisting on a revenue tariff to offset the cost of taking over £100 millions of the British Government's war debt.[8] In 1916 the general tariff on imports, including cotton goods, had been raised to 7½ per cent and in 1921 it was raised still further to 11 per cent. These proposals proved popular in India, though less so in Lancashire.

British cotton manufacturers protested strongly to the Secretary of State, only to be told that the financial and political imperatives of British rule in India now determined that they must be sacrificed for the sake of wider interests. In refusing Lancashire, the Secretary of State could now base his case on the 'Fiscal Autonomy Convention'. This device, which developed out of the need to allow India protective tariffs during the war, had been set out in the 1919 Act as a convention that, in tariff policy, 'the Secretary of State should, as far as possible, avoid interference when the Government of India and its legislature are in agreement.'[9] Although strictly this convention applied only to protective tariffs, not to revenue ones, the Government of India and successive Secretaries of State used it throughout the 1920s as a bargaining counter against Indian and British critics of their tariff policy. However, for the British Government, this attitude of non-interference was based on a simple political calculation, that the deleterious political consequences of Indian tariff policy in Britain would be outweighed by the consequences in India of interference from London. As the events of 1930–1 were to show, in times of crisis the British Government were prepared to reconsider this attitude.

More important than the cotton trade to British Governments of the early 1920s was maintaining the Indian Army's traditional role as a cut-price imperial garrison and expeditionary force. In the closing months of the war the British had found themselves heirs to the old Turkish *vilayats* and Russian spheres of influence in the Near and Middle East. By 1920, however, British policy-makers had found the cost of maintaining a formal presence in these areas unacceptable; particularly burdensome was the garrisoning of Iraq which, it was estimated, would cost £30 millions a year.[10] In December 1920 the British Government decided to withdraw the British garrison and began to cast around for alternatives. It soon became clear that the only way to ensure a British presence in Iraq was to employ the Indian Army. The Viceroy was told to provide a large force for overseas service, at a cost which would push the Indian Army budget up to £60 millions a year (40 per cent of net Indian revenues).[11] Coupled to this specific demand was a more general plan. In 1919 the British Government had appointed an *Army in India Committee* (Esher Committee) to review India's place in the post-war system of imperial defence. This Committee, which reported early in 1920, proposed far-reaching changes designed to prepare the Indian Army as an imperial expeditionary force able to intervene in the Near and Middle East, and even in eastern Europe, under the direct command of the Imperial General Staff.[12]

The Viceroy and the Secretary of State reacted strongly to both these sets of proposals. The Government of India categorically refused to 'accept an obligation to supply permanent overseas garrisons to mandated territories'[13] and pointed out that the Iraq scheme would cause a complete breakdown in the political situation in India since the Central Legislative Assembly would refuse to vote any new taxes and the Indian members of the Executive Council would resign if the Viceroy used his special executive powers.[14] The Secretary of State argued that, for financial and political reasons:

> we must definitely get out of our heads the vague idea too often entertained, that India is an inexhaustible reservoir from which men and money can be drawn towards the support of Imperial resources or in pursuance of Imperial strategy.[15]

In the face of the Viceroy's protests, the Iraq garrison scheme was abandoned. After a flurry of memoranda and bitter arguments between the India Office and the War Office the implications of the Esher Committee report were reviewed by a sub-committee of the Committee for Imperial Defence. This body reported in June 1922, rejecting the Esher Committee's scheme completely. In January 1923 the Cabinet approved this revision, recognising that 'the Indian Army cannot be treated as if it were absolutely at the disposal of His Majesty's Government for service outside India.'[16] This position was held for the next fifteen years. The Indian Army still played a limited imperial role, but at London's expense; Indian troops could still be used to bolster up the British position in the East but, in peace-time at least, they had to be bargained for as mercenaries, they could not be summoned as a right and at no expense. The Indian Army had become a pawn in the political battles waged between London and New Delhi and between the Government of India and its critics.

By 1923, then, the financial and political crisis in India, largely springing from the strains caused by India's imperial role during the 1914–18 war, had forced British policy-makers to drastically reduce India's imperial commitments. The absence of any major imperial military crisis until 1937, or of any major commercial and financial one until 1930, disguised this fact in London. The Indian Army was not called upon again to play a major imperial strategic role until the mid-1930s, but, there again, there were no major strains on imperial defences until then. Similarly, between 1923 and 1930 all London's old taboos about Indian tariff policy were flouted – an avowedly protectionist iron and steel tariff was imposed in 1924 and the cotton excise was abolished altogether in 1926. Yet, although Britain's traditional export staples were becoming uncompetitive in the 1920s and were beginning to require some sort of protection in world markets, all three political parties in Britain were remarkably loath to abandon free trade. India was treated no differently from the Dominions at the Imperial Conference on tariff reform in 1923, while those British policy-makers who looked to the empire to rescue Britain from her economic troubles turned mainly to the colonies of settlement, not

India, for aid. In these circumstances, London's concern about the Government of India's problems in balancing imperial and domestic demands upon its scarce resources died away for the rest of the decade. For the Government of India the changed climate of central administration brought about by the 1919 Government of India Act remained a pressing problem which could not simply be ignored. The Central Legislative Assembly created by the 1919 Act was, in the last resort, powerless; if necessary, the Viceroy could certify any legislation it rejected, refuse assent to any legislation it initiated or simply by-pass it and rule by direct executive acts. However, the C.L.A. did impose the force of Indian opinion on members of the central executive much more than ever before. Although Montagu and Chelmsford had hoped that the all-India assembly would create closer bonds between officials and non-officials, in practice the politics of the C.L.A. revolved around the stances that the various Indian leaders there took up against the Government of India. It became a forum for the dissemination of propaganda, not for a new co-operation between ruler and ruled. As Lord Reading, Viceroy in the early 1920s, complained:

> my task has been, among other difficulties, to govern with a Parliament in which there is always a large majority against the Government.[17]

This exposure to hostile and articulate Indian opinion did have an effect on the policies and attitudes of the members of the Government of India, especially as the major issues on which the M.L.A.s attacked them were 'imperial' ones – tariffs, retrenchment and army reform in the early 1920s, exchange policy and financial autonomy later on.

The attitude of the M.L.A.s was not only another limitation on the ability of the Government of India to play an imperial role; one of their major demands, and a demand of all Indian opponents of the *Raj*, was that the central government should take up active policies to improve the lives of its subjects by 'nation-building' activities, industrial development and protection, expansionist monetary policies and the like. One reason why Government of India officials resisted these demands until the great depression of the early 1930s was a conviction that governments ought not to act in such ways, but another consideration of importance was that, as it was constructed after 1919, the central government was in no position to initiate dynamic policies. Firstly, the provincial governments were jealous of their autonomy; secondly, the Government of India, which claimed to have the interests of the whole sub-continent at heart, in fact represented nobody. Dynamic government policies raised political problems – tariff schemes or monetary policies designed to help the industrialist or the agricultural producer could damage the interests of the consumer and *vice versa*. Active attempts to change the framework of a colonial society could make imperial governments too many enemies and not enough friends. When, for example, Sir Basil Blackett, Finance Member for the Government of India, discussed Keynesian notions of regulating exchange rates to secure an optimum internal price level in the Central Legislative Assembly in 1927, he rejected such ideas as impracticable because they would leave the government in the 'invidious position' of being 'open to violent criticisms from every quarter in every conceivable contingency'.[18] Without some form of popular support central government could never take the initiative. Even such vague ideas as restoring Indian 'confidence' in monetary policy by founding a Reserve Bank in 1927 to control currency and credit[19] proved to be impracticable within the existing structure of central government, since it was impossible to devise a scheme which would satisfy both the C.L.A. and the Secretary of State.

Indian pressures for the reform of central government had begun as early as 1921, when the virulence of the non co-operation campaign and the *khilafat* movement had prompted short-lived consideration of a round table conference to devise new constitutional arrangements.[20] In 1924 Motilal Nehru, leader of the Swarajist party in the C.L.A., asked the new Labour Government in Britain to again consider such a conference, but the Viceroy managed to squash this initiative and, to play for time, appointed instead the Muddiman Committee to review the working of the reformed constitution and to propose amendments that could be made within the framework of the 1919 Act.[21] The majority report of this committee ably supported a policy of prevarication by discussing only provincial aspects of the reforms. However, even government officials were beginning to see the limitations of such an approach: as Blackett pointed out, a genuine objection to the 1919 Act was that 'the line of least resistance is always an advance towards provincial autonomy', leaving central government high and dry.[22]

Paradoxically, it was the accession of a Conservative Government to power in Britain in 1925 that heralded a major constitutional advance. Lord Birkenhead, the new Secretary of State, claimed that he had never seen the need for the 1919 Act,[23] but by the end of 1925 he had decided that it would be better to appoint a Statutory Commission to review the constitution before it became due in 1928 because 'we could not run the slightest risk that the nomination of the 1928 Commission should be in the hands of our successors. You can readily imagine what kind of Commission would have been appointed by Colonel Wedgewood and his friends'.[24] In 1926 it was the new Viceroy, Irwin, who took up this initiative, insisting on a parliamentary (and hence all-white) Commission (the Simon Commission) because to open its ranks to Indians would be to invite bitter quarrels over representation. By this action Irwin hoped to attract the support of at least the Muslims and Hindu

liberals,[25] but this was a massive miscalculation and the announcement
of the personnel of the Commission sparked off a new and dangerous
crisis in India. Sir Tej Bahadur Sapru and the National Liberal Federation joined with the Congress to boycott the Commission and to set up
an All Parties Conference to produce an independent report on future
constitutional reform; the progress of Sir John Simon and his colleagues
through India was marked by a resurgence of political agitation.
Measures to counter this caused increased hostility to the Government
in the C.L.A. and Irwin had to look for a new policy to 'split the present
artificial unity among the Hindu organised intelligensia'.[26] This new
policy, when it emerged, was aimed at securing the co-operation of at
least some of the Congress leaders, who after December 1928 were
committed to a policy of securing Dominion Status within one year or
launching a mass campaign to obtain full independence. In October
1929, with the consent of the Labour government in Britain, Irwin
declared that he had been 'authorised on behalf of His Majesty's Government to state clearly that in their judgement it is implicit in the
declaration of 1917 that the natural issue of India's constitutional progress, as there contemplated, is the attainment of Dominion Status'[27]
and invited delegates from British India and the States to a round table
conference in London to discuss a new constitution.

The exact implications of Irwin's declaration have been much discussed. Irwin himself seems to have been either unclear or devious in
its interpretation. Writing to reassure Baldwin, he drew a distinction
between what Englishmen would understand by Dominion Status – self
government – and what Indians would understand by it – a commitment to some sort of self-government eventually, probably with reservations, but essentially an act of trust. Irwin also had a capacity for
telling different listeners what he thought they would want to hear: he
assured Baldwin that he did not think Indian self-government would be
a possibility for a long time[28] and informed Lord Salisbury that it
would never be practicable;[29] yet, when trying to induce Gandhi to
come to the London conference, Irwin told him that Dominion Status
for India meant Dominion Status in the full sense of the Balfour Declaration of 1926.[30] In an important sense Irwin's Declaration was a
failure, for he did not succeed in attracting Gandhi or the Congress to
the first Round Table Conference, while the ructions it caused in Britain alerted large sections of the Liberal and Conservative parties to the
dangers of a policy of generous constitutional reform.

Making declarations and extending invitations could not solve the
problems which became apparent during the search for an improve-
ment on the 1919 Act. British policy-makers had to devise a solution
that would satisfy the often opposed aspirations and ambitions of the
Hindu Liberals, the Muslims, the Princes and the Government of
India. The Indian non-official opinion that was consulted was incapa-

ble of making constructive suggestions of its own, while the Indian National Congress kept out of the discussions almost completely. Nor was Indian opinion all that had to be faced: public opinion in Britain, and especially within the Conservative Party, was roused on this issue as never before. Although the major problem which faced those concerned with the making of the 1935 Government of India Act was that of central government, this legislation was also responsible for taking the earlier technique of devolution and decentralisation to its logical conclusion by setting up fully autonomous, fully responsible non-official provincial administrations. When the discussions on the new reforms got under way it was clear that autonomous provincial governments responsible to elected legislatures were bound to be established soon. Provincial administration was now seen to be peripheral to the main concerns of British policy-makers.[31] None of the important areas of Indian administration – commerce, finance and the army – had any contact with the provincial arena. Nor was the future of British members of the government Services put in much jeopardy for there had been no recruitment from Britain to the provincial Services since the Lee Commission's report in 1924.[32] The granting of provincial autonomy was a way of appeasing Indian opinion, taking the sting out of nationalist protest and rewarding the sections of Indian society, especially the Muslims, who had remained loyal to the *Raj* during civil disobedience. This last point was an important one, as Hoare stressed in Cabinet:

> One of the basic principles of Imperial policy was agreement . . . with the Moslem world. . . . To say that provincial autonomy would not be granted would put all the Moslems against us.[33]

The setting-up of provincial autonomy did create one headache for the British administrators: it forced them, unwillingly, to find some solution to the communal problem. By the end of the first Round Table Conference in January 1931, it was clear that the Indian delegates would never agree on communal matters. In his speech at the close of the Conference, Ramsay MacDonald promised that the British Government would, if necessary, arbitrate the matter. In private MacDonald was less than keen on doing this. He thought that a Communal Award decided by the British Government was a dangerous step since 'whoever the arbitrator was he would lose all authority in India in future.'[34] The second Conference again failed to produce a solution to the problem and again MacDonald unwillingly agreed to arbitrate if necessary.[35] The Cabinet still hoped that the problem would go away if they did nothing about it, but by March 1932 the Viceroy was warning them that an Award was necessary to keep Muslim support for the *Raj*.[36] Faced with a threatened breakdown in the constitutional discussions, the Cabinet embraced the lesser of two evils and, despite continued misgivings, announced that it would draw up a Communal Award,[37] although still refusing to do more than the bare necessities of the situation warranted. It determined to restrict the Award to the problem of the proportion of seats each community should have in the new provincial assemblies and to ignore the wider 'communal' issues of the relations between the provinces and the centre under the new constitution, the separation of Sindh and the reconciliation of the Muslim demand for one third of the seats in the Federal Legislatures with the Princes' insistence on nominating their own representatives freely.[38] In August 1932 the Communal Award was announced, with a rider that its terms could be altered if all communities involved agreed on any change.[39]

The search for a viable central constitution was inhibited by two complicating factors. The imperial commercial and financial crisis caused by the great depression and sterling's slide off the gold standard reawakened the interest of London policy-makers in India's imperial commitment. At the same time, the attempt to find Indian support for any plan to transfer power at the all-India level was jeopardised by the nature of the colonial response to British rule.

In 1930 and 1931 the Government of India decided to raise the import tariff on cotton textiles to make good the revenue deficit caused by the slump in world trade. These increases in the general rate – from 11 to 15 per cent in February 1930, to 20 per cent in January 1931 and to 25 per cent in September 1931 – alarmed British Governments concerned by the contracting world markets for British export staples. In 1930 the Labour Government confined itself to mild protests but in January 1931 it urged a preferential rate, warning that, without this, home opinion would harden against political reform.[40] In September 1931 the National Government, dependent on the support of the Conservative Party in which the sixty Lancashire MPs were the largest and best organised pressure group, attempted to take a stand. Stressing that as 'an extreme measure in a time of national emergency' the Fiscal Autonomy Convention could be set aside,[41] Sir Samuel Hoare, the new Secretary of State, frequently warned the Viceroy that both he and Baldwin thought that the principle of fiscal autonomy should be radically altered in the new constitution.[42] But in practice the British Cabinet could do little. The Viceroy countered their proposals for a countervailing excise to remove the protective effects of the revenue tariff for Indian cotton goods, and for preference for British imports, by revealing the political consequences – three Indian and two British members of his Executive Council were prepared to resign if London dictated policy.[43] In the face of this opposition, and the budgetary needs of the Government of India, the British Government could only give in gracefully.

By the end of 1931 the National Government had accepted that it

Distribution of seats in the proposed provincial legislatures under the Communal Award

	General	Muslim	Sikh	Depressed Castes	Backward Areas	Land-holders	Christians	Commerce	Labour	Others*
Assam	44	34	—	4	9	—	1	11	4	1
Bengal	80	119	—	(not fixed)	—	5	2	19	8	17
Bihar and Orissa	99	42	—	7	8	5	2	4	4	4
Bombay†	97	63	—	10	1	3	3	8	8	7
Bombay‡	109	30	—	10	1	2	3	7	7	6
C.P.	77	14	—	10	1	3	—	2	2	3
Madras	134	29	—	18	—	6	9	6	6	6
N.W.F.P.	9	36	3	—	—	2	—	—	—	—
Punjab	43	86	32	—	—	5	2	1	3	3
Sindh	19	34	—	—	—	2	—	2	1	2
U.P.	132	66	—	12	—	6	2	3	3	4

* Anglo-Indians, Europeans, University seats.
†1. Bombay including Sindh
‡2. Bombay excluding Sindh

Source: Communal Decision 1931–2 (Cmnd 4147 of 1931–2) p. 7.

Communal Award as modified by Poona Pact

	General Total	Reserved for Depressed Castes	Backward Areas	Muslims	Sikhs	Commerce	Christians	Land-holders	Labour	Others*
Bengal	78	30	–	117	–	19	2	5	8	21
U.P.	140	20	–	64	–	3	2	6	3	10
Madras	146	30	1	28	–	6	8	6	6	14
Bombay	114	15	1	29	–	7	3	2	7	12
Punjab	42	8	7	84	31	1	2	5	3	7
Bihar	86	15	7	39	–	4	1	4	3	8
C.P.	84	20	1	14	–	2	–	3	2	6
Assam	47	7	9	34	–	11	1	–	4	2
Sindh	18	–	5	33	–	2	–	2	1	4
Orissa	44	6	5	4	–	1	1	2	1	2
N.W.F.P.	9	–	–	36	3	–	–	2	–	–

* Anglo-Indian, European, University and Women's seats.

Source: N. Gangulee, *The Making of Federal India* (London, 1936) p. 309.

By the time that the provincial legislatures were actually set up, a number of changes and readjustments had taken place. By the Poona Pact of 1932, the principle of Depressed Caste representation had been changed from separate electorates to reserved seats in the general electorate. The composition of the P.L.A.s in 1937 was as follows:

could not interfere in the tariff policy of the Government of India, and that this method of maintaining a British commercial advantage was closed to them. At the Imperial Economic Conference at Ottawa in 1932 India was treated like just another Dominion;[44] she could no longer be regarded as a Most Favoured Market. Significantly, in a period when British policy-makers were seeing the need for Government action and diplomatic pressure to maintain the position of British heavy industry in world and Imperial markets, they encouraged the Lancashire Chamber of Commerce to negotiate privately, without official help, with the Indian cotton magnates. The result of these negotiations was the Lees–Mody pact of 1933. Under the 1935 Act the Fiscal Autonomy Convention was discontinued, but it was replaced by the complete exclusion of London from any interference in Indian tariff policy and so from any power to manipulate the terms of trade in favour of British commerce. Even the Viceroy could now only intervene if he was satisfied that any discriminatory tariff was being imposed for political, not economic, reasons.[45]

The imperial crisis of 1931–2 was financial as well as commercial. The slump in world commodity prices in the early 1930s hit hardest just those raw materials and items of agrarian produce on which India's export trade depended. As India's balance of trade surplus weakened and as capital movements turned against her, the Government of India found difficulty in purchasing enough sterling exchange to meet the Home Charges in London. Borrowing in London, the easiest way to meet a short-lived failure of remittance, had become virtually impossible by early 1931. As sterling, too, ran into difficulties, the British Government became seriously alarmed lest the Government of India fail to meet its commitments. The India Office had always been convinced that the stability of Indian finance depended on control by London[46] and, in the autumn of 1931, the Secretary of State forced the Government of India to link the rupee to sterling, arguing that a floating rupee would devalue disastrously, and imposed on New Delhi an emergency budget which pushed up taxation to an unprecedented level.[47]

The Government of India had a different set of priorities for financial policy. New Delhi regarded the problem of financial stability as part of the wider problem of finding a political solution for India that would induce influential Indians to support the government. In 1933 Lord Willingdon thought London's control of financial policy to be supplying 'probably the strongest hostile motive in India'.[48] The Viceroy and his advisers insisted on the necessity of concessions over finance, arguing against any overriding control by London and in favour of a non-official Finance Member in the future central government.[49] Their proposals were based on a scheme for a Reserve Bank free from political influences to take over currency and credit policy. Such a bank had been recommended by the *Royal Commission on Indian Currency and Finance* in 1926, and had then been accepted in principle by the Government of India and the Secretary of State. But now the India Office would have none of it, refusing to consider any central banking institution that was not under the control of the Secretary of State.[50]

By the middle of 1932 the immediate crisis was over and, in the short term, London's policy had been vindicated. Massive exports of gold had repaired India's balance of payments, her credit on the London money market was sound again, the rupee had strengthened, remissions had begun and the repayment of short-term sterling and rupee loans had been started.[51] Now the India Office could consider the terms of the White Paper on Indian constitutional reform and the future control-structure over financial policy in the new Government of India Act. It was now that the Government of India had its revenge.

By December 1932 the British Cabinet Committee on India had prepared a scheme for financial control in the future. This proposed the transfer of finance to an Indian minister responsible to the central legislature, with a number of safeguards. The chief of these was that the Viceroy was to be given powers to certify legislation if necessary for 'safeguarding the credit of the Federation'; he was to have the support of a statutory Financial Adviser to help him in this. The supply of the Defence and Foreign departments and the interest and sinking funds on the public debt (80 per cent of the revenues of central government) were not to be subject to the vote of the legislature, the budget proposals of the Indian Finance Minister could not be introduced to the legislature without the Viceroy's prior sanction and a non-political Reserve Bank was to be set up to control currency and exchange matters. The Reserve Bank was to be under the Viceroy's authority and its establishment was made a necessary precondition of any transfer of financial responsibility.[52]

When the Cabinet came to consider the proposals of its Committee, it was only the question of finance that caused any difficulty.[53] Hoare was under fire from the Government of India and from the Treasury's 'rigid view' that if London did not control Indian borrowing her credit would collapse; he had to reconcile 'the demands of political expediency with the needs of sound finance'.[54] Hoare had by now reversed his 1931 stance – he accepted that it was more important to assuage Indian opinion than to insist on the maximum guarantee of financial probity; eventually the Chancellor of the Exchequer also came round to his view. After a good deal of bluster that the Treasury, the Bank of England and the City thought that any transfer of financial responsibility to India would be disastrous and after warning that the Treasury could not be expected to guarantee any loans raised by an Indian Finance Member, the Chancellor accepted that the political situation in India made it imperative to take the risk of transferring control over finance to the Viceroy.

This scheme was passed by the full Cabinet, written into the White Paper of 1933 and eventually passed by Parliament as part of the 1935 Government of India Act. As Hoare pointed out to the Parliamentary Joint Committee on Indian Constitutional Reforms in 1934, all control by the Secretary of State was to be surrendered.[55] Although the Reserve Bank scheme and the safeguards left too little power in the hands of any future Finance Minister to satisfy the demands of many Indian critics of the new constitution, the new proposals did represent a considerable advance. Despite its doubts about the financial wisdom of the Government of India, as revealed by the measures it forced through in 1931, the British Government were now prepared to relinquish all control to the Viceroy. Even the existence of safeguards could not in practice insulate the conduct of financial and monetary policy from the influence of Indian representatives. As the history of central government since 1919 had shown, direct executive rule could never be sustained for long against the wishes of an elected assembly. Nor would the constitution of the Reserve Bank save it from political interference – as Sir George Schuster, the Finance Member, had pointed out to the Viceroy's Executive Council when discussing the Bank in 1930, the government and legislature would in practice retain the final word on monetary and currency policy even with a non-political central bank.[56]

The progress of constitutional advance in India was determined by the need to attract Indian collaborators to the *Raj*, to swell the revenues and maintain political tranquillity, leaving the Government of India free to fulfill its imperial role. Thus changes in the imperial role assigned to India by London policy-makers – these frequently dictated by conditions in India – were the most important single regulator of the development of constitutional reform. The limiting of this role, and the consequent acceptance of further measures of non-official control in Indian government was not a simple evolutionary process. India's true place in the empire was only revealed at times of imperial crisis and the strains imposed by each successive crisis left India's imperial role diminished for the next one. Even before the first world war it had been clear that, to survive, the Government of India had to balance the imperial and the domestic claims upon its resources. The strains caused by India's participation in the imperial war effort of 1914–18 had boosted domestic pressures on government so that a measure of constitutional reform and a serious limitation on India's imperial military role had to be conceded after the war. The strains caused by India's enforced participation in strengthening the British position in the financial crisis of 1931 had a similar effect – now the British Government had to sell its control over commercial and financial policy to buy Indian support. British policy-makers were not just asking for Indian approval for its own sake. By buying Indian co-operation in commercial policy they were making a last, desperate attempt to safeguard the privileged position of British goods in the Indian market; by surrendering finance to the Viceroy they were recognising that it was Indian, not British, confidence in financial policy that was the key to Indian solvency and to maintaining the role of the rupee in the world sterling system. But in seeking a new, indirect, imperial role for India in these fields the British could not simply juggle with safeguards: a corollary of the need to attract domestic opinion to support imperial requirements was the need to create a body of Indian opinion to hand over to. Thus even to secure their limited objectives the British had to find a viable solution to the problem of central government.

The decision of 1929 to hold a round table conference in London at which representatives from India could initiate and discuss plans for constitutional reform marked a striking departure from the precedent established by the formulation of earlier reform schemes. With the help of delegates from the opposition parties in Britain, the Indian Princes, Moslems, Hindu Liberals and, if possible, the Congress, the minority Labour Government hoped to get the new constitution accepted, before it was introduced, by those who would have to work it. However, the conference method was a failure – the Indian opinion consulted was too limited in vision and too parochial in outlook to make a constitution on its own.

The major advance of the first Round Table Conference in 1930 was the development of a scheme of federation, embracing both British India and the Native States, as a way of integrating provinces and centre into a comprehensive reform scheme. The representatives of the Chamber of Princes were responsible for this; however, the Princes were not inspired by idealism or a genuine desire for constitutional change – their basic concern was with the issue of paramountcy and with the fear that the British might hand over power in the centre to Indian politicians who had little time for princely pretensions. The role of the Government of India as 'paramount power', able to overrule a Prince in his own territory, or even to overthrow him altogether, was a long-standing grievance. A federal scheme of central government in which the Princes were equal partners seemed an ideal arrangement to ensure independence from the central government, be it run by Britons or Indians.

When the Chamber of Princes had advocated this solution in 1929 and 1930 the notion of federation had been just a vague blue-print for the future. As the constitutional discussions got under way each State, or like-minded group of States, tried to get the best bargain for themselves, irrespective of any general plan. The largest of the States, notably Mysore and Hyderabad, did not feel the pricks of paramountcy so keenly as their lesser fellows and so were only prepared to put their practical autonomy at risk in return for substantial concessions. Other important rulers, such as Baroda, called for economic rewards as the price of agreeing to federation, while Bikaner and Bhopal, the two Princes most enthusiastic about the scheme, counted on alliances with British Indian politicians to expand their interests at the all-India centre. On the other hand, the host of small States, ably led by the Jam Sahib of Nawanagar and the Maharaja of Dholapur, feared that any federal scheme would increase the status of the larger States at their expense. By the time that the Government of India Bill was published, all the Princes had lined up against it. Paramountcy was still the vital issue and the Bill did not free the Princes from the interference of the Government of India Political Department.

Of the British Indian politicians, the support of the Muslim leaders was the most important to the British. At the first Round Table Conference the Muslim delegates had supported the general demand for federation, but when they returned to India they quickly began to qualify this support. In April 1931 the All-India Muslim Conference passed a series of resolutions clarifying the terms on which they would accept federation. The basis of this demand was for a weak federal centre so that a predominantly Hindu centre could not interfere in the government of Muslim provinces. The Conference set out to guard their sectional interest by calling for full autonomy for the federating units, the vesting of complete residual powers at the provincial level, the same internal powers for provincial governments as for the rulers of the Native States and an assurance that no executive or legislative area should be put under the control of the federal centre without the consent of each province. The All-India Muslim Conference did not represent all Muslim opinion, but it did represent the most important sections of it. For most established Muslim politicians there was little real advantage to be gained from any federation scheme. The influence of the Muslim leaders prominent in central government, notably Fazl-i-Husain, depended on personal and political qualities that could not easily be exploited in any administration responsible to a legislature. Provincial Muslim leaders would only suffer from a closer integration of the local and national institutions of government. Thus although they continued to pay lip-service in public to the ideal of federation, the Muslim delegates to the various conferences after mid-1931 did little but raise difficulties, siding with any party that was being obstructive.

If the British policy-makers had only needed to consult one section of Indian public opinion, they could have done without the federal idea altogether. But the *Raj* could not live by the support of the Muslims alone. It was to placate Hindu opinion that Lord Irwin had first extended the terms of reference of the Indian Statutory Commission to include consideration of an eventual all-India federation, proposed the Round Table Conferences and, eventually, made his declaration on

Dominion Status. Again, in 1932 when Hoare was toying with the idea
of introducing provincial autonomy immediately and delaying any Bill
to cover federation, it was the Viceroy's warnings about the reaction of
non-Muslim opinion that forced him to change his mind.[57]

In November 1929 many representatives of non-Muslim opinion
wrote an open letter to Ramsay MacDonald voicing their concern at
rumours that the British Government was planning to introduce only
provincial autonomy at the expense of any advance at the centre. This
letter was signed by influential individuals – including Sapru, Sir Purshottamdas Thakurdas, G. D. Birla and Sastri – and by all important
non-Muslim leaders of political organisations.[58] But, as with the
Princes, once the detailed negotiations got under way, this united front
pushing for constitutional advance at the centre disintegrated. The
Congress took little part in the discussions in London and India. The
leaders of the Sikhs and the Hindu Mahasabha easily got diverted into
haggling over purely provincial matters. Only the Liberals (although
they were not united) were consistent supporters of the idea of federation as a means of getting some advance at the centre. This support did
little to further the cause; the problems of concessions to the Muslims,
the Princes and the Conservative backwoodsmen frequently made Sapru, Sastri, the National Liberal Federation and the Servants of India
Society protest against federation in its actual, rather than its ideal,
form. In any case, although the British were forced to take account of
the reactions of the Hindu Liberals on occasion, Sapru and his colleagues did not command the sort of support in India that would allow
them to force their views upon the India Office or the Government of
India.

The British policy-makers also had to take account of the opinions of
the Government of India. Both Irwin and Willingdon were consistently
in advance of India Office and Cabinet opinion on the question of the
extent of necessary reform. Although a Conservative, Irwin led the
MacDonald Labour Government of 1929–31 by its nose, forcing it to go
beyond the I.S.C. report, to set up the Round Table Conferences, to
establish the principle of allowing an Indian initiative on the whole
question of constitutional advance and to declare Dominion Status as
the eventual goal of British rule in India. Willingdon's most fiery
exchanges with London were over commercial and financial policy, but
in constitutional matters he constantly demanded concessions to show:

> that you [London] are giving us more responsibility at the Centre,
> more freedom to administer our affairs. . . . Something that would
> show these people out here that you are relaxing control to some
> extent.[59]

As Hoare pointed out to the Cabinet in 1934, the plan of giving Indians
responsibility at the centre 'had been largely adopted owing to pressure

from the Viceroy'.[60]

In 1919 the British Government had not encountered major opposition to their plans either from Parliament or from British public opinion. The policy-makers of 1929–34 were less fortunate. India policy had now become important as an issue in British party politics, and vital as an issue in the internal politics of the Conservative Party. In the bitter months after the electoral defeat of 1929 Churchill had capitalised on Conservative concern about the results of Irwin's policy of conciliation in India to raise his own standard of revolt. While Baldwin wanted to give full support to the Viceroy, a close personal friend, it was the impact of Churchill and the influence of Austen Chamberlain and Lord Salisbury that ensured that the Conservatives adopted the Simon Report, not the Viceroy's Declaration, as the basis of their attitude to Indian reform in 1929 and 1930. Like Joseph Chamberlain thirty years before him, Churchill also wooed the constituency parties to join an assault on the parliamentary leadership. Aided by the India Defence League, the Lancashire interest and such emotive figures as Rudyard Kipling, Lord Lloyd and General Dyer, Churchill almost defeated the party leaders in the summer of 1933.

One might well ask how the British policy-makers managed to find a way through this morass of negative and conflicting opinion. The short answer is that they did not. MacDonald's Labour Government of 1929–31 never got to grips with the India problem; the National Government that followed increasingly ignored Indian opinion in drawing up a scheme for constitutional change. The Labour Government had inherited a policy of keeping Indians out of discussions of reform (as with the Indian Statutory Commission), of planning only for British India and of a studied avoidance of the issue of Dominion Status. While in opposition, the Labour leaders had consistently advocated a more enlightened policy towards India;[61] once in office they eagerly accepted Irwin's plans for a round table conference.[62] As leaders of a minority administration the Labour Cabinet ministers were restrained by the need to prevent a confrontation over India with the parliamentary opposition and, even without this handicap, their position was seriously compromised by the fact that they had no coherent policy towards constitutional change. MacDonald told Government representatives at the first Round Table Conference to sit as 'judges', to attempt only to elucidate the facts and absorb opinions from others, simply because of this lack of a policy.[63] The reluctance of Wedgwood Benn, the Secretary of State, to publish the Government of India's *Despatch* on the reforms before the Conference in case it should turn out that His Majesty's Government's policy was different from that of the Government of India[64] sprang from the fact that the Secretary of State had no idea what the Government's policy would be. At the first Round Table

Conference Ramsay MacDonald accepted the idea of a federal solution
to the Indian problem. The plan had several advantages for him. Firstly, it gave the chance of creating a 'safer' form of central government
which would mollify the opposition in Parliament and in India and so
made the transfer of power easier.[65] Secondly, it gave him an opportunity to drop the contentious question of Dominion Status and so heal the
breach with the opposition. But at the first Conference, few details of
the federal scheme had been thrashed out.[66] MacDonald realised that
federation must be a 'safe' form of government and that some of the
proposals at the Conference had not been 'safe'. He advised Government representatives to stall on these issues until experts had worked
out the details.[67]

By the time of the second Round Table Conference the Labour
Government had gone out of office and the Conservative-backed
National Government had come in. During 1930 the Conservative
Party had taken a cautious attitude to Indian reform, basing their
stand on the recommendations of the Indian Statutory Commission
report.[68] They had welcomed the idea of federation, seeing a federal
centre as a way of bringing 'the stabilizing forces of the Indian
States . . . into the constitutional balance'[69] and making it possible 'to
rescue British India from the morass into which the doctrinaire
Liberalism of Montagu had plunged it'.[70] The first weeks of the
National Government were dominated by the economic crisis in Britain
and its members had little time to consider an Indian policy. Government representatives again played a passive role at the second Round
Table Conference, although less so than the year before. But, by the
end of this Conference in November 1931, Hoare was beginning to
review the situation and consider major changes in the attitude of the
British Government. He decided that there was no future in the consultative conference method; the Round Table Conferences had achieved
nothing of value and Conservative opinion was becoming restless at
what it saw as a defeatist way of going about things.[71] He decided that
the Government must now take the initiative and the Cabinet resolved
to suspend the whole question of all-India advance and concentrate on
bringing in provincial autonomy as soon as possible.[72] Hoare wanted to
get the approval of the Indian Conference delegates for this move and
had succeeded in getting the backing of the minority delegates, when
the plan leaked out and a shrewd propaganda campaign by Sapru and
the *Daily Herald* forced them to retract and the scheme had to be
abandoned.[73] So at the end of the second Conference, as at the end of
the first, the Prime Minister's speech declared His Majesty's Government's belief in an all-India federation 'as providing the only hopeful
solution of India's constitutional problem'.[74]

Most members of the Cabinet were no longer prepared to act on the
assumptions of this speech. They feared the deep anxiety of Conserva-

tive opinion and were especially nervous of the results of any future consultations with Indian delegates.[75] The Cabinet decided that the time had come when it should lay down the main lines of India's future constitution and only allow Indian opinion to intrude on specific points.[76] Against the advice of the Viceroy, Hoare now insisted that, before the Consultative Committee could be allowed to meet in India, the Government of India and the Cabinet should draw up a detailed agenda and plan of discussions for it to follow.[77] The Secretary of State was still unwilling to abandon the idea of dropping any advance at the centre and concentrating on provincial autonomy alone, but this was still unacceptable both to the Government of India and to important Indian opinion.[78] By May 1932, the Cabinet had reluctantly decided that a scheme for reform at the centre was necessary[79] but they would only go through with it if the terms were kept a secret from India and if the Secretary of State did not publicly declare any time limit for the introduction of the Bill, or even that he would produce one at all.[80] The Cabinet was still vehemently opposed to any consultations with Indians. Following these lines, Hoare announced in June that the Government would proceed to formulate plans for a Government of India Bill which would be published in a White Paper and then submitted to a Joint Committee of Parliament at which Indian assessors would be allowed to attend.[81] The reaction in India to this announcement was so severe that Hoare was forced to compromise and allow a third Round Table Conference to meet. However this Conference was not given the same free brief as its predecessors – the delegates were only allowed to discuss specific topics already formulated by the Cabinet. On the basis of these discussions, Hoare proceeded to draft his White Paper.

The year 1933 was dominated by the diehard challenge to the Conservative leadership using India policy as the main issue.[82] The Cabinet now became more obsessed than ever with the need to placate opinion within their party. The Parliamentary Joint Committee became the key tactic in this ploy. Although Hoare had been careful to stress to India that this Committee would give Indians a chance to participate once more in the shaping of the reforms,[83] he sold the idea to the Conservative Party as providing an opportunity for British opinion to rewrite, if necessary, the whole plan of Indian constitutional advance. When, in September 1933, Willingdon made a speech to the Central Legislative Assembly in which he spoke as if the White Paper were the final form of the reforms, Hoare reprimanded him, claiming that his speech had caused embarrassment to several moderate Conservative MPs who had 'been defending themselves [to their constituents] on the lines that the Joint Committee is a weighty and important body, competent to make alternative proposals and to consider the whole question of Indian government'.[84] In the Joint Committee Hoare gave way on a number of points – on demands for indirect election to the federal legislatures, for reductions in the size of these legislatures and for the introduction of specific clauses to safeguard the position of British individuals, companies and goods in India. Thus the principle of free consultation was reintroduced into the constitution-making process, but it was consultation with British, not Indian, opinion. As Sapru wryly commented, 'Baldwin and the others will purchase the solidarity of their party at a heavy price; it will be paid at our expense'.[85]

The plan for an all-India Federation was the key device of the British policy-makers to attract support from Indian opinion and secure a moderate, sympathetic Indian central government. The 1935 Act envisaged a dyarchic federal centre with power over both British India and the Native States. There was to be a Council of State consisting of 172 British Indian representatives, most of whom would be elected, and 104 members from the Native States, nominated by the Princes; and a Federal Assembly of 250 British Indian members and 125 States members. These elected legislatures were to have power only over internal affairs – they could not interfere with the army, defence, external or ecclesiastical affairs. They could only legislate on coinage, currency and exchange policy after getting leave from the Governor-General. The legislatures were also to be powerless over money for the army, the all-India Services, the debt servicing and the sinking funds. In addition the railways, for which a separate administrative board was set up, were not to be under their control.

Baldly stated, these terms of the Act do not seem very liberal, but they did represent a considerable advance over those that had existed before. If London did not surrender control to elected Indian legislatures, it did hand power over to the Government of India. All the former authority of the Secretary of State was to be vested in the Viceroy – even the treaties of the Princes with the British Crown were to be changed into 'Instruments of Accession' to the Federal Government. The apex of the system of imperial control moved from London to Delhi. We have already seen that, by 1933 at least, the British policy-makers had been forced into the realisation that a political solution to the Indian problem was essential to secure even their limited interests in India. The 1935 Act was a genuine attempt to provide such a solution; that it was never fully implemented was not part of its drafters' intention. By 1934 the wheel had come full circle. The constitution-making process that had begun with the all-white Indian Statutory Commission had ended with the Joint Committee; the 1935 Government of India Act was designed to placate British opinion. This was not altogether the fault of the British Government. It has become a truism to say that British politics were more important than Indian in the formulation of Indian policy, but behind this banality lies a significant aspect of the relationship between Britain and India. It was British initiative that commanded an Indian response: none of the Indians who participated in the constitution-making had a positive, constructive notion of what India's new constitution should be. The various sections of Muslim, Princely, Liberal, Hindu, Depressed Caste and Sikh opinion consulted by the British assumed attitudes ultimately based on a reaction to what they knew or assumed British policy to be. The *raison d'être* of these leaders at the provincial and national level lay in asserting the rights, hopes and interests of minority or majority community, large or small State, in response to any scheme devised by the British. The British policy-makers may have hoped for a positive lead from India, but this was not the way in which Indian politics worked. Each section of Indian and British opinion at the first Round Table Conference had had its own implicit interpretation of federation; since the Conservative Party had to provide the Government of India Act it was their view which eventually dominated.

The 1935 Government of India Act was a failure. Designed to safeguard vital British interests by providing a new basis for co-operation between Britain and India, it pleased nobody. Yet although the federal centre never came into existence, the 1935 Act did introduce a new political environment into India as provincial autonomy caused a radical change in the pattern of provincial politics and the possibility of federation influenced even those who had sworn to have nothing to do with it. This changed environment led to the emergence of a new Indian response to British rule, and it is an account of the nature and development of this response that forms the bulk of this book. With the aid of hindsight we can see that the new constitution helped to deliver the political future of India into the hands of the Indian National Congress. However, in 1935, few things seemed less likely either to British policy-makers or to Congress leaders.

2 The Gandhian Ideal and the Socialist Plan: Central Congress Politics 1933-7

As with their opponents in the Government of India, one of the greatest problems faced by the all-India Congress leadership had always been that of central control. The Congress had had a national organisation and discernible leaders and interests at the all-India level since the 1880s. But, once the national movement had developed into more than the representative of small provincial groups interested in influencing opinion in Britain, the devolution of provincial government and the multiplication of political issues within India limited the role of the centre. By the first world war the central organisation of the Congress had become little more than an extension of dominant provincial interests, with no distinctive role of its own. It was Gandhi's rise to prominence after 1916 that swung some of the initiative back to the centre. In 1920 Gandhi managed to forge a temporary alliance of all sections of Congressmen, under his own leadership, to pursue non co-operation as an expression of disgust and frustration at the 1919 Government of India Act and at the politicians able to make use of it.

Gandhi's new role and the resultant resurgence of the Congress centre were underlined by the passing of a new Congress constitution in 1920. This established the Congress as the only Indian political organisation which combined a permanent central executive with a coherent party structure reaching down to the local level. In addition to the annual general session of delegates from all parts of the country there was now an All India Congress Committee, convened several times a year and acting as the subjects committee for the general session, and a small Working Committee, the permanent central executive. The eleven British Indian provinces were divided into twenty Congress provinces, based on language groups. At the head of each of these provinces was a Provincial Congress Committee, with powers to shape policy and supervise all subordinate activity. Below the P.C.C.s were District Congress Committees and, below them, *Thana, Taluka*, City and Town Congress Committees. By the 1930s even smaller units had been provided for with the establishment of *Mandal, Firka* and Village Congress Committees, although these organisations, based like their superiors on units determined by the structure of local administration and land revenue collection, were rarely formalised and were often non-existent prior to independence. From 1920 until the Bombay Congress of 1934 this pyramidic structure was linked by indirect election, each unit acting as the electoral college for its immediate superior, with the annual General Session delegates being elected by the P.C.C.s, the A.I.C.C. members by the Session delegates and the Working Committee by the A.I.C.C. The creation of this institutionalised hierarchy certainly contributed, in the long run, to the success of the Congress as a nationalist movement, but the mere existence of these institutions did not, in itself, convert the Congress into a centralised, coherent political organisation. Constitutions are more usually the slaves than the masters of politicians, and the Congress constitutions were no exception. The central Congress leaders could not lead effectively simply because a Working Committee existed at the top of the organisational pyramid. Even when the Working Committee was a united body, which it often was not in the 1920s, its members needed, at the very least, an exclusive and popular programme for their subordinates if their real status was to match their nominal position.

The grand alliance for non co-operation lasted for little more than a year – September 1920 to March 1922 – and did not survive Gandhi's imprisonment. In 1923 the central leaders split, and provincial and local Congress activists split with them, some forming the Swarajist party and taking up the policy of 'council entry' (contesting elections to the provincial and central legislatures), while others concentrated on local self-government institutions or, if unable or unwilling to seek any executive power, worked on the semi-political 'constructive programme' of encouraging temperance, communal unity, the production and use of *khaddar* and the like. In 1923 the Swarajists left the Congress; disunities, deaths and failures forced them to rejoin in 1926. For the next three years the Congress led a schizophrenic existence, some members concentrating on obtaining parliamentary power, others on following a programme to which the resources of government were irrelevant.

In the country as a whole the Congress was not a constant or self-generating political force in the 1920s. The fluctuations in its influence and importance were spasmodic and often extremely localised. As Congress Committee, Legislative Assembly or Council, or local board elections approached, Congress activity would pick up; specific, limited mass action campaigns – as the Nagpur flag *satyagraha* of 1923 or the Bardoli agitation of 1928 – also gave a fillip to local organisations. But without a single nation-wide issue to buoy it up, the influence of the Congress as a whole declined drastically from the high point of 1921. In the middle of the non co-operation campaign the total membership of the Congress had been at least 1,945,854[1] but by 1925 it had sunk to 18,339.[2] Nor was Congress membership within individual Congress provinces spread evenly: nearly half of the 2374 total in Maharashtra in

1927–8 came from two districts (Satara and Poona),[3] in Tamil Nad in 1929 the provincial leaders estimated that their membership of over 36,000 was drawn from only 310 villages.[4] This decline in the Congress organisations was not altogether surprising, for the parliamentary programme between 1923 and 1926 and the 'constructive programme' for the whole of the 1920s were not even run by the Congress institutions as such; both were farmed out to special agencies, leaving the Congress Committees with no autonomous programme at all.

This disintegration did not particularly matter while the organisation was dormant, but the quickening of the tempo of political activity that followed the arrival of the Simon Commission in India put a sharp focus on the problem. In 1927, while several Congress leaders were involved in the All Parties' Conference that was drawing up the Nehru Report – the Indian reply to the Statutory Commission and to Birkenhead's jibe that Indians were incapable of making constructive constitutional plans – the annual session of the Congress met at Madras. Gandhi and other all-India leaders did not bother to attend the session and its proceedings were dominated by a group of radicals led by Jawaharlal Nehru and Subhas Chandra Bose, who succeeded in passing a resolution declaring the goal of the Congress to be complete independence, not the Dominion Status that the All Parties' Conference were considering. At the Calcutta Congress the next year, Gandhi only managed to secure a compromise by which the Congress would pursue Dominion Status by constitutional means for one year, and would then switch to a mass campaign for complete independence. Irwin's attempts in 1929 to lure the Congress to the Round Table Conference failed and in December 1929 the Lahore Congress decided on a campaign of civil disobedience.

Whatever the benefits it brought to individual Congressmen in certain localities and provinces, the civil disobedience campaign did nothing to improve the internal position of the central leadership. In 1929 Gandhi had been more concerned with the weaknesses than the strengths of the Congress organisation; the reports on provincial arrangements drawn up in that year made 'sad reading' for him and demonstrated 'the extent of our fall'.[5] The negotiations with Irwin failed partly because, as Gandhi finally admitted, 'we [the Congress] are disunited. There are vast differences of opinion amongst us'[6] – which meant that he could not go to London. To the Viceroy, the Lahore decision made it appear that:

> the main idea in their [the Congress leaders'] minds is that the Indian differences are too deep-seated either to be concealed or surmounted at any Conference, and that participation therefore in a Conference would leave them with their platform so badly riddled as to be incapable of reconstruction. It therefore seemed better to their

minds to invent a reason for not taking part in it and thus maintaining themselves in the position of being able to say that the reluctance of Great Britain to give them all they wanted at once was again responsible for all the difficulties of Government and life in India.[7]

Even while giving his blessing to a mass campaign, Gandhi was still convinced that the Congress organisation was too weak to provide effective leadership for it[8] and at Lahore he tried to ensure that independent agencies based on the 'constructive programme' organisation were put in command. But he was defeated on this issue, and the Congress Committees were established as the directing force of civil disobedience. This did not bode well for the future, as the Governor of the Punjab commented:

> The Congress has deliberately elected to use as its tools organisations, which the proceedings of the Congress itself have amply shown to have no respect for the authority or advice of the Congress leaders, when the latter attempt any form of control.[9]

The Congress civil disobedience campaign of 1930 to 1934 was designed as a mass protest against the constitutional discussions going on in London, specifically at the British refusal to consider anything more than Dominion Status for India. Its purpose was the creation of a deadlock in India which would force the British to recognise the Congress claim to be taken as the sole representative of Indian opinion, a position which the Congress leaders had no hope of upholding at any conference table. In these terms the first mass action campaign, that of 1930–1, achieved a measure of success; Lord Irwin's policy of placation raised Gandhi up to the level of a 'plenipotentiary on equal terms with the Viceroy' and allowed him to deal with the British as 'one who was practically the head of a parallel Government' in the negotiations surrounding the Delhi Pact of April 1931.[10] The conciliatory policy of the Government of India, the general frustrations of the dyarchy period, the enthusiasm of the Congress organisations and the wide-spread distrust of British intentions in India enabled the Congress campaign to evoke a wide response and enlist the support of powerful non-Congress leaders. But, by contrast, the second campaign (of 1932–4) never really got off the ground. In 1932 and 1933 the new Viceroy, Lord Willingdon, used all the resources of government to crush the movement. The Congress programme of action, unchanged since 1929, was losing its appeal, growing stale and becoming inappropriate in a changing environment. Civil disobedience had been a reaction against the proposals for constitutional reform in general; but by 1932–3 these discussions had started to bear fruit. It now looked as if a large scheme of reform was definitely on the way, and it seemed to many political groups that the way to influence the specific points now being discussed in London was by specific agitation (such as that of the Bihar Kisan Sabha against the petitions of the Bihar United Party for a second chamber for land-lords in the proposed provincial legislatures), rather than by the vague Congress attitude of rejecting outright any reforms short of complete independence.

By mid-1933 most Congress leaders outside jail were convinced that civil disobedience could go on no longer. The reserves of morale and finance were inadequate to sustain a mass campaign.[11] In these circumstances, the agitation was allowed to run down. When Gandhi declared that he would embark on a twenty-one day fast from jail on the issue of untouchability in May 1933, the then Congress Dictator, titular head of the organisation, called a six-week halt to the mass movement in sympathy.[12] Just before the fast began Gandhi was released. This seemed to give an opportunity for a major revision in the Congress programme and the period of suspension was extended for another six weeks to give Gandhi time to recover sufficiently to consider future policy. Gandhi was now in a strong position, as the inventor of, and hence only expert in, the technique of *satyagraha,* he dominated the discussions of a future programme for the Congress.

The suspension of civil disobedience was not simply a tribute to the efficiency of government repression. During 1932 and 1933 many leading Congressmen had become concerned about the increasing lack of central control over the movement. Since the Congress had been declared illegal, clandestine arrangements had been necessary to carry on the agitation. Such arrangements had eroded control from the top and they had been attacked by one Congress Dictator after another. After his release from prison Gandhi took up the refrain. Congress leaders had already warned against allowing the organisation to fall into 'unwary hands';[13] now Gandhi doubted whether there was a single Congress institution capable of leading a mass campaign correctly.[14]

As in 1922, the ending of a mass agitation gave no clues about how the Congress might be run in future. But there was now one significant difference from the situation existing at the end of non co-operation. Then Gandhi had been behind bars – now he was the only front-rank Congress central leader not in jail. No two groups of Congressmen could agree on an alternative programme, so Gandhi was able to use his unique position to impose on others his own ambitions for the Congress. In July 1933 Gandhi called a conference of Congressmen at Poona and exploited the divisions of his opponents to dominate the proceedings.[15] At the end of this meeting mass civil disobedience remained as the only programme of the Congress, although in temporary suspension. But within a week Gandhi had moved on to the offensive. He now produced plans to call off the mass movement, ordered the Congress organisations to disband and inserted a completely non-political programme of individual protest and social uplift through the 'constructive programme.'[16] Gandhi had now restored the authority of his own leadership from the centre and solved the problem of *de facto* decentralisation with the Congress organisation. But he had only managed this by abolishing the Congress as a political movement. The Congress was no longer to be the political representative of a subject India, or the spearhead of a mass nationalist movement. It was now intended as a centralised, apolitical élite body dedicated to realising the Mahatma's idiosyncratic view of a just society.

Gandhi's plans for the dissolution of the Congress had a galvanising effect. The fear that the Congress might cease to exist spurred all sections of Congress opinion in their determination to restore the Congress as a political force, to relegate religious and social considerations to a second place, to free the Congress from the dangerous 'incubus of Civil Disobedience' and to combat the 'irresponsible and arrogant dictatorship enthroned in the Congress by Gandhiji'.[17] With the organisation dissolved, politicians were faced with the unpalatable choice of either offering individual civil disobedience or else immersing themselves in the 'constructive programme'. Neither alternative had much appeal, but the problem facing those who disliked the situation was how to remedy it. Congress leaders in several provinces exchanged gloomy letters on the subject of what they should do;[18] it was felt that the most simple course, that of calling an A.I.C.C. meeting to discuss a future programme, would achieve nothing, as Gandhi would be able to dominate it as he had dominated the Poona Conference.[19]

It was the lure of parliamentary politics that eventually provided a way out of the dilemma. The initiative came from S. Satyamurthi, the Madrassi Congressman who, in October 1933, founded a provincial Congress Swarayja Party to contest the elections to the local boards and legislatures. He next began sounding out sympathetic leaders in other provinces with a view to holding a nation-wide meeting of 'friends who agree' and founding a party at all-India level.[20] The idea of forming a party of Congressmen to follow a positive political programme was eagerly taken up by other leaders: in January 1934 Dr Ansari (a Muslim Congress leader from Delhi and Gandhi's personal doctor) and Dr B. C. Roy (a prominent figure in the faction-ridden Bengali Congress organisation) began a series of discussions in Delhi about what programme would be suitable for such a party and concluded that only a revival of parliamentary politics and a policy of contesting elections would serve.[21] It was decided to form the New Swarajya Party to contest the Central Legislative Assembly elections due within the next year, and an inaugural meeting was arranged at Ranchi, Bihar.

There were still two major stumbling-blocks for the founders of the new party – the question of how Gandhi would react and the problem of how the Congress leaders who had not taken part in the Delhi discussions would respond. Ansari had taken the trouble to discover Gandhi's opinion before he had suggested a parliamentary programme to his other associates and had received the Mahatma's blessing.[22] Gandhi quickly gave public support to the new party, declaring that although he had no faith in parliamentary politics he had 'no hesitation in welcoming the revival of the Swarajya Party and the decision of the meeting to take part in the forthcoming elections to the Assembly'.[23] This was not really a contradiction of his previous attitude, only an amendment of it. He saw clearly that there was a formidable section of opinion in the Congress who would not be content with his programme and that 'their ambition must be satisfied'.[24] He was quite happy to see the emergence of a political wing for the Congress, in a loosely affiliated relationship to the parent body, which would draw off all those interested in power politics and leave the rest of the organisation free to follow the 'constructive programme'.[25]

The reactions of the Congress leaders who had not been at Delhi presented a much more serious problem, one that was eventually to smash the Swarajya Party and destroy Gandhi's plans for the Congress. The month between the Delhi discussions and the Ranchi conference was full of activity. All over India, Congress politicians were forced to reconsider their positions. At the Delhi meetings there had been, by and large, only one leader or body of opinion from each province. April, therefore, gave the excluded provincial leaders time to jockey for position. It is interesting that the chief point of attack was the Swarajya Party's relationship with the rest of the Congress organisation. There was a general protest that the organisers of the Delhi discussions should not be allowed to establish themselves as the leaders of the political wing of the Congress, and a widespread demand that any parliamentary activity should be controlled by the A.I.C.C. and the provincial organisations, not by the narrow circle of Ansari's and Roy's contacts.[26]

This pressure forced Gandhi and his colleagues[27] to call an A.I.C.C. meeting for mid-May at Patna. It also forced the Swarajya Party leaders to consider what their relationship to the main Congress organisation should be. They had been trying both to have their cake and eat it – they wanted the electoral advantages of using the Congress name but to be free of any supervision of policy or programme[28] – but the events of April caused them to modify their plans. On one hand, Ansari began to sound out prominent non-Congressmen with a view to some sort of alliance should the A.I.C.C. meeting reject the Swarajya Party,[29] on the other, the party leaders entered into a series of discussions with Gandhi just before the Ranchi Conference. As a result of these, Gandhi agreed to recommend to the A.I.C.C. that the Swarajya Party should act as the parliamentary wing of the Congress, on condition that only Congressmen could join it and that the Working Committee retained an over-all control. The Conference accepted this position but, because

of the need to meet a possibly hostile reaction from other Congress
leaders, delayed any major decisions on the constitution or executive of
the party until after the A.I.C.C. had met.[30]
  The A.I.C.C. session at Patna was the first full meeting of a Congress
deliberative body since 1931. Its proceedings were dominated by reactions to the foundation of the new party. At Patna a new group of
Congressmen came to the fore, led by men such as Madan Mohan
Malaviya and Mohanlal Saxena, who were prepared to accept and
even welcome the end of civil disobedience and the establishment of a
political programme of Council entry for the Congress provided that
the Swarajya party (from which they were excluded) was not in control
of the parliamentary programme and that the A.I.C.C. and the P.C.C.s
(in which they had influence) conducted the Central Legislative
Assembly election campaign. Before the formal A.I.C.C. session a new
round of discussions took place between Gandhi, the Swarajist leaders
and Malaviya. Out of them emerged another compromise – the parliamentary programme was to be accepted, but instead of the Swarajya
party executive a new Congress Parliamentary Board was to be formed
to control all election matters. This Board was to have 24 members,
nominated equally by Ansari and Malaviya, who was to be its President.[31]
  Thus a formal institution was set up to work for Council entry with
the blessings of Gandhi, the Swarajya Party leaders and the A.I.C.C.
However, the Central Parliamentary Board was not a stable body – it
revolved around the aspirations and influence of Ansari and Malaviya.
Unfortunately, both had interests outside the Congress which, by pul-
ling in opposite directions, made a split inevitable. Essentially the differences concerned their reactions to the Communal Award. While
Ansari was attempting to form an electoral alliance with various Muslim politicians outside the Congress (who supported the Award),
Malaviya was opening discussions for pacts with Punjabi Hindu and
Sikh provincial leaders and with the Hindu Mahasabha on the basis of
joint opposition to the Award.[32] These tensions were quickly revealed.
Even at Patna there had been cracks in the façade of unity, for Ansari
and Malaviya had refused to accept each other's nominees for membership of the Board and eventually Gandhi had had to make the
appointments himself.[33] The fortnight after Patna saw a battle of
statement and counter-statement as Ansari and Malaviya each attempted to secure their own lines outside the Congress and to destroy the
other's. Ansari was the first to crack and he announced his intention of
going to Europe for the sake of his health. By the middle of June
Malaviya felt his position to be strong enough to let it be known that
the Board would adopt as candidates those who were opposed to the
Award. This led to a major row at the Board meeting of 16 June when,
after Malaviya and Aney, his chief ally, had threatened resignation,

Gandhi had to be brought in to 'imagine away' the difficulties in a moving speech and to propose arbitration.[34] But this compromise did not last for long and early in July Malaviya and Aney made their final break with the Congress Parliamentary Board to found the Congress Nationalist Party on a programme of opposition to the Award.

The problem caused by the Communal Award shows how difficult it was for the Congress leadership at this time to make a clear stand on important national issues. The attitude of the central Congress leaders to the Award, encapsulated in the Working Committee resolution on it which laid down that 'the Congress claims to represent equally all communities composing the Indian Nation and therefore, in view of the division of opinion, can neither accept nor reject the Award so long as the division of opinion lasts',[35] was based on the calculation that they had to duck the whole question of separate representation for Muslims as they could not afford to take sides on an issue which might allow political considerations within the Congress to become influenced by attitudes adopted for the sake of the wider political world outside it. As Rajendra Prasad (Congress President-elect) pointed out:

> We must bear in mind that the Congress cannot afford to do any-thing which will take away from its essential character of being the representative of all communities in the country. It may choose to represent the best opinion in the country [that rejecting separate electorates and special representation for minorities as breeding-grounds of communalism] but then it will cease to represent communities which hold views which are not the best. Any representative institution must truly reflect the best as also the weakest elements in the country unless it is prepared to give up its representative character.[36]

In 1934 and 1935 the Award became the single most important issue in the minds of Muslim politicians in the Muslim minority provinces (who saw it as their only safeguard of continued importance) and of both Muslim politicians (who were granted a statutory majority) and Hindu politicians (who resented this) in the Punjab and Bengal.

Although Malaviya's defection sapped the strength and impaired the unity of the Central Parliamentary Board, the major curb on the Board's activities came not from splits within it but from the continuing distrust of Congressmen in the provinces for control from the centre. At the Patna A.I.C.C. meeting provincial Parliamentary Boards had also been set up and it was on them that the main burden of arranging the election campaign fell. Generally speaking, these provincial bodies included a wide enough spectrum of the provincial leadership to make them acceptable managers of the election campaign and the immediate political programme. But there were still difficulties: some men in the provinces were not yet completely happy with the way in which the

Parliamentary Boards seemed set to control the political activities of the Congress for the foreseeable future.

The most dramatic effect of these tensions was the revolt in the United Provinces led by Rafi Ahmed Kidwai and the 'left-wing' members of the U.P.P.C.C. In early 1934 the 'left-wing' group formed a very important part of the United Provinces Committee, and of the twelve 'District Re-organisers' appointed by the P.C.C. to get the Congress machinery going again in May 1934 eight belonged to this group.[37] But in the crucial selection of the provincial Parliamentary Committee by the executive of the P.C.C. in August, they lost ground: they were outnumbered 4 : 3 on the Committee and 4 : 1 on its executive.[38] When R. A. Kidwai was released from jail in August, the dissidents decided to counter-attack. Kidwai's offensive was directed more against the people in charge of the Council entry campaign than against the policy of Council entry itself; indeed he argued that he had always favoured parliamentary politics and had been an enthusiastic member of the old Swarajya party of the 1920s. His objections now were that the composition and method of selection of the Central Parliamentary Board was not representative, that the Central Parliamentary Board could have too much influence over the selection of candidates in the provinces and that the dominance of parliamentary politics in the political programme of the Congress would alienate many who had little interest in constitutional activities, which were still the only form of political action open to Congressmen.[39]

Kidwai's campaign steadily gained support throughout August and in September Vallabhbhai Patel, acting President of the Congress, brought Kidwai to Wardha to discuss his grievances with the Working Committee. Here the rebel was bought off. He was promised that the forthcoming Bombay session of the Congress would reform the Central Parliamentary Board and that its members would be elected by the A.I.C.C. At the same time, the Congress adherence to the ideal of complete independence would be re-affirmed, symbolically demoting the parliamentary programme.[40] Kidwai now returned contentedly to the fold and the *Pioneer* soon reported that all the groups within the U.P. provincial Congress had smoothed over their differences and ' . . . have joined hands to sweep the polls'.[41]

Opposition to the Central Parliamentary Board was not confined to the U.P. On 30 July the Working Committee had passed a resolution threatening disciplinary action against members of Congress executive bodies who failed to give active support to the Patna resolutions on Council Entry. This caused a considerable stir in Congress circles. By early September there was much talk of revolt against this resolution: among those who protested were Kidwai and Tandon, Malaviya, Aney and J. C. Gupta of the Congress Nationalist Party, Sir P. C. Roy of Bengal, Choithram Gidwani, President of the Sindh P.C.C., and Seth

Govind Das and Dwarka Prasad Misra of Mahakoshal (the Hindi-speaking areas of the Central Provinces).[42] But at the same Working Committee meeting at which Kidwai was mollified the fears of these protesters were also allayed. Patel issued a statement reinterpreting the July resolution – there would be no disciplinary action against those who felt that they could not support the election campaign, only against those who publicly opposed or obstructed it.[43] Thus the Working Committee took a further step in its retreat from an exclusively parliamentary programme for the political wing of the Congress, and it did so in response to pressure from its subordinates.

Since there was so much distrust of the centre, and since the provincial Boards had taken over most of the work, there was little for the Central Parliamentary Board to do. All candidate selection was left to the provincial organisations and the central Board was not even called in to resolve disputes over nominations. The only important function left to the Swarajists, who had once hoped to direct the entire Congress election campaign, was that of finding money to finance the candidates. Here Dr B. C. Roy's contacts with Calcutta businessmen proved invaluable, as did Bhulabhai Desai's in Bombay. But even with this support, and the additional help of Vallabhbhai Patel and Jamnalal Bajaj, the financial strain caused by the election campaign was severe in several provinces. In Bihar, for example, Congressmen quickly discovered how limited their own fund-raising capabilities were – two tours of Calcutta by provincial leaders raised only 'paltry amounts', while the only guaranteed source of finance in the U.P. was the overdraft raised on his personal account by the Treasurer of the Provincial Parliamentary Board, Shri Prakash.[45] Despite contributions arranged by B. C. Roy, the Bihar Parliamentary Board finished the campaign Rs 13,700 in debt,[46] while in the United Provinces Shri Prakash was unable to pay off his overdraft. In March 1935 the Central Parliamentary Board still had a deficit of over Rs 50,000 from the C.L.A. election campaign.[47]

The Congress did well in the Central Legislative Assembly election campaign, winning 44 of the 88 elected seats.[48] Apart from the problem of funds the campaign ran smoothly. The selection of candidates caused few ructions and local Congress committees fell enthusiastically into the task of electioneering. Sir T. B. Sapru, for one, felt no surprise at the Congress success; the Congress was a nation-wide organisation with large resources of men and money and could appeal to the electorate on its record of civil disobedience and anti-British stance.[49] The basic Congress platform was one of opposition to the new constitutional reforms but with a neutral stand on the Communal Award. The only areas in which it did badly or did not bother to contest seriously were those – the Muslim seats in general and the Hindu seats in the Punjab and Bengal – in which the reforms, and in particular the Award, had polarised political passions into attitudes beyond the generalist sweep of the Congress appeal. But the importance of the 1934 elections should not be exaggerated. The electorate for the Central Legislative Assembly was small and the power of elected members was limited by the presence of a large official bloc and the lack of any legislative or executive responsibility for the Assembly. Nor was parliamentary activity yet the dominant interest of the most important central Congress leaders. Gandhi still felt that Council entry was not the key to the Congress's future and his closest associates backed him to the hilt. Vallabhbhai Patel and Rajendra Prasad were particularly emphatic about the limitations of the parliamentary programme – Patel attacking the method and purpose of the Parliamentary Board, and Prasad pointing out that:

> I am one of those who believes that a party engaged in a mass revolutionary movement should not accept positions of honour, responsibility and profit until it has succeeded in capturing power.[50]

Bhulabhai Desai who, as leader of the C.L.A. party, had expectations of a central role, was disgusted to find himself still an outsider.[51] After only twelve months in the Assembly, he had become completely disillusioned. He now saw that the programme of parliamentary political activity based on the Central Legislative Assembly – that he had once thought to be 'the one essential thing after the suspension of the Civil Disobedience movement'[52] – had turned into a sterile dead-end, cut off from the main centre of Congress activity. The members of his party in the Assembly had proved to be more interested in keeping their reputations bright in their home provinces than in providing a lead for the nation.[53] It was not these men who would provide the initiative in the all-India Congress in the next vital years.

Although the particular arrangements for the Swarajya Party and for contesting the C.L.A. elections dominated the Congress political scene for much of 1934, Gandhi had never given up his ideal of freeing the Indian National Congress from the narrow path of a purely political programme. His plans for individual civil disobedience had been overtaken by the march of events in 1934, yet he still held to his distinctive purpose throughout the tortuous negotiations over the Council Entry programme. Having recognised, in March 1934, that those who wished to contest elections from within the Congress would have to be satisfied, he modified his plans to allow for a separate Swarajya Party to draw off all the disruptive tendencies of party politics, leaving the rest of the Congress sufficiently pure and apolitical to follow his leadership.

At the Patna A.I.C.C. Gandhi had been forced to modify his plans further. His programme to turn the Congress organisations into vehicles for the constructive programme and the village uplift movement remained unchanged, but the role cast for the Swarajya Party now had to be given to the Congress Parliamentary Board. Thus the Parliamentary Board was established as an autonomous body 'with a view to achieving the greatest amount of solidarity in the Congress',[54] leaving Congress itself free for the mass action programme. But as the election campaign developed, it became increasingly obvious that the Parliamentary Board could not, in practice, work on its own. Gandhi now tried the more ambitious plan of removing party politics from the Congress, since he had failed to remove the Congress from party politics. He did this by proposing radical changes in the structure of the Congress organisation.

As the Congress machinery began to turn over again in the summer of 1934, factionalism and internal strife became obvious in the elections to the various Congress organisations. Although there was general agreement about the cause of these evils − 'intrigues, filth and petty quarrels resulting from a greed to [sic] power'[55] leading to a rush to take over Congress bodies as a stepping-stone to securing election to Councils, Corporations and local boards − only Gandhi was clear about a solution. Congress membership, according to the Mahatma, was the clue: he condemned the enrolling of members simply to get their votes (or even a signed, marked ballot paper) at the next Executive elections; he claimed that a simple four anna subscription was too loose a qualification for Congress membership, and recommended a stiff *khaddar*-wearing qualification also.[56] In Gandhi's final proposals (which were put before the Congress session at Bombay in October) the *khaddar* clause, spinning franchise and six-month membership qualification to vote were all designed to combat corruption and to secure discipline and quality at the expense of mere numbers of Congress members.

Up until the Bombay Congress in October 1934, apart from contesting the C.L.A. elections, there was no clear programme laid down for Congressmen to follow. This was seen as another reason for the growing corruption.[57] Gandhi, again, was the only one with a clear idea of what a new programme for the Congress should be. In mid September, soon after the final breakdown of negotiations with M. M. Malaviya over the Congress Nationalist Party, Gandhi announced his plans to convert the Congress into a '*Satyagraha* organisation'. He followed this with schemes for changing the Congress constitution: a change of creed substituting 'truthful and non-violent' for 'peaceful and legitimate' to describe the means by which *purna Swaraj* (complete independence) was to be attained, an insistence on a'*khaddar* clause' which would exclude all those who did not regularly wear hand-spun cloth from Congress membership and a spinning qualification for voting in the Executive and delegate elections. Gandhi threatened that if these ideas were not accepted at the Bombay session in October he would leave the Congress.[58] This first statement received a mixed reaction: some groups, notably the Congress Socialists, condemned them outright, claiming that they would divert the Congress from politics into ethical and metaphysical abstractions,[59] other Congress leaders, while approving of Gandhi's ends, had reservations about the means. Thus Rajagopalachari admitted that the spinning and *khaddar* clauses had not proved very popular[60] and Vallabhbhai Patel actually denounced the *khaddar*-wearing qualification – saying that it had proved unworkable and it was better that Gandhi should leave the Congress than that the Congress keep the *khaddar*-wearing clause.[61] Lala Dunichand, a minor Punjab leader, correctly predicted that the *khaddar*-wearing clause would lead to vote manipulation (since the reigning Congress Executives were to be the arbiters of who was a *khaddar* wearer),[62] while R. A. Kidwai saw that most Congressmen would oppose a measure that would cut down Congress membership.[63]

On 16 October, on the eve of the Congress session, Gandhi published his full proposals for the Congress constitution. These had two basic features. First, membership was to be strictly controlled – with a six-month probation period between a member's enrolment and his entitlement to vote in a delegate or Executive election (designed to eliminate the buying of members for the sake of their votes), a *khaddar*-wearing clause and a spinning franchise qualification that before any Congress member could vote in a delegate or executive election he must have spun 500 yards of yarn a month for the six months preceeding the election. Secondly, the Executive bodies of the Congress were to be made more compact and efficient. The number of delegates to the annual session were to be cut down to 1000, elected by constituencies of 1000 primary members each. These 1000 delegates were also to become the P.C.C.s for the provinces from which they were elected. This would provide a powerful incentive to the P.C.C.s to keep their recruiting up to the mark, since the only way to ensure 1000 Congress delegates was to enrol 1,000,000 members. That the A.I.C.C. was to be abolished and P.C.C. and session delegate elections combined into one was designed to cut down the amount of time wasted on canvassing and holding elections.[64] Gandhi's aim was to create a 'permanent elite' of 1000 full-time political workers, elected by a body cleansed by *Khaddar* and *Charka*. They would get to work in the districts, have a greater impact upon the Congress at the centre and would be able to prepare the country for a new *satyagraha* campaign based on Gandhi's principles.[65]

Gandhi's plans were essentially the same as they had been in July 1933 – he wanted the Congress to be an organisation of high spirituality, strong in quality rather than quantity and dedicated to a programme which eschewed ordinary political activity, whether electoral or agitational. In July 1933 his attempt to divert the Congress permanently from the political path had led to a powerful reaction. The reaction of most Congressmen now was not so intense, but it was just as critical and almost as effective. Some Congress leaders agreed that an

annual session of 6000 delegates was inefficient and tended to the
'merely spectacular,[66] and some leaders, such as S. K. Patil of Bombay,
concerned to exclude their local rivals, welcomed the proposals to
tighten membership and limit the franchise.[67] But generally it was
thought that a strict spinning qualification would make Congress
membership so small that half the seats on the all-India and provincial
bodies would be vacant.[68] The proposal to make membership of the
P.C.C.s and the A.I.C.C. identical provoked the most opposition. Provincial leaders feared that they, or their henchmen, would be excluded
from the élite that would dominate provincial and national politics.

Gandhi swiftly recognised this lack of enthusiasm for his policies; on
17 October he announced that he would leave the Congress and set up
an independent association, the All India Village Industries Association, to carry out his scheme of rural uplift.[69] Appeals were made to
him to stay, but Gandhi and his two chief lieutenants, Vallabhbhai
Patel and Rajendra Prasad, were adamant.[70] Thus, as the Congress
Socialists (who had hoped to mount a concerted attack on the parliamentary programme and the 'Gandhians') cynically pointed out,
Gandhi's role in the Congress was made the main issue at Bombay.[71]
Technically, Gandhi ceased to be a Congress member in 1934 but, in
practice, his influence remained paramount.

Although it had been hoped that the Bombay session would give the
Congress a clear programme for the coming year, the session simply
discussed Gandhi's proposed changes in the Congress constitution. At
the Working Committee meeting before the session a drafting committee was set up to frame Gandhi's proposals into specific constitutional
amendments. To the proposals that have already been mentioned this
committee added some 'transitory provisions' designed to make the
changes more appealing to the Subjects Committee (which was the
A.I.C.C. under another name) – the existing 350 members of the
A.I.C.C. were to be assured of places on the 'permanent executive' and
the other 650 members were to be elected by the delegates gathered for
the General Session.[72] However, these sops had little effect in mollify-
ing the assembled delegates and, before the Working Committee resolutions were ever brought before that body, Rajagopalachari had successfully proposed a compromise restricting the *khaddar* and spinning
qualifications to voting in delegate elections and as a qualification for
membership of Executive committees.[73] When these modified clauses
were moved before the Subjects Committee, an amendment to have
them all referred back to the P.C.C.s was only narrowly defeated, while
the proposed change in the creed was referred back.[74]

Gandhi himself put his proposals about changes in size and composition of the provincial and central deliberative bodies to the Subjects
Committee, but there was deadlock over these as well. To overcome
this, Gandhi proposed the compromise solution of a 'revising commit-

tee' spontaneously elected from the floor, from which he banned all members of the Working Committee except himself. This committee, after meeting overnight, recommended that the A.I.C.C. should remain intact and consist of 166 members, elected from the provinces by the delegates elected to the General Session, who should number 2000. It cut out the 'transitory provisions' of the earlier drafting committee, restoring the P.C.C.s also, with the proviso that they should cut down to 100 members maximum by 15 January 1935.[75] The committee also introduced a few small innovations, notably the provision of other forms of manual labour as a qualification for those who objected to spinning, and the 'rural/urban ratio' by which three-quarters of the 2000 delegates had to be returned by the 'rural areas' and the remaining quarter by 'urban areas' (defined as a town with a population of over 10,000)[76]. These proposals were put before the Subjects Committee, and later the General Session, and passed without further amendment.

The Bombay Constitution has often been regarded as of major importance in shaping the Congress during the 1930s. Certainly it is true that a number of its provisions provided a striking contrast with what had gone before. Briefly, the main points of the 1934 constitution were the following: the creed was unchanged; the only limits on membership of the Congress were being 18 years old and paying 4 annas (2p.)[77] annual subscription (Article IIIa); no member could vote in a delegate or Executive election before he had been a member for six months (Article Va); to qualify for the membership of a Congress Committee or Executive, the member had to be a regular wearer of *khaddar* and have performed manual labour equivalent to spinning 500 yards of yarn a month for the six months previous to his election (Article Vb); the Working Committee had the right to bar from election to any committee Congressmen who were also members of other political organisation which it regarded as 'anti-national and in conflict with the Congress'.[78] Each P.C.C. was to send a list of its members to the Working Committee, who would assign to it a quota of delegates to the Annual Session on the basis of one delegate per 500 members. These delegates were to be elected by single member constituencies in the rural areas (plural in urban) and would also constitute the P.C.C.s (Articles VI and VIII). These delegates were to meet before the annual session to elect a President and an A.I.C.C. of 166 members. This election of the A.I.C.C. was to be by proportional representation with a single transferable vote system[79] (Article VII).

Superficially, the Bombay Constitution made radical changes in the Congress structure.[80] However, in practice, this constitution was less of an innovation than it seemed. The hopes that the new provisions would cut out corruption were not fulfilled – Congress institutions under the 1934 constitution provided just as fertile a ground as their predecessors for manipulation, bogus enrolment, etc. In any case, the weight of Congress opinion had watered down Gandhi's most radical proposals, re-instated the P.C.C.s and the A.I.C.C.and doubled the number of delegates he had proposed. Furthermore, the provisions of spinning and manual labour and the six-month enrolment qualification were amended after only eighteen months and so governed only one set of Congress Committees and executive elections (those of July–December 1935) and the 1 : 500 ratio for P.C.C. and the annual session membership and the 166 member A.I.C.C. applied to one year only (1935–6) and one Congress Session (Lucknow, April 1936).[81]

In one other respect the Bombay Constitution made a significant departure from established practice. More power than before was given to the Working Committee, which was now formally recognised as what it had in practice been from the mid-twenties on, the controlling group in central Congress politics. The Bombay Constitution provided for the Working Committee to be nominated by the President (Article XII), and shortly afterwards the Working Committee passed a resolution restating the disciplinary powers which it had first been given in 1929. However, the role of the Working Committee could not be assured simply by theoretical provisions. If it was effectively to dominate the Congress, then it had to win that dominance in competition with dissident groups at the centre and the desire for independence of action of the provincial organisations. As we shall see, victory in these fields depended far more on favourable circumstances than on constitutional powers.

In some ways the Bombay Congress session had greatly strengthened Gandhi's position. The challenge of the Socialists, the Congress Nationalist Party and those opposed to contesting the C.L.A. election had been overcome, some of his schemes to combat corruption had been passed and his retirement into the All India Village Industries Association left him free to build up a base for the constructive programme. But what the Bombay Congress failed to do was to establish a clear policy for the movement. The divergent elements in the Congress were still within the organisation and members remained free to follow whatever line of action they pleased. The events of 1935 show that the 'Gandhian' leadership had no effective programme; for this reason they lost the initiative in all-India Congress politics and were forced on to the defensive by groups that had more attractive plans for the future.

The problems facing the 'Gandhians' in the sphere of political activity pure and simple were shown by their reaction to the publication of the Joint Committee Report on the Government of India Bill late in 1934. One suggestion was that the Congress should ally itself with the Liberals and other moderates opposed to the Report, to conduct a campaign against it short of mass or illegal activity. Although

Rajagopalachari and Patel seemed at times to favour this course, it came to nothing as the leaders realised that no effective joint activities were possible other than a 'wordy protest'. By getting involved with constitutional reforms the Congress might again get entangled with the tricky question of the Communal Award and this would demonstrate once more to London that the Indian politicians were still incapable of reaching a solution among themselves.[82] On the other hand, a mass campaign was out of the question since the leadership realised that neither the enthusiasm nor the organisational preparations for such a campaign existed. Also, even at this time, they feared that they would be unable to control a mass movement and prevent it taking a leftwards turn under the more effective agitational leadership of their opponents within the Congress.[83] So, on the issue of the Joint Committee Report, the Working Committee contented itself with a resolution condemning the terms of the Report but offering no programme of opposition to it beyond the pipedream of preparing the country for a Constituent Assembly that could decide a better constitution for India.

The 'Gandhian' leadership were now forced back onto their 1934 programme of parliamentary work (for the party already in the C.L.A., and support for them in the country at large) and the constructive programme. The speeches and statements of the President of the Congress, Rajendra Prasad, and other leaders make this quite clear. 'The essential factor in the battle for freedom is constructive work' declared Prasad in a speech at Delhi in January 1935. 'You cannot always live on condiments and stimulants. You must have staple food. The constructive programme . . . was in the nature of staple food for the nation'.[84] The Working Committee meeting of December 1934 laid down a three-month programme of an intensive recruiting campaign and of extending the organisation of the Congress, but, as Prasad pointed out, 'the influence of the Congress cannot be judged by the number of members on the rolls only, it depends more largely on the service and sacrifice which those members and others can put forth' through the constructive programme.[85] Even the solid political activity for the Assembly election was only allowed to continue if it were 'harnessed and turned into good and solid constructive work'.[86] In its extreme form, this stand reflected Gandhi's position on the Swarajya Party in March and April 1934 when he denied that Congress had a political role of its own, but saw it simply as a manpower reserve to be led in the political field by the Congress Parliamentary Board (with all the limitation of activity implied by that) and in all others by the All India Village Industries Association.[87]

The major flaw in this plan, however, was the lack of appeal of the constructive programme. Most provincial Congress leaders did not see the need for any special programme at all, being mainly concerned with events inside the Congress. In so far as they wanted guidance, or were

interested in policy, what concerned them was the relationship of the
Congress to other bodies, such as the Kisan Sabhas, and the problem of
working the 1935 Act – rather than how to make molasses from toddy
wine or to improve the efficiency of bullock carts (subjects with which
the All India Village Industries Association was pre-occupied). The
village uplift programme never really got off the ground. Even in Bihar
(a province in which Gandhi was highly respected) six months after the
All India Village Industries Association was set up, it still had no
provincial organisation or co-ordination, and its activities were limited
to the initiative of local Congress committees. Two-thirds of the Bihar
districts reported no activity at all. Funds were also a problem, since
such money as the local Congress organisations possessed had been
spent or confiscated during Civil Disobedience and the All India Village Industries Association had no money to splash around.[88] Where
money was allocated for the constructive programme, it was often mis-
appropriated by local politicians desperate for resources to use against
their opponents within the Congress.[89] Indeed the All India Village
Industries Association was most effective in the U.P., where its branch
was improperly used in place of the banned Congress volunteer organisation, the Hindustan Seva Dal, to organise meetings of peasants and
workers in support of the 'socialist' faction of the P.C.C.[90] Although
both Gandhi and Prasad professed to believe that the All India Village
Industries Association was preparing the country for a mass campaign,[91] other Congressmen had a more realistic view. As K. B. Sahai,
the Bihar leader, cannily observed in April 1936, the constructive programme was languishing, the Harijan movement dying and the All
India Village Industries Association still-born.[92] W. B. Brett of the
Government of Bihar and Orissa Political Department was even more
blunt: in December 1935 he noted that the All India Village Industries
Association had turned out to be 'a very damp squib'.[93]

The failure of the constructive programme marks the end of the total
dominance of the 'Gandhians' within the national level of the Congress.
In the late 1920s their main strength had been that they alone had a
coherent, practicable programme of mass action. But by 1934 there was
a rival group with a programme that appealed to the economic, not the
spiritual, condition of the Indian people. It is to this group, the Congress Socialist Party, that we must now turn.

The Congress Socialist Party was officially inaugurated at Patna on
17 May 1934. The formation of this party was not a sudden step. In the
late 1920s much of the dissent and dissatisfaction with the old Congress
leadership had been expressed in socialist terms, especially in youth
and student politics. Many of those who were to become the leaders of
the new party were incarcerated together in Nasik Jail in 1933 – Jai
Prakash Naraìn, Ashok Mehta, Achhut Patwardhan, Yusuf Meherally
and M. R. Masani among them. From its germination here, the idea of

forming a party was nurtured by a series of conferences culminating in the inaugural meeting at Patna.[94] A second meeting, at Benares in October, laid down a policy and programme. The object of the party was here stated to be '. . . the achievement of Complete Independence in the sense of complete separation from the British Empire and the establishment of a workers' society'. Membership was restricted to members of the Congress, excluding Congressmen who were members of communal associations, or groups opposed to the Party, but the relationship between the Party and the Congress was treated rather ambivalently. One section of the programme stated the need to 'rescue the Congress from the hands of the right wing by educating and organising the rank and file on the basis of a clear-cut programme of national revolution and also . . . to carry on a constant propaganda for the exposure of the reactionary aims, policies and programme of the right wing group'. The most controversial of the resolutions banned any Party member from holding office in the Congress (except on a body committed to the Party programme).[95] But another resolution laid down that the Party should launch its programme immediately, without waiting for the Congress to adopt it, and that it should work with any other group willing to co-operate, whether or not it was inside the Congress.[96] There was a logical flaw here: on the one hand the C.S.P. was only to be open to Congressmen and not to members of groups opposed to the Party, while on the other the attitude of the right-wing Congressmen seemed to designate them as a group opposed to the Party. Again, the C.S.P. was only open to members of the Congress, but it was to work in alliance with groups whose members were not necessarily Congressmen. This contradiction runs through the history of the C.S.P.; thus while the 1937 Party constitution again stressed that only Congressmen could join the Party, the 'thesis' that accompanied it claimed that one of the important tasks of the Party was to organise 'workers and peasants' independently of the Congress because the official policy of the Congress was incompatible with that of the C.S.P.[97] The root of this dichotomy lies in the true nature of the C.S.P. It was not, in reality, a party in the formal sense at all; it was more of a ginger group of leaders who needed the name and structure of the Congress to retain any organisational solidarity and whose only effective function was as a focus of opposition within the Congress rather than as a creative political force outside it.

The ideology of the Congress Socialist Party was as unclear as its role. As J. P. Haithcox has pointed out, socialism was in vogue among young, educated Indians but it 'represented an ill-defined sentiment' rather than a clear-cut ideology.[98] The theoretical preferences of the C.S.P. leadership reflected this vague attitude; although Marxists formed a majority of the most influential members, they did not have complete control and the Marxist terminology of many C.S.P. pronouncements gave them a more radical appearance than was, in fact, the case.[99] But by the end of 1934, some sort of programme was emerging. The Congress base among workers and peasants was to be extended to prepare for a new agitational movement. Although the Party leaders denied that the C.S.P. was a class-based organisation, they did tend to look exclusively to the 'masses', criticising the Congress as a 'middle-class organisation' which did not care for these 'masses' and could never win freedom without turning itself into a 'real mass movement', thus incorporating the historical and economic necessity of mass struggle into its programme.[100] In practical terms the C.S.P. leaders set themselves to 'democratise' the Congress constitution by ensuring representation for 'the masses'. They also planned to decentralise the Congress by giving the initiative to primary committees. They hoped to make the freedom struggle more radical by developing an anti-imperialist 'united front' of all those who were politically or economically oppressed – be they labourers, peasants, States' subjects, students or traders.[101]

The Congress leaders took up the Socialist challenge and, from mid-1934 onwards, a propaganda war developed. With the exception of Gandhi and Prasad, all the main leaders of the Congress '. . . considered the Congress Socialist Party a challenge to their authority, and did everything in their power to reduce it to impotence'.[102] In June 1934 the Working Committee criticised the language of the C.S.P. resolutions, and warned that 'loose talk' about the abolition of private property might lead to violence.[103] In July, Vallabhbhai Patel described the Socialists as a group of young men with brain fever who knew nothing about the real needs of the peasantry.[104] Patel, in particular, was nervous that the rise of the C.S.P. might damage the delicate relationship between the Congress and Indian capitalists.[105] By the time of the Bombay Congress he was looking for a showdown with the C.S.P.; P. Sitaramayya wrote to Patel of 'the scum [that] may gather to the surface' during the shake-up in the Congress expected at Bombay.[106] Even Gandhi, who was later ready to make some concessions to the Congress Socialist Party in his constitutional proposals (as over the principle of proportional representation), made public his 'fundamental differences' with the C.S.P. programme, attacking the idea of the necessity of class war as 'not sound'.[107] The Congress Socialists responded to these attacks by planning to take over the Congress and mould it into 'a Soviet of the representatives of the revolutionary classes and a true instrument for the attainment of independence and Socialism'.[108]

C.S.P. leaders argued that while they could not take over the Congress by 'parliamentary methods' they should represent the 'official opposition' within the movement. Although the Congress Socialists never succeeded in carrying any of their resolutions or amendments

against the wishes of the right wing in any Congress central deliberative body, they did provide a focus for discontent against the 'Gandhian' leadership. Even though the C.S.P. leaders had neither the
strength nor the inclination to force a split within the Congress,[109] they
could, on occasion, compel the 'Gandhian' leaders to compromise. The
Congress Socialist Party certainly did provide a consistent opposition.
The voices of its members were raised in dissent at the Swarajya Party
Conference at Ranchi in May 1934 (over the economic programme of
the Party), at the A.I.C.C. meeting at Patna (especially over the resolution giving Gandhi sole right to carry on civil disobedience independently of Congress control) and at the Bombay session. Here the
Socialists were the only group who were not bought off by Gandhi's
compromises in the Subjects Committee on the constitutional changes,
and moved resolutions condemning the constitution as a whole and the
spinning and *khaddar* clauses in particular.[110] All these were defeated,
however. The C.S.P. continued its opposition at the national level
throughout 1935, 1936 and 1937. In these years they had rather more
success. Although they never managed to defeat the 'Gandhians', they
did force a discussion on some of the major issues at the central Congress meetings.

The greatest strength of the Congress Socialist Party was not at the
centre, however, but in mobilising within the Congress workers and
peasants who had previously organised outside it. The relationship
between the Congress Socialist Party and the Bihar Kisan Sabha pro-
vides a good example of this. In Bihar in the late 1920s, various Kisan
Sabhas critical of the position of the great Bihar zamindars had been
organised. These included a group from Darbhanga who had fallen out
with the Maharaja of Darbhanga over local board politics, members of
the Bhumihar Brahmin Sabha who distrusted the dominance of Sir
Ganesh Dutta Singh in that body and in the P.L.C., and large tenants
from Gaya District who were concerned about the political pretensions
and economic exactions of the Tikari *Raj*. Agrarian politics in Bihar
were further complicated by the insistence of the Government of Bihar
and Orissa that evidence of support by both tenants and landlords was
necessary before they would allow any Tenancy Bill to be passed by the
P.L.C. Thus in 1932 when the Bihar United Party, led by the
Maharaja of Darbhanga, wanted to introduce a Tenancy Bill it also
had to set up a 'Kisan Sabha' of its own to convince the Government of
tenant support. In the early 1930s, the anti-zamindar groups combined
to oppose this Tenancy Bill and also the United Party's proposals,
designed to safeguard landed interests, for a second chamber for
Bihar's provincial legislature under the new reforms. However, the
leaders of the opposition, Dhanraj Sharma and Jamuna Karjee in Darbhanga, Swami Sahajanand Saraswati of the Bhumihar Sabha and
Jadunandan Sharma of Gaya, had little in common with each other

except their opposition to certain zamindars. In 1929, Swami Sahajanand had admitted that he could not establish even a Patna District
Kisan Sabha, let alone a provincial organisation, because of the factionalism of Bihar politics. Yet, at the Sonepur Fair of November 1929,
a rudimentary provincial organisation was established with the help of
a number of Congressmen – notably Kailash Behari Lal, Ram Brikash
Benipuri and Ramcharitra Singh – who were later to be prominent in
the Bihar Congress Socialist Party. But during Civil Disobedience,
especially from 1932, the Kisan agitation began to take a line of its own,
concentrating on the details of the future reforms and the district board
elections of 1933. In 1934 the 'socialist' Congressmen again became
interested in the Kisan Sabha. In April 1934, members of the Bihar
C.S.P. were elected in a 21/4 majority to the provincial Kisan Sabha
executive. The Socialists needed such a base as this for their assault on
the Congress leadership. They also wanted the Bihar Kisan Sabha to
come into line with a 'united front' of all leftist elements, by pressing for
the complete abolition of zamindari. This they achieved, somewhat
against the wishes of the purely Kisan leaders, at the Hajipur Conference early in 1935. In return for this, the Kisan leaders got welcome
support against the United Party's 'false' Kisan Sabhas. Also, guided
by the Congress Socialist Party leaders, the Sabha leaders began to
enter the Congress organisations, so that by 1936 factions dominated
by Kisan leaders had control of the Patna and Gaya D.C.C.s, and
formed sizeable minorities in the Champaran, Darbhanga and Saran
D.C.C.s. By January 1935 the influence of the Kisan Sabhas in provincial Congress politics was already sufficient to have Swami Sahajanand
appointed to the Working Committee of the B.P.C.C.[111]
     The Congress Socialist Party leaders in Bihar showed great astute-
ness in allying themselves with the Kisan Sabhas. Since the 'Gandhian'
programme had little popular appeal, the initiative in politics switched
to men like Swami Sahajanand with his network of political contacts
and influence over such potential agitators as sugar cane growers and
cane-crushing factory workers. One consequence of this was that the
'socialists', and also the 'right-wing' leaders, had to time their own
political conferences to coincide with meetings held by the Swami, who
alone could guarantee a good attendance. The effectiveness of the links
between the Congress Socialist and the Kisan Sabhas was noticed in
other provinces also. The U.P. Government commented:

> Actually this party is the only section of the Congress which seems to
> be thinking on concrete and practical lines; and if politics in India
> were realistic, it might command a considerable following.[112]

     The Congress Socialist Party leaders did not limit their alliances to
provincial agitation groups; they also tried to create viable national
organisations of trade unions and Kisan Sabhas. Here their efforts met

with less success. The extreme factionalism in the trade union groups, polarised into internecine conflict between the largest, the All India Trades' Union Congress, based mainly in Bombay, the 'moderate' National Federation of Trades' Unions, based mainly in South India, and the communist dominated 'Red Trades' Union Congress', consisting mainly of the members of the Girni Kamagar Union, defeated even the attempts of a special sub-committee of the Congress Socialist Party to find a common platform. Many Kisan leaders were extremely parochial in their outlook and were suspicious of the intentions of P. D. Tandon and J. P. Narain, who were trying to establish an All India Kisan Sabha. In December 1936 the first meeting of the All India Kisan Sabha was held at Faizpur, but by then Kisan leaders such as Swami Sahajanand and Professor Ranga of Andhra had been excluded from taking a hand in the selection of Congress candidates for the P.L.A. elections, and had lost faith in the tactics of the Congress Socialist Party.[113]

During 1935, the Congress Socialist leaders were mainly concerned with using agitations to create a base for themselves within the Congress. In 1936, however, with Jawaharlal Nehru as President of the Congress, they moved into the mainstream of nationalist politics. From April 1936 there were three members of the Party on the Working Committee and they hoped to influence Congress policy from the inside. This, in turn, provoked a reaction from the 'right wingers' of sufficient violence to shake them, at least temporarily, away from the stale dogmas of 'Gandhi-ism'. Because the Congress Socialists and Nehru attacked the vague expectations of Council Entry this issue became a trial of strength between the two groups in 1936. Council Entry was no more part of Gandhi's ideal than it had been of the Socialists' plan. But the direct Congress Socialist threat to the position of the 'Gandhians' in the Working Committee made them turn to Council Entry and to office acceptance as a means of winning back the support of provincial and local Congress leaders, who had had little enthusiasm for the orthodox Gandhian constructive programme.

The question of parliamentary politics had played a minor role in the events of 1935. At the Bombay session of 1934 the principle of an elected Parliamentary Board had been established, but the Board was still dominated by the old Swarajist rump of Ansari, Desai, Satyamurthi and Khaliquzzaman. When the Congress Socialists attacked the conduct of the Assembly party at the Jubblepore A.I.C.C. meeting of May 1935, the Working Committee sprang to the defence of the parliamentarians, but the top leadership did not change their attitude that the question of contesting elections and accepting office in the provinces was not relevant since the elections were such a long way off.[114] In August 1935 a Working Committee resolution deferred the issue until the next session of the Congress; at the Madras A.I.C.C. meeting in October another attempt to get a decision one way or the other was defeated on the grounds that it was still 'premature'. Those opposed to the established leadership saw in the deferment of the issue the sinister prospect of eventual Working Committee support for a full parliamentary programme. But in fact the Working Committee had not been won over. Although the old Swarajists, notably B. C. Roy, Ansari, Asaf Ali and Khaliquzzaman, campaigned actively for office acceptance, their advice was ignored by the Working Committee.[115] The 'Gandhian' leadership's stand on this issue was explained by Prasad in December 1935:

> It has been wrongly and unfairly assumed that the Working Committee has been thinking of nothing except offices under the New Constitution. We have not as a matter of fact given the matter any importance. On the other hand it is others who have been trying to force our hands to come to a decision.[116]

Early in 1936 Bhulbhai Desai still believed that the Congress would enter the Provincial Legislative Assembly election with no clearer policy than it had had in 1934. He complained to his diary that nobody seemed to think of the 'bother' of organising the elections and collecting funds as very important to the future of the Congress and that he did not want to be stuck with the job again himself.[117]

In 1935 Jawaharlal Nehru had been released from prison to accompany his dying wife to Austria. After her death he remained in Europe until February 1936. During his absence, both the 'socialists' and Gandhi looked to his return to India as the solution of their difficulties. As early as 1934, the Congress Socialist leaders had planned their strategy (the withdrawal from all Congress institutions) in the hope of joining with Nehru in a drive to take over the Congress.[118] In the brief period between his release from jail and his departure to Europe in 1935, Nehru had had talks with a number of 'left wing' leaders, notably P. D. Tandon, at which they decided to concentrate on a campaign to prevent the Congress accepting Ministries under the 1935 Government of India Act.[119] Gandhi also looked to Nehru, but as an ally against the Congress Socialists; he had several times publicly announced that Nehru was his heir and successor within the Congress. Much could be gained, Gandhi believed, by now giving Nehru the leadership of the Congress. On one hand, he would serve as a link with the socialist group and help to integrate them into the Congress, on the other, making Jawaharlal President might temper his radicalism. So Gandhi appealed to Nehru to take the helm as 'it was the only way in which much of the difficulties of the Working Committee and the bitter controversies of today could be avoided'.[120] Gandhi also admitted that Congress policy had run out of steam and needed the injection of new life and new ideas which Jawaharlal alone could give it.[121] Other Con-

gress leaders were not so sure on this point. The 'parliamentary' leaders – Ansari, Satyamurthi and Bhulabhai Desai – viewed Nehru's
re-emergence on the scene with suspicion, and resented the fact that a
man who had never made any secret of his opposition to constitutional
methods should be ushered so assiduously to the Presidential *gaddi* just
when the P.L.A. elections were to be held.[122] Ansari, Satyamurthi and
Desai all attempted to persuade Rajagopalachari to contest the Presidentship; however, they received little support from other leaders[123]
and Rajagopalachari, while admitting his concern at having 'dreamers
and sentimental men' in charge of the Congress,[124] refused to take such
drastic action.[125] Of the inner circle of 'Gandhians', Prasad, while
acknowledging that there were 'fundamental differences' with Jawaharlal, claimed that these had not prevented full co-operation before and
would not again, unless very radical changes were made in the Congress programme.[126]

Before Nehru returned to India, the 'Gandhians' thought that his
Presidentship would make little difference to their plans for the Congress. Despite his radical talk, they believed that Nehru would toe the
line and accept Gandhi's programme.[127] But the Working Committee
had to find some consensus on the twin issues of council entry and office
acceptance which were to be considered by the Lucknow Congress in
April 1936. Before this Congress met, new factors made a clash on these
questions almost inevitable. While in London, Nehru had made it clear
that he would only allow the Congress to contest the Provincial Legislative Assembly elections on the understanding that it did so only to
wreck the constitution from the inside.[128] In a series of letters to members of his family written from England, Nehru stressed that while he
would accept council entry he would have no truck with office acceptance. Nehru saw his most urgent task to be bringing Gandhi back into
the Congress to launch a new civil disobedience campaign.[129] While
Nehru was forcing the issue from one side, provincial opinion was
mobilising on the other. At a meeting of the Congress Parliamentary
Board in February 1936 the issue of office acceptance was again discussed. Almost all the members of the Board, representing important
opinion in most provinces, announced that they were in favour of contesting the elections. A majority also reported their provinces as want-
ing office acceptance too. Only the Punjab and Bengal were firmly
against accepting office; in the U.P., G. B. Pant was in favour of acceptance but had to propose the compromise of Congress refusing office
but supporting another ministry to keep in line with R. A. Kidwai who
was against a Congress ministry. But even Kidwai's objections were for
public consumption only; he admitted in private that he would be
happy to see a Congress ministry if his own influence on it were assured
and if Nehru gave it his blessing.[130] This strong indication of provincial
opinion took the Working Committee by surprise. Kripalani wrote to

Prasad that 'no-body could have imagined that there was such a strong opinion for accepting office' and predicted that Nehru's attitude would make the situation 'a little difficult'.[131]

With their calculations upset by the conflicting attitudes of Nehru and the provincial leaders, the 'Gandhians' began negotiations with Nehru on his return to India. The vehemence of his ideas and the willingness of Gandhi to humour him alarmed several members of the Working Committee. A series of talks took place throughout March and early April. At the New Delhi Working Committee meeting at the end of March, Jawaharlal insisted that no decision on office acceptance be taken at the Lucknow Congress. Gandhi agreed with this and no other member of the Working Committee felt confident enough to oppose them. After this meeting, G. B. Pant and B. Desai of the Parliamentary Board, who had attended the meeting as advisers, succeeded in convincing Patel that a stand had to be made somewhere, before Nehru's technique of creeping socialism entwined them fully. However, when Patel appealed to Gandhi to have the resolution reconsidered because he had been unable to attend the Working Committee meeting, Gandhi refused, saying that to do so would amount to a resolution of no confidence in Nehru.[132]

At the Lucknow Congress session of April 1936, Nehru succeeded in thoroughly annoying and alarming the right-wing leadership. His presidential speech was full of the language of revolution, if lacking in concrete ideas for carrying it out. Before the session he gave his support to resolutions seeking to further the Socialists' plans for the Congress, suggesting 'functional representation' for workers' and peasants' organisations in the Congress and an extension of the agrarian programme to include the abolition of zamindari. His Working Committee included three members of the Congress Socialist Party – J. P. Narain, Narendra Dev and Achhut Patwardhan – and, worst of all, he broke with convention by speaking against the Working Committee resolution on the parliamentary programme. In fact, the 'right-wing' countered these attacks effectively. Although they commanded a majority in the Subjects' Committee and the General Session, they could not risk appearing to split the Congress by their intransigence. So they were careful not to offer too drastic a snub to the newly-elected President. However, they did restrain Nehru somewhat. On the issue of 'Mass Contacts' the original Socialist suggestion for direct representation of workers' and peasants' organisations on Congress committees[133] was neatly side-stepped and instead a sub-committee of Prasad, J. P. Narain and J. Doulatram set up, to suggest ways in which, by amending its constitution, the Congress could 'develop closer association' with the 'masses' and establish links with existing peasant organisations.[134] When the Congress Socialists proposed an amendment in the Subjects Committee seeking to restore this resolution to their original intention, they were defeated 35/16.[135] Much the same watering-down process took place with the Agrarian Programme resolution. The original resolution, drafted by Nehru and P. D. Tandon, included recommendations for the abolition of zamindari, a 50 per cent reduction in rent and a moratorium on all agricultural debts. Despite the protests of a majority of the Working Committee, this resolution got as far as the Subjects Committee. Here, however, it had to be withdrawn and in the open session a much milder resolution was passed, which merely attributed the poverty, unemployment and indebtedness of the peasantry to faults in the tenancy and revenue systems and set out a questionnaire for P.C.C.s to recommend proposals.[136]

The resolution dealing with the Congress attitude to the new Constitution presented a more difficult problem. On the eve of the Lucknow session, Working Committee opinion on this matter was divided. Nehru was definitely against office acceptance – he thought it would be reactionary; since the Congress could not possibly win a majority in any province without seriously compromising itself, it was a waste of time and money to organise a large campaign – all that was needed was a small number of candidates controlled by the Working Committee and elected for propaganda reasons. The Prasad/Patel group were tentatively in favour of office acceptance, but only as a means to an end. They feared that if the Congress did not take full advantage of the opportunity offered by the P.L.A. elections, then other groups would make use of the ministries to harrass the Congress organisations and under-cut the appeal of a future agitation by piece-meal reforms.[137] The wording of the resolution underwent many changes as the members of the Working Committee tried to reach common ground. Jawaharlal's first drafts include several ideas he shared with the Congress Socialists, notably the running of a token campaign by the Working Committee alone, a definite commitment for the Congress to take all steps necessary to prevent the introduction of the new Constitution and an insistence on a special or general session of the Congress to decide the office acceptance question. The resolution actually introduced was milder. This merely laid down that the Congress would contest the elections 'in accordance with the mandate of the Congress and in persuance of its declared policy'; the A.I.C.C. was to to issue an election manifesto, the Working Committee was to appoint a new Parliamentary Board and the question of office acceptance was to be decided after the elections, by consultation between the A.I.C.C. and the P.C.C.s.[138] In the Subjects' Committee this resolution was passed easily by 48/5, despite Nehru's unprecedented action in speaking against it, as the socialists did not bother to vote; in the General Session, despite concerted Congress Socialist opposition, it was again passed.[139]

In repulsing the challenge of Nehru's socialist ideas, the 'Gandhian' leaders had drawn heavily on the support of the provincial leaders. The main concern of these men was to maintain, or improve, their position built up through internal politics within the P.C.C.s and to extend such a position into dominance of all politics in their provinces or districts. Any radical change in the rules of the Congress political game, such as the functional representation of workers' and peasants' organisations, or any strictures that would materially damage their prospects in the P.L.A. campaign, such as a radical agrarian programme or a merely symbolic election campaign, were opposed strenuously. However, the 'Gandhians' could not just capitalise on these hopes and fears for the Lucknow Congress, and then revert to an equally inimicable programme; the counter to the socialist challenge had now become the parliamentary not the constructive programme. This was clearly indicated when, in July 1936, the Working Committee appointed the Congress Parliamentary Board Executive. This Executive, consisting of Vallabhbhai Patel as President, Prasad and Pant as Secretaries and one representative from each major province, declared that its main purpose was to transform the Congress organisation into an electoral organisation, and to revitalise and reorientate it to this end.[140] Thus, temporarily at least, the Congress was not to be an organisation for revolution or an organ of the constructive programme, but a vote-getting machine.[141]

The issues at stake in central Congress political manoeuvres in 1936 now become somewhat blurred by a personal quarrel within the Working Committee. Although Nehru had appointed three members of the C.S.P. to his Working Committee, he had also included Patel, Prasad, Azad, Desai, Jamnalal Bajaj, Doulatram and Rajagopalachari, who had all opposed him at the Lucknow session. The tensions remained after the session ended. Although Gandhi was sanguine about the future of the Working Committee, feeling sure that Nehru would 'accept the decisions of the majority of his colleagues',[142] the next three months belied his expectations. Nehru did not accept that events at Lucknow represented his failure to convert the Congress to his own ideals, while the 'Gandhians' on their part became more over-suspicious than ever of his every move and utterance. The first clash occurred at the Working Committee meeting at the end of April. Here Nehru proposed to reawaken the 'mass contacts' issue by appointing special committees, composed largely of non-Working Committee members (or, in other words, Congress Socialists) to investigate and report on the problem of industrial labour and *zamindari* and *ryotwari* tenants. The discussion of this suggestion revealed what Nehru described as a 'difference of outlook which resulted in an ideological tug of war', and he offered his resignation. Only the personal intervention of Gandhi succeeded in papering over the cracks. A labour sub-committee (containing one Congress Socialist member out of five) was set up, but the agrarian committees were scrapped.[143] The next crisis occurred in late May and June when Nehru claimed that the Working Committee was not of his choosing.[144] Although he was simply defending himself against complaints that he had not included any women on the Committee, the 'Gandhians' took it as an unfair attack by Nehru upon themselves. It brought an immediate response. Gandhi replied to Nehru that his letter on this point had caused pain to himself, Patel, Prasad, and Rajagopalachari, while Patel assured Prasad that they had been placed in a 'humiliating position in which I for one would not agree to stay at any cost'.[145] The rift continued to grow, and even Gandhi proved powerless to heal it. Eventually the 'old guard' decided to use shock tactics; on 29 June a letter of resignation was sent to Nehru, signed by Prasad, Patel, S. R. Deo, Bajaj, Rajagopalachari, Kripalani and Doulatram. This had the required effect, Nehru appealed to Gandhi for help and by 1 July the resignations were withdrawn.[146]

Although by August Patel was commenting on the 'smooth and harmonious working' of the Working Committee,[147] the differences between Nehru and the majority had not been fully ironed out. But the election campaign could now proceed. In August the Working Committee passed a resolution (endorsed by the Bombay A.I.C.C. of the same month) that a decision on office acceptance would not be made until after the elections, but by now the 'right-wing' leadership was coming to regard office acceptance as inevitable if the Congress did well in the elections. Patel, admittedly, had only declared himself in favour of office acceptance in order to force an immediate constitutional crisis with the *Raj*, but Prasad favoured it because 'the people today, as I see it, want small good things done for them; they would not like complete deadlock or mere obstruction'. He thought that reforms could be made by Congress ministries in education, land revenue and in pushing on the constructive programme.[148] By December, Prasad was saying that if the Congress controlled Government and the legislatures it would be much stronger.[149]

The chief reason for this attitude on the part of the leaders was the inexorable pressure of provincial followers,[150] but the threat from Nehru and the Congress Socialists had also influenced them. The tensions between Nehru and the other members of the Working Committee came into the open again before the Faizpur Congress. Since the Lucknow and Faizpur Congresses were only eight months apart, Gandhi was anxious that Jawaharlal should be allowed another term in office in order to keep a contact with the 'left-wing' during the first difficult months of the new Constitution. However, Nehru's public and private statements that if he were re-elected it would amount to a public affirmation of support for his policies and programme, annoyed Patel and his colleagues. As early as September, Prasad, Patel and

Desai were trying to persuade Rajagopalachari to run as presidential candidate. However, Rajagopalachari consistently refused[151] and Gandhi supported his refusal. By November Patel was desperately casting around for a candidate, asking Prasad to stand and finally deciding to accept nomination himself. Gandhi, however, was adamant that there should be no contested election and so, despite their fears that Nehru's re-election would 'mean a substantial weakening of the Congress and a disturbance of the present programme',[152] the right-wingers grudgingly agreed to leave him a clear run.[153]

At the Faizpur Congress in December 1936 the Working Committee resolution to again defer the decision on office acceptance until all the election results were available was passed without difficulty.[154] The A.I.C.C. meeting was arranged for March, and in early February a circular was issued to all P.C.C.s asking them, after consulting district opinion, to report their views on office acceptance. Within the Working Committee Nehru, Dev and Patwardhan still opposed office acceptance, while the majority were in favour. At the meeting held at Wardha on 27 and 28 February 1937 Gandhi, who regarded such a concession to political materialism as retrograde, set himself to find a compromise. This he did by suggesting that the Congress should declare itself in favour of accepting ministries, in provinces where it had a majority, only if the Governors of those provinces agreed not to make use of their special executive powers under the 1935 Government of India Act, and thus tacitly accepted the Congress as the real voice of the Indian people. Although the majority of the Committee regarded this proposal as 'impractical and difficult', it was accepted to preserve unity.[155]

Before the next Working Committee meeting, called to frame the resolution to be put before the A.I.C.C. at the end of March, the views of the provinces had become known. Of the eighteen Congress provinces who replied, thirteen expressed themselves as fully in favour of office acceptance, eleven of them with no mention of any special conditions.[156] Among the leading Congressmen of the six British Indian provinces (thirteen Congress Provinces) in which the Congress had secured a clear majority in the elections, there was little doubt about whether office should be accepted. Of these provinces, only Maharastra and the U.P. voted against a ministry, while in C.P., for example, rumours filtering down about conditional acceptance came as 'a great shock'.[157] The Working Committee met at Delhi from 15 March. Here Gandhi formally introduced his plan for conditional acceptance,[158] and was supported by Patel, Prasad, Khan Abdul Gaffar Khan, Bajaj, Doulatram, Desai, Pant and Kripalani. Mrs Naidu, despite her reservations, voted with the majority, leaving only Nehru, Dev and Patwardhan in opposition.[159] At the A.I.C.C. meeting, these proposals were attacked by the socialists, and by Satyamurthi's followers who wanted ministries at any price. Only the Congress Socialist amendment got as far as a vote, however, and was defeated 125/78, leaving the Working Committee resolution to be passed 127/70.[160] The Congress conditions, as stated in the resolution, were that 'the Governor will not use his special powers of interference or set aside the advice of the ministers'; not surprisingly these proved too stiff for the British to accept. By the end of March, the Congress had refused to form ministries in any province and the Governors were looking for substitute ministries among minority parties in the P.L.A.s.

The Congress leaders were now faced with the problem of what to do next. Although Nehru happily wrote to Prasad and Patel after the A.I.C.C. meeting that 'it is clear now that there is going to be no Congress Ministries anywhere',[161] none of the leaders were prepared to act on that assumption. The next two months saw a series of statements and counter-statements from the Secretary of State for India and the Viceroy and the Congress leaders. The British were determined not to give way on what they saw as an attempt by the Congress drastically to revise the 1935 Act by political blackmail.[162] The weakening came, in fact, from the Congress. Immediately after the breakdown of negotiations with the Governors, Gandhi, somewhat to the surprise of other Congressmen, stated that all the A.I.C.C. resolution required was a 'gentleman's agreement', not a formal commitment by the Governors,[163] while by June, statements by Patel and Pant had indicated that the only major issue at stake was that in the event of a crisis the Governors should dismiss the Ministers, not ask for their resignations.[164] By the Working Committee meeting of 5 to 7 July, it had become obvious even to Nehru and Gandhi that they could hold out no longer against the pressure from the local and provincial leaders to accept office. The feeling among local Congressmen was 'very strong' on this issue, even in Nehru's home town of Allahabad,[165] while five of the six P.L.A. Party leaders in the majority provinces also stressed the necessity of acceptance.[166] Within the Working Committee, Nehru, Dev and Patwardhan still held out in opposition, but the majority felt that, although the required assurances had not been given, the weight of opinion within the Congress should be respected and offices accepted. It was even decided that, since the vast bulk of the A.I.C.C. would favour office acceptance anyway, there was no need to summon that body to ratify the decision.[167] Even Nehru came to accept the necessity of this position, and wrote soon afterwards that the Working Committee decision was 'inevitable under the circumstances'.[168] So, taking what skimpy cover they could behind an unofficial statement by the Liberal peer, Lord Lothian, that the governors would not use their 'special powers' to interfere with the day-to-day administration of the Provinces,[169] the Working Committee bowed to the inevitable, and allowed Congressmen to enjoy the full fruits of their victory.

Contemporary observers, both Indian and British, had claimed as
early as 1934 that the policy of Council Entry would lead inevitably to a
policy of office acceptance. Undoubtedly the desire to enjoy the fruits of
power had played a great part in provincial and district Congress
politics since 1934. That office would be accepted in 1937 was the
underlying assumption which governed much of the internal factional
fighting in the provinces, the Congress election campaign and the relationship between the Congress and other political groups. Although
provincial opinion had some effect on the decisions of the national
leaders, especially in 1937, it does not wholly explain their attitude.
The national leaders did not always follow the wishes of their counter-
parts in subordinate Congress organisations. Local Congress bosses
were concerned to build a party – a caucus or machine to consolidate
their local position; the national leaders, both 'Gandhians' and Nehru,
were concerned to build a national movement, held together by obedience and self-sacrifice. Discipline, they realised, was the key to an
effective mass movement, and such a movement was essential since
parliamentary activity alone would strain the unity of the Congress and
would not advance the struggle with the British. If the Congress
worked inside a political system imposed by the British it could never
effectively overthrow it. Since no one believed that the British would
ever voluntarily give up India, it was necessary to devise some way of
keeping pressure on them.

What the national leadership of a national movement needed above
all was a common strategy for the movement. Between 1934 and 1936
the 'Gandhian' leaders lost their way. Once they had failed in 1934 to
convert the Congress to their plans they had no effective programme
with which to lead the movement.[170] The irrelevance of the constructive programme isolated them from the bulk of Congressmen. Their
role as the formulators of ideology was threatened by the Congress
Socialists. For these reasons they turned to the parliamentary programme. By adopting the parliamentary programme as their own, and
protecting it against attacks from within the Congress, they re-
established their position between 1937 and 1939. But they achieved
this only at a price; once Congressmen were established in the provincial governments it was their wants and needs that dominated even
central Congress politics. The activities of Congressmen in the provinces now became the single most important determinant of the political life of the Congress. So to understand even events at the national
level for the rest of our period, we must now look at what was happening in the Congress organisations in the provinces, districts and
localities of British India.

3 Provincial Congress Politics 1934–9

This book is a study of policy and politics at the all-India level. Only by looking at the activities of the national leadership of the Congress can we secure an overall view of Indian politics in this period, a picture that cannot be pieced together from provincial studies alone. However, as we have already seen, the Congress national leadership did not operate in a vacuum; an all-India history of the Congress would be meaningless if events in the provinces and localities were ignored. To understand events in the provincial Congress organisations we must first elucidate the ground-rules of Congress politics, which were those set out by the Bombay Constitution of 1934. These new arrangements balanced greater popular participation with greater hierarchical control. Previously the organisation had run on a system of indirect elections; now a single annual election was held at which the primary members elected the delegates to the annual Congress session, and the same men served on the P.C.C., the D.C.C. and the local Congress committees. Thus the provincial level of the Congress was thrown open to those who could enrol members and mobilise their votes in the localities.

These elections were not quite a free-for-all. Six months' membership was required as a voting qualification and anyone standing for election had to have a certificate proving that they wore *khaddar* regularly and had completed the spinning or manual labour qualification. The annual elections took place on the basis of one delegate per 500 primary members. The size of each province's quota of delegates and of its P.C.C. and subordinate committees was fixed in ratio to its membership enrolment. The full 2000 Congress delegates could not be elected unless one million primary members were enrolled; in fact only 473,000 were enrolled in 1935 and 636,000 in 1936,[1] and about half the places in the Congress hierarchy in the provinces were vacant in 1935. The Congress Socialists and many provincial leaders protested about this state of affairs and the Working Committee was forced to set up a Constitution Sub-Committee to reconsider the offending clauses. After consulting with the P.C.C.s, this Sub-Committee recommended various amendments which were passed at the Lucknow Congress of April 1936. The membership qualification for franchise at the annual elections was reduced to three months, the manual labour and spinning clauses were removed and the ratio of delegates to members reduced to

1 : 250, with a ceiling of no more than one delegate for every 100,000 population of the province. The maximum sizes of the annual session, the A.I.C.C. and the P.C.C.s were also increased by one-third.[2] These amendments, forced on the Working Committee by provincial opinion, increased participation in Congress politics to the level of incipient anarchy.

Since the constitution laid such stress on direct elections and mass participation, the business of enrolling members became a dominant feature of political activity. Despite all the paraphernalia of rules and regulations, in practice it was not possible to prevent bogus members being enrolled and votes being bought and sold, even when the members of the executives wished to do so. As the frequent investigations of election complaints make clear, forgery and connivance in P.C.C. and D.C.C. offices made the rules little more than hurdles over which the nimble politicians had to leap. The task of checking rolls and forms was a forum for constant struggle between leaders who understood how important this was in influencing who got elected. To secure a seat on a Congress body was rapidly becoming a full-time battle for these freedom-fighters:

> As for the elections, the Congress workers have no other work throughout the year except that of keeping an eye on their seat on the Congress body. Three or four months before the last date of enrolment they get about from village to village and door to door and complete the quota for getting [a] delegate's seat. . . . After the closing date, the candidate makes a tour with the Congress money if he is in office in the name of propaganda, but really for the purpose of canvassing votes. . . . Out of 12 months 7 or 8 months are spent for election purposes alone. For the remaining four or five months he takes a rest.[3]

The 1934 constitution had also given new powers to the Congress Executives. The P.C.C. Executive Committee (and in some places the D.C.C. Executive Committees) had the power to issue the membership forms, scrutinise them and reject those found invalid, to issue certificates of *khaddar*-wearing and of completion of the spinning or manual labour qualification, to fix the constituency boundaries for the annual elections and to hear complaints and decide disputes arising from subordinate committees. These provisions, which were designed to eliminate corruption and establish standardisation, in practice gave the executive committees of district and provincial Congress organisations great control over the election of their successors. As the competition for dominance of the subordinate Congress committees hotted up, these powers were greatly abused and members were accepted or rejected arbitrarily, the *khaddar* and spinning clauses waived or imposed according to circumstances, and gerrymandering and conniving in the enrolment of bogus members became common.

It was in Mahakoshal (the Hindi-speaking areas of the Central Provinces) that the art of the manipulation of Congress institutions found its most talented practitioners. There were two rival groups of provincial Congress leaders. One set, based on Jubblepore District in the north of the Province, was headed by S. G. Das and D. P. Misra. The other was based on the eastern Chhattisgarh Division and led by Ravi Shanker Shukla of Raipur. In the reconstruction of the Congress organisation after civil disobedience, Shukla had been elected President of the P.C.C. with Misra as a vice-President. The next two and a half years were to be dominated by Shukla's attempts to maintain his pre-eminence by exploiting his executive powers under the 1934 constitution.

The constitutions of each P.C.C. had to be revised to bring them into line with the new rules laid down at Bombay. Shukla made a determined attempt to rewrite the Mahakoshal provincial constitution in such a way as to ensure permanent control by his own faction. Under the Bombay regulations D.C.C.s were allowed to extend their influence over adjacent areas of Native States. For every 500 members enrolled in these States one delegate to the Congress could be elected (even if there were no Congress organisation there). So district Congress leaders were keen to make use of adjacent States as a vote bank to increase their following on the P.C.C. In Mahakoshal there were two such areas of Native States – Bundlekhand, bordering Jubblepore District, and the states of Chhattisgarh Division. Under the new P.C.C. constitution published by Shukla in February 1935 the Bundlekhand States were to have a separate D.C.C. but the Chhattisgarh States were to be divided up among the D.C.C.s of Chhattisgarh Division. The boundaries of the Raipur D.C.C. were also to be extended to absorb the two *teshils*, Dhamtari and Mahasamund, that in 1924 had been allowed to set up as an independent D.C.C. to escape Shukla's dominance. Thus, of the projected 88 places on the P.C.C., 24 were to go to the districts of Chhattisgarh Division and another 11 to the Chhattisgarh States. Despite a lot of sharp practice Shukla was unable to get this constitution ratified by the P.C.C. and, after the A.I.C.C. office had been called in to arbitrate, a compromise was reached by which the Chhattisgarh States were given a separate D.C.C.

Shukla also used his powers as P.C.C. President to strike at his opponents' home base in Jubblepore. The minority faction within that district was led by Dr George da Silva. In September 1935 Shukla declared 3500 of the members enrolled by Das and Misra to be invalid because their forms were not returned in time and because unofficial membership forms had been used in some places. Shukla had played a part in causing these breaches in the enrolment regulations – his P.C.C. Secretary had been very slow in sending authorised membership forms to Jubblepore. The President of the P.C.C. was also allowed to select his own Executive Committee and Shukla used this power to form alliances in districts where he had no direct influence. Both in selecting his P.C.C. Executive in January 1936 and in appointing the Provincial Parliamentary Board in May of the same year, Shukla gave places to the minority faction leaders of several districts, whose influence was thus dependent on his patronage. The most striking example of this was in Jubblepore, where Das and Misra were so busy complaining to the A.I.C.C. office about the exclusion of the 3500 members that Shukla was able to appoint da Silva as his vice-President on the P.C.C. without interference. But control based on an alliance of out-groups could not be secure; if the majorities in the D.C.C.s were to ally against him, Shukla would have to compromise. Once Das and Misra reasserted control over the Jubblepore D.C.C. in the elections of April 1936 (their new power being based on the control of local patronage that they had secured through their victory in the Municipal Council elections a few months before), the writing was on the wall. After a series of petitions by his opponents to the Congress President, Shukla was forced to compromise in August 1936 and consent to the establishment of a composite Parliamentary Board with a neutral Chairman, Makhanlal Chaturvedi. This compromise survived, and the Mahakoshal leaders closed their ranks to fight the P.L.A. elections without factional dispute.[4]

The events in Mahakoshal demonstrate both the strengths and weaknesses of the provincial leaders' ability to build up a political machine within the Congress using the new powers granted to them under the 1934 constitution. In Mahakoshal Shukla needed allies in the districts to secure his control over the provincial centre. Since he was trying to establish a unitary, not a coalition, control he had to deal with minority faction leaders who were not in a position to demand any independence as the price of their support. But this system was unstable simply because his local allies were not in control of their own localities. The particular developments in each provincial Congress were firmly tied to the peculiar circumstances of each province. As a broad generalisation we can, at least, say that in large provinces, where the local Congress organisations were the most extensive and vigorous, the twin strands of centralisation and decentralisation in the Congress constitution met at the district, not the provincial level. In many respects it was the district that became the basic unit of the Congress faction-system.

Just as there was a leadership vacuum at the Congress centre during the mid-1930s, so there was in many provinces as provincial leaders wrestled for control and for the political initiative. Such splits in the provincial leadership were at their most destructive in the United Provinces. In 1934 several of the provincial leaders in the U.P., notably C.

B. Gupta of Lucknow and Dr Murarilal of Cawnpore, lost out in factional battles in their home areas over the selection of candidates to fight municipal and district board elections on the Congress ticket. Both men then escalated these local rivalries to the provincial level and tried to manipulate their power on the P.C.C. and the Lucknow Congress Reception Committee against their rivals in the localities. Other provincial leaders took sides in these personal vendettas and the day-to-day administration of the P.C.C. was brought to a standstill. Although these squabbles put the arrangements for the Congress session at Lucknow in jeopardy, even the all-India leaders were powerless to intervene. Eventually, order was restored only by the decision of the Provincial Executive to suspend the entire P.C.C. and to set up a small 'Board of Control' to manage provincial affairs. This Board had to remain in existence for seven months (November 1935 to May 1936) until the passions of the provincial leaders had cooled down.[5]

Even in provinces where they could co-operate without tearing the P.C.C. apart, provincial leaders could not find a programme of Congress activity to keep their subordinates usefully employed. In several provinces, attempts were made to implement the 'constructive programme' and to build up the influence of the Congress in preparation for the next mass action campaign. In the U.P. in 1934 attempts were made to found a permanent, paid corps of Congress activists. In Bihar the P.C.C. tried to set up a province-wide network of *ashrams*, one to each *thana*, manned by a permanent staff of Congress organisers. In Gujerat Vallabhbhai Patel drew up plans on similar lines – a series of *ashrams* to serve as centres for Congress activities. All these schemes failed for want of funds or lack of enthusiasm.[6] Lacking resources and a clear lead from above, and unsure of their hold over their subordinates, many provincial leaderships surrendered the initiative in provincial politics to others. In Bihar, for example, it was the Kisan Sabha leaders who dominated politics from 1934 to 1936. With the Congress programme still becalmed in the doldrums of Gandhi-ism[7] British officials noted that:

> . . . the Congressmen are now trying to associate themselves with the Kisan Sabha movement to restore their waning influence . . . .[8]

and that:

> . . . other parties seem to be realising that politics is not a live issue in the muffosil and they are all showing a tendency to link up their work with that of the Kisan Sabha to whose meetings Swami Sahajanand can attract audiences because he deals with grievances in which there is a live interest. . . .[9]

Even the provincial Congress acknowledged this debt, admitting that in 1934 and 1935 it was the Kisan Sabha that had kept the name of the Congress in the popular mind.[10]

After the end of civil disobedience the all-India Congress leaders were unable to provide an effective policy for the movement. Provincial leaders in their turn could not supply the vital spark needed to keep the flame of sacrifice burning in the hearts of their subordinates. Factional conflict and accommodation became the main activity of Congressmen. But the statement that factionalism dominated the Congress institutions must not be taken simply as a slur on the moral integrity of the nationalist movement, or as no more than a proof that the devil finds work for idle hands. The growth of faction-systems within the Congress had a positive, as well as a negative, effect. We have seen that success in these internal battles depended on Congressmen's contacts in the wider political world (in particular, on their ability to enrol new members) and on their relationship with other groups in the higher and lower echelons of the organisation. To maintain or improve their position within the Congress, politicians were encouraged to look outside its confines and to build vertical relationships within it. These relationships, based on the driving force of mutual political benefit, could build up strong links within the provincial organisations founded on considerations more powerful than the old ones of respect, deference and the formal chain of command of the institutional structure. The new regulations of the 1934 constitution helped to make the faction-system more coherent and more intense. To understand the actions of any group of Congressmen, inside or outside the Congress, it becomes increasingly necessary to assess their position in this faction-system. These conflicts became the chief dynamic of Congress activity. As the Congress came to dominate the provinces more and more, the role of faction within the Congress grew to dominate the politics of most of British India.

Of course politicians were only prepared to fight hard to create or maintain influence in the Congress when such influence could bring them some long or short term benefit. It was the victories in the Provincial Legislative Assembly elections in the winter of 1936–7 that brought the biggest rewards for Congressmen. These elections were fought under new conditions; the electorate was five times larger than the electorate for the old Provincial Legislative Councils of the 1919 Government of India Act and the new Assemblies had direct control over the entire executive government of the provinces. The Congress successes were striking – in five provinces (Madras, Bihar, Orissa, the Central Provinces and the United Provinces) it won a clear majority, in Bombay it formed easily the largest party in the P.L.A., in Assam and the North West Frontier Province it could only be kept out of power by an uneasy coalition of its opponents. Only in Bengal, the Punjab and Sindh did the Congress seem to have no hope of ministerial power.[11]

Province	Total Seats	Seats won by Congress	Percentage won by Congress
Madras	215	159	74
Bihar	152	95	62·5
Orissa	60	36	60
C.P.	122	70	57
U.P.	228	134	59
Bombay	175	86	49
Assam	108	35	32
N.W.F.P.	50	19	38
Bengal	250	60	24
Punjab	175	18	10
Sindh	60	7	12

Source: P. Sitaramayya, *History of the Indian National Congress Vol. II* (Bombay, 1945) p. 39.

Contemporaries all stressed the strength of the Congress as a 'movement'[12] in explaining this success. The United Provinces Government, for example, gave the reasons for the Congress victory as its army of canvassers, the exploitation of Gandhi's name, speaking tours by all-India leaders, 'wild promises' of reductions in rent and agricultural debt, the lack of organisation of the rival parties and the clever exploitation of the new electoral rules by the Congress.[13] The lowering of the franchise, especially, was greatly used by loyalists as an excuse to explain their poor performance. As the Nawab of Chhatari, an ex-minister in the United Provinces dyarchy administration, wrote to Sapru:

> . . . although we used to advocate lowering the franchise . . . I am sure that we have lowered the franchise too much, having regard to the condition of our electorate.[14]

The new voting qualifications increased the electorate from 7,049,372 for the whole of India – 2·75 per cent of the total population and an average of 9421 electors to every seat – to 35,982,000 – 13·3 per cent of the total population and an average of 25,406 electors per seat.[15] The new qualifications had been arrived at almost by accident. Taking its cue from the report of the Indian Statutory Commission, the Franchise Sub-Committee of the first Round Table Conference had suggested, arbitrarily that 10 per cent of the population should be enfranchised under the new constitution.[16] The Indian Franchise Committee, appointed by Parliament in 1932, was given instructions to implement this. This Committee then asked Provincial Governments to submit proposals. Rather unwillingly they did so, by simply extending the existing property qualifications to bring the electorate to the required level.[17] The Franchise Committee then supplemented these with additional qualifications designed to create an electorate representative of 'the various classes of the population',[18] increasing the numbers of Depressed Caste members and women and including an educational qualification (completion of upper primary school level).[19]

Much work still needs to be done to determine the composition of these new electorates. At present it is impossible to estimate the new interests which were brought into formal politics by the 1935 Act, or even to establish who exactly was enfranchised. But clearly a large number of people who had had little or no previous direct contact with the electoral governmental institutions were now given the vote. In the 1920s the franchise qualifications for the local boards had been considerably lower than those for the provincial legislatures, but, in most provinces, even these limits were higher than those introduced for the provincial elections in 1937.[20]

In these circumstances Congress politicians, skilled in the mass canvassing techniques of agitational politics and in getting out the votes for the Congress elections, and supported by an army of political workers, had an immense advantage. In a country such as India – with a largely pre-industrial, peasant economy, slow communications and a low literacy rate – merely printing new franchise qualifications was no guarantee at all that a significant number of the new electorate would be aware of their powers, much less use them. So the first priority of the Congress campaign-managers was to ensure that as many as possible of the voters were informed of their rights by Congress workers.[21] This accomplished, the canvassing machine went into top gear and bands of white-capped, *khaddar*-clad volunteers became a feature of the rural landscape.[22]

In rural areas the Congress leaders were able to cash in on their past opposition to the large zamindars in local and national agitations and to reawaken the bad feeling that had arisen between landlord and tenant at the time of the agrarian slump of the early 1930s. Especially in the U.P. the Congress workers were able to revive their role as 'peasant's friend'. Wild election promises were coupled with enquiries into grievances and propaganda urging tenants to petition the Congress, not the zamindars, for redress. The ties between local urban Congress leaders and the rural areas that had been developed for different ends during Civil Disobedience were also re-established.[23] Various legends have grown up about the feats of some Congress campaign-managers. One biographer of Rafi Ahmed Kidwai, who had overall charge of the Congress campaign in U.P., has claimed that Kidwai had a complete list of the number of voters in each locality and of the number expected to vote for the Congress. According to this account, Kidwai also managed to commandeer all vehicular transport in the U.P. and Bihar for the Congress on election days, not so that the

Congress could use it – their sturdy peasant supporters marched happily to the polls – but so that effete zamindars could not transport toadies to vote for them.[24] This strength in canvassing and organising was certainly one reason for the Congress success. As the Commissioner for Nagpur Division in the Central Provinces reported:

> In fact every contest has been the contest of an individual against a highly organised party with a wide-spread sentimental appeal. The Congress candidate everywhere has been supported by a host of voluntary workers, while the canvassers of independent candidates have been for the most part salaried workers, who have by no means always been faithful to their paymasters.[25]

It was not only in rural areas that the Congress techniques were effective. In his diary for the period, Dr Moonje, the Hindu communalist leader based in the Marathi-speaking area of the Central Provinces, gives a clear picture of the problems of mobilising even sophisticated urban politicians against the Congress. Moonje's (unsuccessful) campaign on behalf of Dr Paranjpye for Nagpur City constituency consisted of strengthening his colleagues' resolve against the organised destruction of their public meetings by hooligans imported by the Congress, and of desperately interviewing local men of influence to persuade them to vote for his nominee. In this he was consistently disappointed. When, for example, he went to see the managers of a local temple trust, the Shraddhanand Peth, who had about 500 votes under their control, he found that he had been forestalled – their support had already been promised to the President of the Civil Station Municipality in return for a grant for a school and to Dr Khare (the Congress candidate) who had offered to get them a cut in their rates for electric lighting.[26] It is this extreme parochialism that is the mark of the election campaigns for many seats, and only the Congress could combine sufficient knowledge of local conditions with a province-wide organisation.

Behind any explanation stressing the strength of the Congress as a 'movement' in accounting for its electoral victory hangs the shadowy spectre of nationalism. It is, of course, impossible to prove that nobody voted for Congress simply because they wanted to see the end of British rule, but also it cannot be accepted that this was the only reason for the Congress victories. No explanation of the 1937 elections based solely on the power of the emotional appeal of the Congress can be very satisfactory. It is true that the main plank of the rhetoric of the Congress campaign presented the elections as a clear fight between the *Raj* and its collaborators on the one hand and the Congress and nationalism on the other. But this propaganda, which equated being anti-goverment with being anti-British and being anti-British with being pro-Congress, had a specific relevance in the system of local politics which had grown

up in the 1920s in most provinces, where those who had been excluded
from loyalist ministerial patronage, or who had been attacked in their
localities by the ministers' use of their provincial power, far outnumbered those who had benefited from the system. In Madras, for example, the Raja of Bobbili's ministry had mobilised for the P.L.A. elections by using all the punitive powers of provincial government (suppression and bifurcation of local boards etc.) against its opponents in
the districts.[27] Thus the Congress was swept to power on a wave of
disaffection, but it was a disaffection born of frustrated ambition and
one that could later be raised against a Congress ministry in its turn.

The weakness of the political systems that had grown up under
dyarchy also aided the Congress victory by making any opposition
ineffective in most provinces. One of the main features of the 1920s had
been the lack of stability of the provincial ministries – only in two or
three provinces could any sort of joint ministerial responsibility be
established at all.[28] By 1936 these incipient rivalries resulted in the
fragmentation of any opposition to the Congress as each ex-minister
looked to his own salvation at the expense of his erstwhile colleagues.
In the United Provinces, successive Governors had worked hard to set
up a 'conservative' opposition party to the Congress, using the large
landlords and prominent members of the business community.
Founded with the help of Sir Malcolm Hailey between 1932 and
1934,[29] the National Agriculturalist Party was led by two of the most
important politicians of the dyarchy period, the Nawab of Chhatari
and Sir J. P. Srivastava. When the Party came to organise for the
P.L.A. elections, however, factions and rivalries destroyed its effectiveness. The Hindu and Muslim leaders kept a second string to their bows
by building up the provincial Hindu Sabha and Muslim League
respectively and the rivalry of Srivastava and Chhatari, expressed in
communal terms, prevented the creation of any strong single leadership
or organisation. In August 1936 the party was unable to elect a new
Executive,[30] while the only Parliamentary Board that could be
appointed was one consisting of 112 members.[31] With its top leadership
so split, it is not surprising that the N.A.P. did so badly in the elections,
winning only eight of the 66 Muslim seats and nine of the 144 General
seats.[32] In the constituencies that they contested against the Congress,
the N.A.P. candidates could rely only on their own influence and that
of their personal followers; in the new electorates they were sunk without trace.[33]

One of the problems in discussing the 1937 elections is that much of
the basic material is not available. It is difficult enough to find a
complete and accurate statement of the results, let alone any of the
information needed for the more sophisticated techniques of election
studies.[34] But if we turn to studies based on elections in India after
independence (for which more information is available) we find that

although efficiency of organisation and lack of opposition are given
some weight in explaining victory at the polls, a quite different scheme
of analysis is also suggested. Elections in modern India, it is claimed,
are won by the Congress not as a 'movement' but as a 'machine';[35]
success is dependent on careful candidate selection, vote manipulation
and links with dominant groups in each locality.

Most students of post-independence India have a poor opinion of the
electorate; it is, in Kothari's words, 'politically speaking . . . an
amorphous mass, unorganised and undifferentiated.'[36] In these circumstances the vital role is given not to ideology but to the 'inter-
mediaries' or 'brokers' – local magnates who can control and mobilise
votes by dominance of local government, development agencies and
informal systems of influence and linkage.[37] The message of the best of
recent Indian election studies is that party performance at the polls
depends on a complex system of factional interplay and rivalry both
within the local party and within the electorate.[38] In this analysis, the
electoral success of the Congress since 1947 is based on the party's
ability to draw into it, and keep within it, the maximum number of
local magnates. Conversely, where the Congress is weak it is because
the local party has been unable to balance the demands of enough of
the important factions. The internal politics of the Congress organisation is the key to this; as P. R. Brass has put it:

> a remarkable feature of the functioning of the Congress is the extent
> to which variations in its strength from state to state depend upon
> internal factors such as factionalism and leadership within the party
> rather than upon differences in the patterns of local inter-party
> competition.[39]

How much of this analysis is relevant to the 1937 elections? Political
scientists have, understandably enough, paid little attention to the pre-
independence period and its elections; the Congress before 1947 is seen
as a broad-based national movement in which sectional interests were
subordinated to a higher goal and kept under control by strong central
control and a quasi-military discipline.[40] The rise of the professional,
careerist political entrepreneur is seen as a post-independence
phenomenon.[41] But a close look at the internal politics of the Congress
at the local and provincial level in the 1930s reveals that it was almost
as much of a 'party system'[42] before independence as it was to become
afterwards. In view of this, it is worth trying to push some of the
analysis of the political scientists back into the period before 1947.

Of course the elections of 1936–7 differed from those after independence in that they were fought on a limited electorate, not on universal
adult suffrage. But in view of the proportion of those who actually voted
in 1937,[43] we can assume that the limited electorate contained a fair
sprinkling of the politically unsophisticated, while the political

operators of the later period were more likely than not to have been among the 14 per cent enfranchised in 1937. Recent work on Madras Presidency has revealed that, in some areas at least, local-level leaders similar to the 'brokers' of post-independence India had already emerged. These men, their power based on control of local government institutions, co-operative banks and the networks of marketing and agrarian credit, had taken on a vital role in local and provincial politics by the 1920s. Driven by the impetus of local and provincial faction-systems and by a desire to secure and extend their influence, such men had come into the Congress by the 1930s.[44] In his survey of Congress members of the *Lok Sabha* in 1952–62 and of the Council of Ministers in selected States from 1945–65, S. A. Kochanek discovered that the most significant group to join the Congress in the 1930s were middle-level agriculturalists and professional men with strong links to rural areas.[45] According to recent work by C. J. Baker on the 1937 elections in Madras, it was such men, who had often been active in local board politics in the 1920s, who joined the Congress between 1935 and 1937 to fight the P.L.A. elections and who ensured the success of the Congress. Of the 137 Congress M.L.A.s elected from the Madras constituencies in 1937, 77 had been involved in local government, nearly half of them over ten years, and 31 were also prominent in co-operative societies and local banks. One-third of the M.L.A.s can be identified as recent adherents of the Congress, either time-servers or local politicians from remote areas who had never previously felt it necessary to identify with any provincial party.[46] This analysis is supported by the remark of Dr Rajan, a Madrasi Congress leader, to Bhulbhai Desai, warning him not to be misled by the spectacular successes of the Congress in the district board elections of 1935 and 1936 because:

> success has been possible because a considerable number of men who are not really Congressmen have, to serve their own purpose, adopted the Congress because it suited them as well as local Congressmen with a view to secure support.[47]

These men remained in the Congress to fight the P.L.A. elections too.

Examples from other provinces confirm this impression. The political antecedents of a few of the Congress candidates from the United Provinces serve to show the same pattern – in Banda District one Congress nominee, Keshav Chandra Singh, had previously been a Liberal Party M.L.C., a Congress Nationalist and a member of the anti-Congress faction of the U.P. Hindu Sabha (that led by Vikramajit Singh and Sir J. P. Srivastava), yet his candidature was approved. Sitapur District was dominated by one of the provincial landlord leaders, Raja Maheshwar Dayal Seth, who had set himself to build up the district as a model of organised landlord power. The Congress candidate against him was B. Jagannath Prasad Agarwal, who had been a

supporter of the Raja until a quarrel in 1936. The most prominent
Congress worker of the district, B. Narendra Dev Verma, who happened to be a socialist, was forced to stand as an independent.[48] In the
Central Provinces, of the 70 Congress M.L.A.s elected, at least 18 had
been members of a local board executive in the previous decade; only
19 were elected as Congress delegates to the Lucknow Congress (1936),
21 to Faizpur (1936), 24 to Haripura (1938), 25 to Tripuri (1939) and
19 to Ramgarh (1940).[49]

Two of the three criteria for the selection of candidates laid down by
the Congress Central Parliamentary Board were that those chosen
should have a chance of winning the election and be able to provide
their own finance.[50] These conditions favoured men of local standing,
substance and influence. But the story of Congress candidate-selection
is not simply one of local magnates knocking on a door opened to them
by an all-India policy decision. The integration of the Congress into the
wider world of local and provincial politics was a complex process, one
in which the dynamics of internal Congress factional conflict, at the
local and provincial level, played the main part.

The Congress election campaign in Bihar supplies some clear examples. We have already noted that it was the Kisan Sabha, not the
Congress leaders, who had taken the initiative in provincial politics.
Men connected with the Kisan movement had also reached positions of
importance in the Congress organisations; in alliance with the Congress Socialists they controlled the Patna D.C.C. and, for a time, the
Gaya D.C.C.; they were a substantial minority in the Darbhnga,
Champaran, Muzaffarpur and Monghyr D.C.C.s and were also important in the P.C.C. itself.[51] Not only 'left-wingers' but also established
Congress leaders allied with the Kisan Sabhas. Men like Shri Krishna
Singh (who had had a long association with Swami Sahajanand since
the days of the Bhumihar Brahmin Sabha in the 1920s) spoke at Sabha
meetings and adopted the Sabha organisations in their home districts
as their own. But in late 1935, under the influence of the Congress
Socialists, the Kisan Sabha made zamindari abolition the main plank
of its platform. As the P.L.A. elections approached, other Congress
leaders began to feel the need to assert themselves on this issue. In
January 1936 the P.C.C. set up a Kisan Enquiry Committee. Nominally this committee was formed to gather the information needed to
formulate a detailed Congress agrarian policy, but in practice it operated as a propaganda device against the Kisan Sabhas, to win the
support and trust of the landed classes for the Congress. Committee
members toured the province encouraging local Congressmen, making
speeches and attempting to assure local zamindars that the Congress
was not a party to the Kisan Sabha's attacks on them.[52] The Committee's report, which was never published, included several disparaging
references to the Kisan Sabha, its leaders and its programme.[53]

The development of this propaganda war increased tension in the provincial Congress, but it did not lead to a clear break. It was over the selection of the candidates for the P.L.A. elections, and from pressure from the district not the provincial level, that the split occurred which forced Sahajanand's resignation from the P.C.C. Working Committee and drove him into direct opposition to the established leaders. The machinery laid down for the selection of Congress candidates in Bihar was simplicity itself – no separate committee was formed, the P.C.C. Working Committee being given complete control. Each Congressman who wished to stand for election was to write to the Committee which would then send out representatives to assess the local standing of each applicant and then make the decision. Sahajanand, with his position on the Working Committee, seemed assured of a good deal of influence over this process of selection.

Provincial leaders made it clear that, in theory, all powers of selection would rest with them; no local Congressmen, not even D.C.C. Presidents, were to have special influence.[54] But in practice it was at the district level that most candidates were selected. A Congress ticket for the elections was greatly sought after – in October 1936 the P.C.C. office in Patna was surrounded by over 300 mutually hostile groups of potential candidates and their supporters.[55] The new M.L.A.s would have great power in their home districts and every district Congress faction leader strove to get his followers nominated. As factions within the district Congress organisations fought for dominance, their political horizons were forced outwards. They forged alliances with local magnates and local agitators and so, by internal factional struggle, brought a large slice of the local polity into the confines of the freedom movement.

Events in Darbhanga district give a good idea of what went on. The major political force in district politics was the Darbhanga *Raj.* In 1936 the *Raj* controlled the District Board under the chairmanship of the Maharaja's brother, Kumar Visheshwar Singh. The chief opposition group on the Board was led by Maheshwar Prasad Narain Singh, one of three brothers who owned extensive lands in Darbhanga and adjoining districts. There was also a small Congress group on the Board, led by Jagdish Narain Sinha, the brother of Satyanarain Sinha who led the majority party in the D.C.C. The minority party in the district Congress organisations was the Kisan Sabha group led by Jamuna Karjee and Dhanraj Sharma, which had been founded to oppose the *Raj* on tenancy and District Board matters and was aided and abetted in this by Maheshwar Prasad Narain Singh. The two main parties on the Board, those of the *Raj* and of Maheshwar, were fairly evenly matched, with the Congress group of five holding the balance. While the Kisan Sabha group on the Board consistently supported Maheshwar, the Congress group had switched its allegiance between the two major parties as circumstances and advantage dictated.

In March 1936 a major row blew up on the Board, as a result of which the Chairman decided to resign to test his support. The Congress group on the Board, which had up to then supported the Chairman, went to the Maharaja and offered renewed support only if Satyanarain Sinha, the D.C.C. President, was made Chairman with the support of the *Raj*. The Maharaja refused these terms, so Satyanarain Sinha and his brother turned their attention to a deal with Maheshwar. They succeeded in making an arrangement that covered not only the District Board, but the P.L.A. elections and the control of the D.C.C. as well. In return for disowning Jamuna Karjee and Dhanraj Sharma and for throwing all his support in the district behind Satyanarain Sinha, Maheshwar got support in the Board and a Congress P.L.A. nomination for his brother, Rameshwar Prasad Narain Sinha, and one of his agents, Suryanandan Thakur.[56]

When the P.C.C. Working Committee came to consider the arrangements for this district, they were confronted by a *fait accompli*. As a result of Satyanarain Sinha's dealings, they had to accept two non-Congressmen as candidates and, despite determined efforts by Sahajanand and Shri Krishna Singh, they could not repair the position of Karjee and Sharma.[57] This pattern was reproduced in other districts – the provincial leaders were largely powerless to reverse the *ad hoc* arrangements of a dominant district faction. Sahajanand actually resigned from the Working Committee over events in Muzaffarpur District when he found himself unable to counter the D.C.C. President's coup of excluding Kishori Prasana Sinha, a leading Congress Socialist and member of the provincial Kisan Sabha executive, from nomination as a P.L.A. candidate.[58] Overall, twelve Kisan Sabha candidates were selected in the province,[59] while Sahajanand was defeated over about a dozen more.[60]

Anugrah Narain Sinha, who took on most of the work of organising the election campaign, freely admitted that most of the Congress P.L.A. candidates were of the 'zamindari class' and that many zamindars had turned to the Congress as a result of the Kisan Sabha agitation.[61] But the candidate selection process was not simply a plot devised by the provincial leaders to rid themselves of the challenge of the Kisan Sabha threat.[62] Although the events of late 1936 came to be seen in ideological terms, at the time they were conditioned much more by the interaction of factional conflict within the Congress, at the district as well as at the provincial level. Kisan Sabha leaders at the district level were usually in a minority in the D.C.C.s and were not able to draw in such powerful outside allies as were their opponents. It was for these reasons that they tended to do so badly in the selection of candidates.

A study of the candidate selection process of any political organisation can give a good indication of its internal structure and centres of power and of the effective relationships between its various echelons. An analysis of the Congress selection process on these lines will be valuable. An all-India Parliamentary Committee composed of Prasad, Patel, Azad, Rajagopalachari, B. Desai, Narendra Dev, G. B. Pant and the Presidents of each P.C.C. had been founded in April 1936 'to take such steps as may be necessary in connection with the organisation of elections to the Congress'.[63] But so large a body was too unwieldy in practice and most of its business was carried out by Patel, as President, with the occasional assistance of Nehru or another of his colleagues. This Committee had complete supervisory control over all the selections made by provincial authorities of candidates for Congress tickets. Its task was thought important: Pant, who had been Secretary of the old Congress Parliamentary Board, had welcomed it:

> The work that lies ahead of us is almost stupendous and unless vigorous measures are taken forthwith in this direction the success of the Congress candidates in at least some of the provinces will be seriously jeopardised.[64]

But in practice, the all-India leaders did little to direct the election beyond making campaign speeches. The national leaders felt strongly that only good Congressmen should be rewarded with nominations,[65] but they could not do much to enforce their wishes. As Patel later assured a questioner on this point:

> It is impossible for me to interfere in the selection of candidates proposed by the Provincial Congress Committees, unless it is alleged and proved that the candidate so recommended is not a genuine Congressman or that there is something against that candidate that would justify his disqualification by the committee.[66]

Even within these boundaries, the all-India leaders were unwilling to delve into the murk of sub-provincial politics. Just as the provincial bodies, in practice, left much up to the district leaders, so the national Committee left provincial bosses to sort out their own affairs. The All-India Parliamentary Committee confined itself to hearing appeals against the provincial nominations; if the provincial list had caused no serious protests they let it past.[67] Even where alterations in the provincial lists were ordered, each case was considered on its merits – there was no consistent attempt to balance factions in the provincial body or to exclude Congressmen of whom the national leaders disapproved.[68]

Of the provinces with which we are dealing in detail, the all-India leaders gave their closest attention to Berar. Here the aberrations of Congress factionalism had resulted in an alliance between Biyani, head of the majority faction on the P.C.C., and the anti-Communal Award Democractic Swaraj Party under M. S. Aney. The members of the

Parliamentary Committee were very concerned that such a deal might
lead to the presence of Congress M.L.A.s who would fail to follow the
party line on the Communal Award. Both Patel and Nehru were convinced that an alliance with the Democractic Swaraj Party would be a
retrograde step and Patel refused to accept the Berar list of candidates.
But such negative sanctions were of little use and the national leaders
had to accept the alliance eventually, and be content only with a promise by Biyani and Aney that the Democratic Swarajists would follow
the Congress line on the Award and that none of them would be given a
ministry.[69]

The relationship between the provincial and district levels were
rather more complex. We have seen that, in Bihar, district leaders
could exert a good deal of autonomy in practice. In the United Provinces the same sort of pattern emerged. Here the supervision of candidate selection fell mainly to Nehru and Pant. Little of their correspondence has survived, but what there is indicates that the provincial
leaders' role was limited to filling the gaps left after the dynamics of
district-level factionalism had done their work.[70] In other provinces, in
Berar and Mahakoshal for example, the provincial faction-leaders had
much closer contacts with the districts and were able to control their
choice with more ease. There was still local factional conflict in these
provinces, but it was expressed in terms of the provincial factional
battle, not autonomously. A. Gaffar Khan, a pro-Misra leader of
Saugor District, Mahakoshal, wrote of the participation of the provincial leaderships in local affairs:

> Mr Shukla's attitude seems so hositile [sic] and with the present
> spirit it seems unavoidable [?] to give any co-operation to a party the
> leader of which has some ulterior motive behind everything.[71]

In Berar, Biyani felt sure enough of his position to cement his deal with
Aney by completely ditching the dominant Congress faction in one
district, Yeotmal, and allowing Aney to nominate his followers as Congress candidates for all seats of the district.[72]

The sources of finance drawn on by a party fighting an election are
another good indicator of the relationship between the various levels of
that organisation. Not only is it important to discover simply who pays
the piper, but also the degree of centralisation or decentralisation in the
funding of a campaign can reflect the amount of central authority and
local initiative at work. The methods used to finance the Congress
P.L.A. election campaign demonstrate again what the study of the
process of candidate selection has already told us – that although large
powers nominally lay with the central leaders, in practice it was the
local level that was most important. Taken as a whole, the Congress
expenditure (or rather the expenditure of Congress candidates) was
vast. Rajendra Prasad estimated that at least Rs 3–4000 would be

needed for each seat contested;[73] in practice this figure was fairly accurate. The election expenses of the eight Congress M.L.A.s in Berar averaged out at Rs 4500 each;[74] in the U.P. the amount spent by Congress candidates varied from under Rs 500 in some Scheduled Caste constituencies to the Rs 11,399 spent by the nominally socialist C. B. Gupta in Lucknow City. The average expenses of Congress candidates in the U.P. was only Rs 2667, but in absolute terms the Rs 376,068 they spent in the 141 seats they contested was a fabulous sum.[75] It is true that, in many cases, the expenses of Congress candidates were less, sometimes a great deal less, than their opponents; but it is also worth noting that of the 129 Congress M.L.A.s who won contested seats about one third spent more lavishly than any of their opponents.[76]

Overall, the Congress won 719 P.L.A. seats in the elections, and contested several more. The amount of money spent by Congress candidates on the elections was enormous, much too much for any single centralised agency to provide the resources. The Central Parliamentary Board realised this at its very first meeting and suggested to the provinces that every candidate should bear his own election expenses as far as was possible.[77] The only commitment which the Board accepted was to find money to help candidates who could not be expected to pay their own way – notably those contesting Scheduled and Backward Caste seats.[78] The central leaders looked to the Indian capitalists for money. But, as in 1934, such fund-raising was not easy. In February 1936, Bhulabhai Desai had noted how little the Indian business community was prepared to do for the Congress in terms of financing the P.L.A. election campaign. Although G. D. Birla was ready to pay his share and use his influence to raise the estimated Rs 500,000 that the Parliamentary Board would need, the most influential of the Bombay capitalists, Sir Purshottamdas Thakurdas and Sir Chunilal Mehta, refused to provide any money at all, leaving Desai's hopes resting on the Ahmedabad industrialists Ambalal Sarabhai and Kasturbhai Lalabhai.[79] Later on during the campaign the central leaders, chiefly Patel, Desai and Bajaj, were able to persuade some businessmen with special interests in certain provinces to give money to those provinces, but they acted only as brokers and had no say at all in how the money was spent. Even when they did give direct handouts to provincial leaders the effect was not always what they had intended – when Desai gave one of the Utkal leaders, Nilkantha Das, Rs 8000 for the election campaign it was used to pay for the expenses of Das's newspaper and to bolster up his position in provincial Congress politics.[80]

The provincial Congress organisations had little money of their own. Some of the P.C.C.s wanted to act as paymasters for the election campaign but their aspirations were defeated by lack of funds. The U.P.P.C.C., for example, suggested to the Parliamentary Board that they should be allowed to raise cash for the elections since otherwise some Congressmen would not be able to afford nomination for a Congress ticket. This suggestion was met by polite disbelief[81] – a disbelief well founded since the U.P.P.C.C. found that after making an initial payment of Rs 3500 to its provincial Parliamentary Committee it was unable to meet its day-to-day running expenses of the office.[82] The provincial organisations simply did not have enough money to finance the campaign – they could spare a few hundred rupees here and there but nothing more.

But some provinces did receive substantial sums from outside, the money raised by Patel, Desai and Bajaj from business men with local interests. One of the areas in which such money was needed most was Bihar. Here the provincial organisers spent at least Rs 37,000 in the election campaign.[83] Of this Rs 37,000 at least Rs 30,000 was arranged by Patel, Desai and Bajaj[84] – and at least Rs 27,000 of it came from one man, R. K. Dalmia.[85] Dalmia was a Marwari businessman and financier with extensive interests in cement manufacture, sugar mills and insurance, much of it in Bihar province. Dalmia's financial assistance was not disinterested; he was backing both sides anyway by giving an equal amount of money to Sir Ganesh Dutta Singh's election fund.[86] He also insisted on vetting the lists of Congress candidates and demanded, much against Prasad's wishes, the removal from the Congress ticket of at least one man – Bhuddan Ray – who had organised a labour agitation in one of Dalmia's mills.[87]

The Congress won 95 seats in Bihar; even taking a low estimate of Rs 2000 per seat, Dalmia's Rs 27,000 represented only a drop in the ocean of money spent by Bihari Congressmen on the election campaign. In any case, most of his money seems to have been siphoned off to pay for Muslim and, perhaps, Depressed Caste campaigns rather than those of regular Congressmen.[88] The bulk of the money spent came, in Bihar as elsewhere, from the candidates and their local supporters. As Anugrah Narayan Sinha, who did much of the detailed work on the provincial campaign in Bihar, later admitted, although the Congress leaders did not like having the newly converted nationalist zamindars standing in person for the P.L.A., they gave their consent in return for a substantial contribution to the campaign chest.[89]

In a study of the candidate selection process in Bihar and Rajasthan in 1957, 1962 and 1967, Ramashray Roy has drawn a number of general conclusions about the effect of various factional situations on the degree of centralisation or decentralisation at work.[90] His main finding is that, while the provincial leaders generally defer to the lower levels of the party in selection, where a provincial leadership feels unstable it will tend to impose, or seek to impose, its supporters on the district leaders.[91] In view of the scarcity of information and the variations in the methods of candidate selection, it is difficult to draw conclusions even as general as this for 1937. It does appear, however, that something of the reverse of Roy's finding applied; where the provincial leaders had little direct contact or control over the districts and where their position was made insecure by multiple factional rivalry and the threat of an alternative agitational organisation at the provincial level, as in Bihar, they could not do much but rubber-stamp the selections of the lower echelons. Where the provincial leadership had been able – thanks to closer physical contact and constitutional chicanery – to make itself indispensible to district-level leaders, as in Mahakoshal, it was able to take a larger part in the selection process. In any case, such speculation is not central to our argument; all that it is necessary to make clear is that the selection of Congress candidates for the 1937 elections did not simply follow the chain of command laid down by the Congress hierarchy. The considerations which influenced selection were the interplay of various factions within the district and provincial Congress organisations, and the interaction between these organisations. Success in such struggles did not only depend on any one faction's strength in internal politics, it was also decided by its ability to draw in forces from the wider political world outside the boundaries of the Congress.

Obviously the Congress's skill in canvassing, as well as its ability to make alliances with local magnates, was important in securing its electoral success. But the two phenomena cannot be clearly separated; one reason why so many local men of influence were eager to join the Congress was because it would make such a formidable opponent in the elections, one reason why the Congress vote-getting techniques were so effective was because they were supported by the influence of powerful local magnates. What is important about the 1937 elections is not merely that the Congress won so many convincing victories, but that, by its candidate selection processes and still more by its handling of the ministries, the Congress internal faction-system spread outwards to become the chief dynamic in local and provincial politics as a whole. It is this phenomenon that we must study most closely because it is by this that the local and provincial Congress organisations made their greatest contribution to the development of Indian politics. During our period, many Congressmen still had a romantic picture of themselves as members of 'a fighting machine . . . functioning on a high moral plane . . . an army following a strict moral discipline . . .' made up of men 'dedicated to the cause of freedom and to the cherished principles of the Congress'.[92] But by 1936 a new sort of Congressman was seen emerging. As one observer put it:

> You can find instances of one and the same individual being a member and office-bearer of a Taluq Congress Committee, a District Congress Committee and the Provincial Congress Committee,

a member and office bearer on a District Board, a member and office bearer in a municipal Corporation and with all these having a sure chance of being selected for a seat in the Legislative Assembly elections.[93]

This archetype was much nearer to the modern Congress boss than he was to the idealised freedom-fighter.

The 1937 election campaign had, for the first time since the end of civil disobedience, given the provincial and local Congress organisations a full-time and attractive programme. The electoral successes had at last made real the potential strength of the Congress and its ability to dominate the political stage. Now Congress and government were linked inextricably, with profound effects on both. The road to power and influence now lay through the Congress. Once in office, the Congress ministers were able to influence local administration and dispense governmental patronage. The ministers, M.L.A.s and D.C.C. leaders had the power to select the lists of candidates to be given Congress tickets for local board elections and nominations. Since the Congress now had an immense advantage in these elections, in the provinces in which the ministers were Congressmen, the real battle was not for election but for the Congress ticket, not at the hustings but within the Congress institutions.

But although Congressmen now controlled government, the Congress organisations also remained the most useful and influential political institutions open to those who were opposed to government in general, or to particular pieces of legislation. Thus the whole gamut of political activity in the provinces, districts and localities – competition to enjoy ministerial patronage or to obtain local legislative and executive power, as well as competition to lead agitations and to capitalise on real and imagined grievances against the government – all became expressed as competition within the Congress and for control of the Congress legislative and executive institutions. Between 1937 and 1939 Congressmen clearly dominated the political life of most provinces. They ran both the politics of the establishment – the search for power and influence through control of government institutions – and the politics of dissent – agitational movements against government power. The chief arena of political conflict now became not the provincial political scene as a whole, but the Congress institutional structure within it. The political life of the Congress became the political life of the provinces, and both local magnates and local agitators, whether established Congressmen or parvenus, were drawn into the net of Congress institutional politics. The Congress became more than a nationalist movement or a political party, it became the whole provincial political environment. The full range of provincial politics became expressed through its institutions and within its membership. This process enormously increased the status and influence of the Congress and Congressmen within local and provincial politics, but at the same time it stretched the unity and homogeneity of the movement almost to breaking point.

The Congress had always been a very open institution and one of the most striking features of the ministry period was the dramatic increase in its membership – an increase far greater than any that had resulted from the deliberate membership enrolment drives of the anti-government agitations. As the following figures indicate, a Congress that controlled government was far more attractive than one in revolt against the *Raj.*

Congress membership, all-India and certain provinces 1935–41

Province	1935–6[a]	1936–7[b]	1937–8[c]	1938–9[d]	1939–40[d]	1940–1[d]
Bihar	78,305	104,743	462,787	575,139	276,704	183,731
Utkal	6,819	5,760	87,857	197,201	126,126	45,792
Mahakoshal	24,527	35,986	85,607	126,554	110,119	n.a.
Nagpur	8,164	6,961	26,912	44,854	42,418	22,638
Vidarbha	7,054	11,692	46,728	78,396	44,733	14,878
U.P.	62,703	65,733	939,340	1,472,456	833,830	258,826
All-India	473,336	635,504	n.a.	4,511,858	2,973,452	1,481,616

a AICC P 31 1935
b AICC G 72 1936
c AICC G 78 1937
d I.B. circular memo no. 37/Cong/40 dated 24.5.41 in G.o.I. Home Department (Political) 4/6/41.

These figures clearly demonstrate the dramatic rise in Congress membership during the ministry period and the almost equally dramatic fall after the ministries had been abandoned. It must be stressed that this dramatic rise in membership in the ministry period was not simply caused by politicians who had previously been outside the Congress rushing to be numbered in its ranks. It also represents the efforts of Congress politicians to win new voters who would give them control over the Congress institutions. The Bombay constitition allowed 'a free pass into the institution on a payment of four annas'[94] and established Congressmen as well as parvenus took full advantage. The annual elections to the various Congress Committees now became the major political event of the year in many areas. As the local power and influence of the subordinate Congress Committees grew, so the effort to control them became more intense. The A.I.C.C. General Secretary, in his report to the Haripura Congress of February 1938, noted that:

> Our elections have become more elaborate than elections to local, provincial or central legislatures of the Government.[95]

Keeping the wheels of the Congress machinery running was often a full-time job. In Andhra province, for example, there were elections to over 12,000 different seats on Congress Committees and on local boards between July 1938 and June 1939. The business of selecting candidates, contesting elections and settling disputes took up most of the time of Congressmen in the province. What was left over was used to enrol members to influence the elections.[96]

One of the important stimuli to such activity as this was the approach of elections to local self-government bodies. If the P.L.A. elections had hinted that the high road to governmental power lay through the Congress institutions, the subsequent elections to district boards and municipal councils confirmed it. In many provinces, mobilising for these elections was the major activity of local Congress organisations during the ministry period. The inspectors sent out by the A.I.C.C. office to check on provincial and local Congress activities regularly commented on this in 1938 and 1939. The inspector sent to the Karnatak, for example, reported:

> Unfortunately I could not meet with any solid work, political or constructive, in the province. Wherever I went, I was told that they were doing nothing beyond enrolment and local bodies elections.[97]

In Berar it was the same story,[98] while in Bihar:

> Nothing in particular has been done except elections to local bodies being contested by the Congress in certain districts.[99]

Standard Congress activity, such as the extension of the organisation and campaigns to enrol members, was often linked directly to these elections. In Berar the village Congress Committees were only established to canvas for Congress candidates in the district board elections.[100] Of membership fluctuations in Andhra the inspector wrote:

> The relation between the District Board election and figures of enrolment of primary members makes interesting reading. Whenever the elections of the District Board were over last year, the enrolment went down considerably. On the contrary where the elections have to take place this year, under the guidance and control of the new D.C.C. that will be formed this year, the figures have swollen to a great extent.[101]

But while local self-government election campaigns increased the influence and importance of the Congress in political life, they also increased factional conflict and discord. The approach of these elections caused struggles within the Congress institutions to control the Committees that would make the nominations for the Congress ticket, and attempts by provincial leaders to minimise this competition by mediation and the imposition of control from above often merely resulted in increased bitterness and fragmentation at all levels of the organisation. In Bihar the provincial Congress leaders attempted to impose some sort of control as early as May 1937 by appointing a four-man committee to guide and supervise local board elections.[102] But this action caused an immediate reaction, and several district leaders who feared the consequences of control from above tried hastily to persuade the provincial leaders to back their own factions in the districts.[103] Some D.C.C.s, notably Gaya – which was controlled by an alliance of C.S.P. and Kisan Sabha men who were unlikely to get much sympathy from the provincial bosses – demanded that the districts be left free to nominate their own candidates.[104] In December 1938, with the elections imminent, the P.C.C. Working Committee compromised by setting up Divisional Committees for each of the four divisions of the province to arrange the campaign and recommend candidates to a P.C.C. Working Committee Sub-Committee. Some attempt was made to make these four-man committees representative of the different shades of opinion within the Congress – for example in Patna Division, where the 'left-wingers' were strongest, Jai Prakash Narain was given a place. But, in general, the committees still reflected the established Congress factions in each area.[105]

The Divisional Committees, far from removing rivalries, splits and revolts at the district Congress level, merely succeeded in bringing these squabbles into the provincial arena.[106] Usually, the Sub-Committee of the P.C.C. Working Committee simply rubber-stamped the recommendations of the Divisional Committees. These in turn generally just accepted the nominations of the D.C.C. Presidents, with no attempt to investigate the claims or standing of those candidates, or were used by the members of the Committee to push the interests of their friends.[107] The result of this was more strife in the local Congress institutions, which were already at sixes and sevens over the Bihar Government's deal with the large zamindars over Tenancy legislation. No D.C.C. was free from the accusation of 'corruption' as factions jockeyed for control. Disappointed Congressmen fell out of line and set up as candidates against the official party nominees. Thus in Muzaffarpur District, where Mahesh Prasad Narain Singh[108] controlled the D.C.C., the 'left-wing' Congressmen, identified with the Congress Socialists and the Kisan Sabhas, stood as Independents against the Congress candidates, and succeeded in winning five seats.[109] The work of the Patna Divisional Committee was nearly brought to a halt by the situation in Shahabad District. Here the rivalry in the D.C.C. between Sardar Harihar Singh, a member of the Committee, and Pt. Hargobind Misra, a member of the P.C.C. Working Committee, resulted in Misra's faction setting up candidates to oppose the official Congressmen – just the reverse of what had happened during the P.L.A. election campaign, when Harihar Singh had set up a non-Congress candidate against Misra.[110]

This pattern was followed in many districts; complaints flooded in to the P.C.C. and A.I.C.C. offices from disappointed applicants for the official ticket. In April 1939 the P.C.C. office replied to the A.I.C.C. General Secretary about the alleged 'groupism' in the selection of Congress candidates:

> The candidates who have not been selected . . . are creating disturbance and defying Congress Authority in many places. The Party whose favourites have not been selected are dissatisfied with the decision of the Working Committee [of the P.C.C.] and often write to the papers through their agents to vilify the Working Committee.[111]

As in the P.L.A. elections, candidates were nominated if they fell in with the dominant factions within the Congress; being a good Congressman was of little importance.[112] In effect, the district board elections in Bihar were not fought by the Congress as a party or a movement, but by factions of local politicians posing as the Congress.

In 1939 the Congress won control of all the Bihar district boards except one, but the disunity caused by the Congress participation in the boards did not end there. The Bihar Congress Government had not taken away the minister's power of nomination to the boards, despite their promise to do so in their election manifesto. When the Minister of Local Self Government began to consider these nominations, every one who felt himself to have been wronged in the elections petitioned for redress and asked to be nominated. All the heads of factions in Congress district boards parties called for the nomination of their supporters, whether they were Congressmen or not.[113] So instead of doing something for Moslems and members of the Depressed Castes who appealed for more seats, the Congress gave its places to men who mattered – such as the interim Minister Kumar Ajit Prasad Singh Deo (Manbhum District) – to square the localities.[114] This power of nomination proved to be a stumbling block for all Congress governments: Prasad declared that ' . . . I am taking no interest in the matter . . . for the obvious reason that I do not like to get involved in a matter which has created much local feeling'.[115]

In many ways the complications caused by the district board elections in Bihar and elsewhere were similar to those that had arisen at the time of the P.L.A. campaign. Yet the new opportunities of the ministry period also rise to quite new stresses within the Congress institutions. One of the major sources of influence which had been opened up by the acceptance of office was the personal patronage of the ministers. They could now appoint or promote their clients to jobs in the public services, to vital posts such as public prosecutorships and to the managerships of estates administered by the Court of Wards. Ministers were under constant pressure from their followers to hand out favours. As

D

Syed Mahmud, Education Minister in Bihar, complained:

> many . . . want me to provide posts for them whether it is possible or
> not. They seem to think that I have power to give them even Gov-
> ernment money . . . Those friends who call themselves Congressmen
> bother me more than others and bring out all sorts of impossible
> requests.[116]

Such requests echoed not only the demands from individual Congressmen for their sacrifices to be rewarded, but also pressure from various
factions in the local Congress organisations to have their standing
confirmed by a seal of power. As Dr Khare, Chief Minister of the
Central Provinces, discovered:

> The ministers are much harassed by local Congress Committees and
> Congressmen in the matter of these appointments [public pro-
> secutorships], nominations to local bodies and other such things.
> Every group in the Congress organisation wants to have its own
> nominee.[117]

The distribution of ministerial patronage did more than open the
eyes of the Congress provincial leaders to the mendicant skills of their
supporters. Jealousies and rivalries between individual ministers also
led to major rows within the new governments. Congressmen in Bihar,
for example, protested vigorously when the Chief Minister, Shri
Krishna Singh, appeared to reward his followers with appointments to
the public prosecutorships of Chapra District, the managerships of
Muksudpur and Palaman estates under the Court of Wards, the Assistant Directorship of Agriculture and the Deputy Superintendantship of
the Government Printing Press.[118] When Shri Krishna Singh and
Anugrah Narain Sinha clashed over the claims of their rival candidates
for the Court of Wards managership of the large Bettiah estate the
whole of the machinery of government in Bihar virtually seized up.[119]
Ministerial favouritism was an accepted fact of political life in all provinces and was in no sense an invention of the Congress ministers. But
the irresponsible and partisan use of ministerial patronage was a new
factor in Congress politics and an immensely dangerous and destructive one. This was shown most clearly in the 'Khare affair' that brought
to an end the first Congress ministry in the Central Provinces in July
1938.

Like the ministries in Madras and Bombay, the stability of the C.P.
ministry was put under strain by the fact that one British province was
made up from a number of Congress provinces. Soon after the elections
it became clear that the C.P. Congress leaders had strong parochial
loyalties. In March 1937, the Mahakoshal members of the P.L.A. (who
held 42 of the 72 Congress seats) formed a separate party to protect
regional interests in the Assembly and force Dr Khare, Chief Minister

elect, to co-operate with them.[120] But the Working Committee Parliamentary Sub-Committee (by now known as the 'High Command') gave Khare full powers to select the ministers. Khare picked himself, the Muslim Yusuf Shareef, P. V. Gole and R. R. Deshmukh from Berar and R. S. Shukla, D. P. Misra and D. K. Mehta from Mahakoshal.

Once the Congress had taken office, tension was caused by personal rivalries made worse by the way the ministers arbitrarily used executive power. Khare had won the Chief Ministership with the help of D. P. Misra, who was a useful ally against their common rival, R. S. Shukla[121] but Khare and Misra soon fell out when Khare began to place his men in the police and judiciary of Jubblepore. Misra had once been mayor of Jubblepore and was Minister for Local Self-Government so he, too, had his allies to reward[122]. Misra complained about Khare's inefficiency and neptoism to the 'High Command' – Khare retaliated by ordering the C.I.D. to look into allegations that Misra was corrupt and immoral and by making overtures to Dr da Silva's group who were Misra's enemies in Jubblepore[123]. Other ministers squabbled over patronage – the appointments of a Nagpur University law lectureship (where the rival candidates were Shukla's son and the junior partner of one of Khare's prominent supporters in Nagpur), the public prosecutorships of several districts, the appointment of a forest officer in Sodhi and the accommodation of Dr Khare's brothers – one as an Honorary Surgeon and the other as an Auditor of Joint-Stock Companies – all caused bitterness.[124] Khare did not endear himself to his colleagues by the way he over-ruled them in matters which came under their ministries. In May 1938, for example, he went over Misra's head to order the Deputy Commissioner of Nagpur to investigate the election of Seth Poonamchand Ranka (a local rival of Khare's) to Nagpur Municipality.[125] Khare also used the police to fight his political battles and this too caused resentment.[126]

The actual crisis was precipitated in March 1938. Yusuf Shareef, the Minister of Law and Order, summarily ordered the release from prison of Zaheer Ahmad, serving a four-year sentence for rape, in circumstances which aroused the suspicions of the Congress Assembly Party. The party hurriedly passed a resolution of no confidence in Shareef.[127] The 'High Command' now had to step in. It summoned Khare and Shareef for questioning and set up an enquiry committee.[128] This 'interference' was apparently resented by the Cabinet, but the P.L.A. party welcomed it.[129] However the ministry itself was beginning to fall apart. In May 1938 Shukla, Misra, Mehta and Gole asked to be allowed to resign. This would have led to the collapse of the ministry and only Nehru's intervention won them round.[130] The provincial Governor had also appointed an enquiry into the Ahmad affair, which reported that the Minister had acted legally but unwisely.[131] The Working Committee now demanded Shareef's resignation.[132] Khare regarded this demand as a personal affront and announced that he would seek a vote of confidence in himself from the P.L.A. party.[133] The Hindi-speaking members took this opportunity to issue a statement that they would resign if a vote of confidence in Khare was passed.[134] Vallabhbhai Patel now intervened – he smoothed over the difficulties and warned both parties that since they could not keep their own house in order he would do so.[135] The party meeting demanded and accepted Shareef's resignation and passed a vote of confidence in Khare and all the remaining ministers.[136]

The matter did not end here. Khare still felt himself to have been slighted and his relations with the Hindi-speaking ministers deteriorated. Even before the Shareef affair a Joint Parliamentary Board, with Jamnalal Bajaj as President and the President of each P.C.C. as a member, had been set up to try and get some co-operation within the ministry.[137] In July 1938 a mounting series of complaints about Khare's abuse of his control over the police and bureaucracy led the Joint Parliamentary Board to order him to give up his portfolios of Home Affairs and of Law and Order (which he had taken over from Shareef) and remain in office simply as Chief Minister without portfolio.[138] Law and Order was given to Shukla and Home Affairs to Misra.[139] At this the two Berar Ministers, Gole and Deshmukh, resigned.[140] Khare issued a statement that he would call on all the ministers to resign, do so himself, and then put the whole matter before the Working Committee for arbitration.[141] But the Mahakoshal men refused to stand down.[142] So Khare persuaded the Governor (who was trying to ensure some continuity of administration) to dismiss them and call on himself to form a new ministry.[143] Again the 'High Command' tried to arrange a compromise, but even after extensive interviews with all eight ministers they could not find an acceptable solution.[144] Faced by the threat of revolt from Mahakoshal, they called for Khare's resignation from the ministry and the Assembly.[145] At the meeting of the P.L.A. party to elect a new Chief Minister, Shukla secured 46 votes to Deshmukh's 18.[146] After consultation with the Working Committee, Shukla appointed a new ministry consisting of himself and his two Mahakoshal colleagues plus three Marathi speakers – C. Bhakara of the Commerce Constituency, M. P. Khole from Yeotmal and S. V. Gokhale from Amraoti.[147] Khare could do nothing; in October 1938 the Working Committee passed a resolution expelling him from the Congress P.L.A. Party and calling on him (in vain) to resign his seat.[148]

This involved and unsavoury crisis has been seen as an example of 'regionalism' in Congress politics and of the dictatorship of the Congress Working Committee Parliamentary Sub-Committee over the Congress Ministries. Admittedly the official excuse used when the Working Committee smashed Khare was that he had ignored party discipline by selecting a new ministry without their consent. But, as we have seen, this was not the crux of the matter. Factional and personal rivalry in the C.P. was so intense that some crisis was inevitable. The 'High Command' only intervened when it became clear that this was the only way to maintain even a semblance of unity. Although the inter-ministry struggle came to be portrayed in terms of a division between Hindi and Marathi speakers, this was done deliberately by Khare himself. As P. V. Gole complained to Shukla, Misra and Mehta, he was forced to throw in his lot with Khare because the Chief Minister had threatened to undercut his position in Berar by representing the dispute in regional terms.[149]

In several provinces the destructive effects of the ministries did not end with ministerial rivalries and increased competition for Congress tickets for the district board elections. The Congress ministers and their policies now provided the provincial programmes of the Congress organisations; the Congress M.L.A.s, who helped to make ministerial policy, used their power to try and cement the control of their home areas that they had established by winning nomination as Congress candidates. But, as we have seen, there were many Congressmen who had been excluded from the P.L.A.s by the operation of factional struggles within the district and provincial Congress organisations. These men were not now prepared to sit back and allow those who had beaten them a clear run; to assert their influence they began to mobilise within the Congress organisations and, as it was the P.L.A. elections that had seen their downfall, they began to mobilise against the ministries.

In 1936 the Congress in the United Provinces had been completely disrupted. After the factional disputes of 1935 and 36, the 'left-wing' Congressmen had managed to regain control of the P.C.C. but they did not dominate the election campaign. The district was the key to the elections and, except in a few Congress strongholds (Allahabad, Lucknow and Cawnpore for example), Congress nominations went to men who mattered in the locality. And even at the provincial level Nehru and G. B. Pant were left in charge of the elections. The 'left-wing' leaders managed to get elected easily enough, but in the Congress P.L.A. party as a whole they were out-numbered by men who held no brief either for their ideals or for their methods. As the 'left-wingers' were weak in the Assembly party they had little influence over the ministers. Not a single 'left-winger' was given a place in the ministry consisting of G. B. Pant, R. A. Kidwai, Dr Katju, Mrs Pandit, Pyarelal Sharma and Mohammed Ibrahim (a convert from the Moslem League).[150] With the 'left' entrenched in the P.C.C. and the 'right' in the ministry, the stage was set for a battle between the organisational and the parliamentary wings of the U.P. Congress.

Their first collision was in November 1937 over the election of a new President for the provincial Political Conference. Three candidates for the post were nominated, all from the left – Sampurnanand, Damodhar Swarup Seth and Dr Murarilal. Sampurnanand and Damodhar Swarup Seth then stood down to clear the way for Murarilal. At this stage the right wing put up Mohanlal Saxena to contest the election. The D.C.C.s were the electoral colleges, and so both sides wooed the district Congresses vigorously. The P.C.C. Executive openly supported Murarilal – they even sent out circulars to the D.C.C.s recommending him.[151] The first count gave victory to Muralilal by twenty-four votes to Saxena's twenty-two. But the election was challenged; it was alleged that the P.C.C. Executive had rigged the result.[152] Allegations and counter-allegations grew more and more strident[153] and eventually Nehru arbitrated the dispute declaring Saxena elected.[154]

The next round was in December when the members of the P.C.C. had to elect a new executive and President. The battle for control was now made more intense by the ministry's plans to introduce a Tenancy Bill. The Congress Government did not control a majority in the Provincial Legislative Council, the second chamber, and so could push through agrarian relief quickly only if some of the large landed magnates who controlled the upper chamber co-operated. But the stock-in-trade of the 'left-wing' Congressmen in the P.C.C. had been rural agitations for radical changes in the tenancy laws. Their programme was too drastic even for many Congress M.L.A.s, let alone the magnates in the P.L.C. Since tenancy legislation was bound to be a major issue, both the ministerialists and the socialists wanted control of the P.C.C. The ministry supporters backed Saxena again but the socialists could not find a candidate. Murarilal had been so tarred with the corruption of his abortive bid for office that he could not stand again, and Narendra Dev, their best man, was too ill to stand. They had no choice but to turn to Jawaharlal Nehru, who had once led agrarian agitations, but now they found him sobered by office and eager for a compromise. In December 1937 and January 1938, Nehru called Congressmen of all shades of opinion to a series of unity conferences.[155] The result of these meetings was that Saxena was grudgingly allowed to become President of the P.C.C.; but Nehru and Dev insisted on having a say in selecting his Executive, which now had a slight majority of 'leftists'.[156]

Tenancy legislation had been an issue even before the Congress had accepted office. During their election campaign the Congress had been accused of promising the millenium to the peasantry, with talk of a mortatorium on debts and drastic reductions in rent. At left-wing Political Conferences and Kisan meetings in 1935 and 1936, there had been a call for the abolition of zamindari without compensation. After the ministry took office, this cry was maintained by the 'left-wing'; but the ministers refused to be bullied. The Cabinet recognised the official wisdom of not interfering too much with the land revenue arrange-

ments; as government they realised how much the finances of the province depended on this source.[157] So ministers called for harmony
between zamindar and tenant.[158] Even Nehru had changed his tune.
The hammer of the zamindars now became their mild critic. No longer
was Nehru primarily concerned with the lot of the tenants, which he
did not think to be too bad, but rather he wanted to trim the wings of
the zamindars because they were reactionary in politics.[159] When a
resolution calling for the abolition of zamindari was introduced to the
Political Conference in December 1937, the new President, Mohanlal
Saxena, intervened. The resolution was dropped and the Conference
appealed to the peasantry to pay their rent in full.[160]

But pious exhortations would not solve the problem of the land. By
1937 it had been generally recognised that some tenancy reforms were
necessary. In May 1937 the Revenue Commissioners had recommended certain modest reforms to the interim ministers. Statutory
tenants were to be given occupancy tenancies (which were hereditary)
and *begari* and other illegal arbitary exactions by the landlords were to
be stamped out.[161] The Congress Agrarian Programme Sub-
Committee – appointed by the Assembly party before the Congress
took office – also wanted all statutory tenancies to become hereditary
ones.[162] Even more extreme elements saw this as a step in the right
direction – 'left-wing' Congressmen such as Narendra Dev, Mohanlal
Gautam and Damodhar Swarup Seth agreed that hereditary tenures
were the solution to most of the agrarian problems of the province.[163]
In March 1938 the ministry's tenancy proposals were set out. Not
surprisingly, the provision of hereditary tenures was the main plank.[164]
The rights of landlord and tenant on *sir* (demesne) land were clearly
defined for the first time[165] and new rules were proposed to deal with
the thorny problem of a tenant's not paying rent.[166] All extra fees,
charges and imposts on the tenants over and above the rent were
declared illegal. These restrictions on landlords were to apply equally
to tenants when they sub-let. Landlords, in return, were given security
against arrest for non-payment of revenue and tenants were given an
inducement to pay up their current rent demands in full by the promise
of a 25 per cent reduction in the next demand.[167]

What did these provisions mean in practice? Agrarian relationships
in the U.P. were complex. Terms such as 'landlord' and 'tenant' give
no idea of the subtle gradations that existed. Legislation which might
hurt the landed magnates could benefit the more numerous petty landlords, who were characteristic of the rural scene.[168]

The 1938 Tenancy Bill was designed to benefit these small and
medium-sized zamindars. Indeed, the Congress P.L.A. Party Sub-
Committee on the Tenancy Bill made more concessions to them by
amending the Bill to allow zamindars paying less than Rs 100 land
revenue to hold fifty acres of *sir* land and to eject tenants if necessary to

make their *sir* holding up to fifty acres.[169] When the Bill was discussed in the Assembly these concessions were also granted to zamaindars paying up to Rs 250 land revenue.[170] The Tenancy Bill successfully appealed to a wide section of rural society, from the medium-sized zamindars to the new hereditary tenants, without humbling the mighty or exalting the very humble.[171] But it did still leave an opening for radical Congressmen to mobilise against the ministry on behalf of the poorer class of peasant.

The ministers were now on the horns of a dilemma. To disarm their critics within the P.C.C. they had to get their Bill passed swiftly and thus be seen to be bringing real relief to the tenants. But to get the Bill passed swiftly the large landowners who dominated the P.L.C. had to be squared. Squaring the big zamindars would in turn infuriate the ministry's critics within the Congress.[172] Negotiations with the zamindar associations were begun in August 1938 and went on until November.[173] Although the Agra zamindars at first seemed ready to do a deal, the *taluqdars* of Oudh refused to have anything to do with the Bill. The Agra zamindars were glad to have this opportunity to show themselves to be independent of their Oudh brethren, but they were by no means prepared to give anything away. As they plodded, point by implacable point, through the Bill they threatened the ministers' plan for a quick solution. In November Vallabhbhai Patel called off the negotiations.[174]

If the zamindars' associations disappointed the minsters' hopes, the P.C.C. Executive justified their fears. As soon as the Bill was introduced into the Assembly, the P.C.C. Executive tried to dynamite its principles by calling for rents in the province to be halved. After Pant had pointed out that this proposal was, to say the least, impracticable since on rent depended revenue for a government that was now their own, the Executive modified its demands to a reduction of one-third in the rent – a little matter of eight million rupees.[175] The Executive also set up a Sub-Committee on the Tenancy Bill, headed by Narendra Dev, which called for zamindars to be defined in the Bill as the tax-gatherers of government, not the proprietors of the land.[176] This Sub-Committee was suspicious of the ministry/zamindar negotiations and condemned the Bill as falling short of the 1936 Agrarian Programme of the Congress.[177] This attack by the P.C.C. Executive continued even after the Bill was passed by the P.L.A.; Pant was now denounced as 'the new Chhatari'.[178]

The Kisan Sabhas agitated even more violently against the Ministry. In the U.P. the Kisan Sabhas were dominated by Congressmen and thus could be used either to support or to attack the Congress from within, depending on the needs of their leaders. When the Tenancy Bill was published, the P.C.C. leaders lost no time in mobilizing the kisans for the attack. In April 1938 A. N. Dev and Mohanlal Gautam organised several demonstrations to protest against the Bill.[179] The ministers plaintively requested that the kisans should put their complaints through the proper channels – the D.C.C.s and the M.L.A.s[180] – and Nehru angrily attacked the disloyalty of Congressmen to a Congress government.[181] The kisan leaders were not cowed; at a Political Conference in Lucknow District Dev and Gautam urged the kisans to organise themselves to force the necessary reforms through and not to wait for relief from the ministry.[182] The P.C.C. Executive, under Nehru's influence, had to resort to threats – any Congressman who used the Kisan Sabhas against the ministry would be disciplined or thrown out.[183] In a tactical retreat, Dev now changed his tune and called for the ministry's initiative to be respected.[184] By October, with the P.C.C. elections coming up, it was time for another advance; Dev began making speeches attacking the Tenancy Bill and calling for the abolition of zamindari.[185] Saxena had such a rough ride when he called upon Congressmen to respect law and order under a Congress ministry and to toe the party line, that he thought of resigning.[186] By early January, when the Provincial Political Conference was held at Ajodhya, matters came to a head. At meetings before the Conference the Kisan Sabha leaders reiterated all their demands – the Tenancy Bill should be speeded up, ejectment or distraint for non-payment of rent abolished, the rent demand cut by half and the threats of discipline against the Kisan leaders should be withdrawn.[187] At the Conference itself only Nehru's influence prevented a vote of censure on the ministry. Even so, resolutions were passed which demanded the abolition of zamindari and a large remission of rent.[188] The governor thought that cutting the rent demand by half would be an economic disaster for the province, but Pant reassured him that no notice need be taken of this as 'people at Conferences are not very strong in arithmetic'.[189]

The Ajodhya Conference in January 1939 proved to be the high point of the crisis. After it oil was liberally poured on troubled waters. The new P.C.C. Executive had a left wing majority, but Nehru, as President, was a moderating influence. Although disgruntled Congressmen continued to whip up kisan campaigns against the Tenancy Bill, Nehru had enough influence to keep these isolated and sporadic.[190] When the Tenancy Bill came before the P.L.C., the ministry managed to buy off the '*bania* vote' by legislation on agricultural indebtedness and the other members of the Council were so divided among themselves that they could not even agree on which amendments to the Bill to vote for.[191]

In the United Provinces the battle over tenancy legislation had been between ministry and P.C.C. Executive for the provincial political initiative. In Bihar tenancy legislation also caused conflict within the provincial Congress organisation. Here again the divisions were apparently between two sides separated by ideology and principle. In fact the real causes had little to do with divisions of this sort – they were a series of struggles between politicians, regardless of political complexion, for the control of district level Congress organisations.

The P.L.A. election campaign had brought the tensions in the Bihar Congress to the surface. Swami Sahajanand Saraswati, disappointed by his failure to get his followers nominated for the Congress ticket, had resigned from the P.C.C. Working Committee in pique. In 1937 Congressmen with kisan connections made it clear that a Congress Ministry which excluded them would not be treated with kid gloves. Propaganda and agitation were used in their attack – at the Provincial Political Conference in July 1937 they pushed through a resolution calling for the abolition of zamindari without compensation;[192] in their direct action campaigns they led the kisans, in the name of the Congress, against medium-sized zamindars who were the traditional Congress supporters.[193]

Ever since 1920 the issue of tenancy legislation had divided Bihari Congressmen. The Bihar Congress Ministers faced the same problem as their colleagues in the U.P. They were committed to introducing some agrarian legislation and were under pressure from the 'left-wing' within the Congress, but they also needed the support of Congress zamindars in the P.L.A. and of rural magnates, who were not Congress supporters, in the Provincial Legislative Council. The Bihar ministry decided to deal with this dilemma by concentrating more on bringing immediate relief to the tenants than by attempting any radical changes. Their Bill reduced the amount of rent paid by the tenants to the level set in 1911, set up some machinery to settle a 'fair rent', abolished arbitrary imposts by the landlords, forbade the arrest of tenants for arrears in rent and limited the interest on unpaid rent to six per cent.[194] What was lacking from these proposals was any attempt to solve the problem of the *bakasht* lands – the land that had been re-possessed from hereditary tenants during the agricultural slump of 1932 and 1933 and let to different tenants on an occupancy basis. The tenants thus dispossessed had been the mainstay of the kisan agitations since the early 1930s and continued to be so during the period of the Congress ministry.[195] But in contrast to their fellows in the U.P., the Bihar ministers' tactics brought them great success. Helped by Rajendra Prasad they opened negotiations with the zamindar associations of Bihar and, after several false starts, achieved an agreement that was ratified by the passing of the Tenancy Bill by the P.L.C. in August 1938.

Almost as soon as the Congress Ministry took office, Swami Sahajanand led the Bihar Kisan Sabha in a move to win the leadership for himself. He appealed to all those dissatisfied with the Tenancy Bill – landless labourers, ex-tenants of *bakasht* and even the small zamindars (who feared that their interests would be sacrificed in a deal between the Congress and the magnates). These activities became concentrated around the control of the D.C.C.s. The Congress election campaign had been dominated by a series of struggles in different districts, roughly divided between those Congressmen who based their strength on an alliance with the important landed magnates outside the Congress and those who relied rather on agitational politics. This tension continued during 1937 and came to a head at the end of the year at the annual Congress elections to choose the delegates to the Haripura Congress and the membership of the P.C.C. and D.C.C.s.

A brief examination of a few of these conflicts will show what was happening. In Saran, Rajendra Prasad (whose home district this was) had managed to unite the factions led by B. Mahamayya Prasad and Pt. Girish Tiwari, who had quarrelled over the P.L.A. elections.[196] But a new challenge to the joint dominance of these groups was led by socialist Congressmen under Ram Binode Singh and Ram Raksha Bramachari. By 1937 Saran Congressmen of all shades of opinion had allied on the District Board to form an opposition party to the Chairman of the Board. But the ties of their unity were not very strong – they began to quarrel over who should be supported in the nominations made by the District Board to the subordinate Union Boards. One faction of the Congress District Board party (loyal to the D.C.C. President Mahamayya Prasad) now formed an alliance with non-Congress Board members to get their men elected on to the Union Boards. The other faction in the Congress District Board party reacted to this by allying with Ram Binode Singh and Ram Raksha Bramachari to fight the D.C.C. elections against Mahamayya Prasad. Since they were weak on the Board and in the Congress Committee, they turned their attention to leading a kisan agitation as an electoral device. When Swami Sahajanand arranged a tour of the district to support this campaign, Mahamayya Prasad banned it. What appeared to be a clash of ideology at the D.C.C. elections between the spokesmen of landlords on the one hand and the spokesmen of tenants on the other, was in reality nothing more than tactical manoeuvres, and on the District Board the men who had talked of socialism and gone out to lead the peasantry in the D.C.C. election campaign forged an alliance with the largest zamindar of the district.[197]

In Darbhanga District the two rival groups were those that had clashed over the Assembly elections – Satyanarain Sinha and his zamindar allies against Jamuna Karjee and Dhanraj Sharma with their Kisan Sabha. The Kisan Sabha had been rushed into existence in 1933 as a lever in the District Board elections; now the same lever was employed by its leaders against their opponents in the Congress. This factionalism was decently clothed in talk of class interests with Sataynarain Sinha being described, by the self-appointed leaders of the masses, as the tool of the magnates who had sold out the district Congress. But this was an over-simplification. Satyanarain Sinha, it is true, had the two largest zamindars of the district – Maheshwar and Rajeshwar Prasad Narain Singh – on his side, but the kisan party had the support of several zamindars who feared the dominance of the bigger landlords.[198] In Muzaffarpur District the election seemed to have been a full-dress battle between Socialists and Gandhians. But what really divided the leaders (Thakur Ramnandan Singh and Dr Ramashish Thakur) was mere faction, as some of the more sceptical onlookers realised.[199] When, a few months later, the two leaders buried the hatchet of principle to join forces to repulse the challenge of a third group to their dominance,[200] they showed that ideology was the handmaid of circumstances.

These divisions all took place at the district level. But the locality was now more fully linked to the province, and it is not surprising that these tensions were exported (bearing the same trademarks) to the provincial market. This happened in December 1937 when the Saran and Champaran D.C.C.s banned a tour by Swami Sahajanand and the Monghyr D.C.C. expelled eleven members of the District Kisan Council who were on the D.C.C. and its Executive. The P.C.C. Executive backed these actions by its local supporters and ordered all Congressmen to 'keep aloof' from the Kisan Sabhas.[201] This order was supported by the national Working Committee resolution on Kisan Sabhas and the Congress which was passed at the Haripura Congress in February 1938.

During 1938 and 1939 the Bihar Kisan Sabha inevitably drew apart from the Congress. Those Bihar kisan leaders who still managed to keep a place in the Congress – men like Kishori Prasana Sinha and Awadeshwar Prasad Singh – called on their followers to obey the Haripura resolution and join the Congress, where they would be the most use to their embattled leaders. But most of the Kisan Sabha leaders – Swami Sahajanand, Jamuna Karjee, Jadunandan Sharma and Dhanraj Sharma – were not so well placed. They began an all-out agitation against the agrarian policy of the ministry and their triumphant rivals in local and provincial Congress politics. When the Kisan Sabha men lost control of Patna and Gaya in 1938 their antagonism to the P.C.C. Executive and the Ministry increased. By 1939 there had been several direct action campaigns to restore the *bakasht* lands to their original tenants.[202] With this treadmill of more and more agitation turning over steadily, the Bihar Kisan Sabha came to represent an alternative road for political advance at the provincial level for those who had lost out in the regular Congress; 'a forum where disgruntled men labouring under a sense of personal and party grievance' could lead 'a campaign that has proved in practice and effect to be a campaign against the Congress.'[203]

During the period of the Congress ministries, the Congress became the most important ladder to political success at the local and provincial level. Provincial Congress politics now revolved around a scramble for provincial influence by all the politicians who had been in the Congress before the 1936 elections or had joined it then. Control of the P.C.C. became vital for those excluded from the ministries and from the Assembly parties. In the U.P. the 'left-wing' groups managed to retain a dominant position within the provincial level organisation and therefore put pressure on the Ministry from the inside. But in Bihar the 'left-wingers' had lost their footing in the P.C.C. in 1936 and were unable to regain it. The elections at the end of 1937 became vital to them since control of the D.C.C.s was the surest way to build up influence to take over control at the provincial level. But their defeat shut this door also. Therefore many 'left-wingers' in Bihar had to rely on agitation to have any importance in the politics of the province. Thus in the U.P. and Bihar political struggles that were expressed in terms of ideology and economic class were also struggles for the control of the provincial Congress, and thence the dominance of the politics of locality and province.

By accepting office Congress gave some of its members wide power and influence, but threatened the unity and homogeneity of the movement as a whole. Office did no good to the Congress organisations. The all-India Congress leaders had hoped that its ministers would act as loyal subordinates in the struggle for *Swaraj*, ably assisted by the provincial organisations which would act as 'an effective link between the people and the Ministers'.[204] But it was the ministers, not the provincial organisations, that came to be the real heart of the movement. Once the Congress was in office, the P.C.C.s had neither programme nor role, while the ministries had all the power of the *Raj*. In these circumstances, it is hardly surprising that most provincial Congress politics were mainly concerned with influencing the ministries. The obverse of this was that the provincial and district committees were now important only in so far as they were the road to office and influence or the means of mounting an opposition campaign within the Congress.

Ever since 1934 rivalries between Congressmen, fought out within the Congress institutions and under the rules laid down by the Congress constitution, had been the major dynamic of development in the politics of province and locality. The competitiveness of Congress politics had been a source of strength as much as a cause of weakness: unlike its rival political organisations the institutional structure of the Congress was open enough to attract and accommodate widely divergent leaders and interest groups, and at the same time competitive enough to ensure that each level of the organisation could contain a consensus of Congress opinion from its catchment area. But such consensuses were endangered once the Congress began to participate in the search for governmental power, for the nomination of candidates

for the P.L.A. or local board elections or for executive posts under
Congress ministries, while the need for the Congress ministers to compromise their avowed principles by limited tenancy legislation
increased the bitterness of factional dispute. But the great strength of
the Congress was that such disputes did not necessarily lead to the
disintegration of the organisation. The ladder of Congress institutions
was still vitally important to those who had been excluded from the
rewards of the 1937 election campaign or from the networks of ministerial patronage. The tactics of the Congress critics of the tenancy legislation of the U.P. and Bihar Governments illustrate this: in the U.P. the
Kisan Sabha agitation against the Tenancy Bill seemed to have a
distinctive class basis, yet it died away after the Ajodhya Conference
which confirmed radical Congressmen's control of the P.C.C. but did
not affect the terms of the Bill; in Bihar, as the *Searchlight* pointed out,
the Kisan Sabha was:

> a platform where disgruntled men labouring under a sense of per-
> sonal and party grievance [can pronounce] . . . judgement . . . on the
> conduct and action of the Congress office bearers. The truth of the
> matter is that consciously or unconsciously most of them were
> swayed by the thought that they were in a position now to dictate to
> and displace the Congress leadership.[205]

The political priorities of the controllers of provincial and local governmental power in India had always influenced the types of political
response that emerged to meet them. The British concern to attract
support from what they saw as important interests in local society –
castes, communities and economic groupings – had resulted in the
mobilisation of organisations to take advantage of these openings. By
1937 the British had abdicated control in the provinces and had
retreated to the all-India level. The Congress ministries that succeeded
them in most of the provinces had a different political vision. Partly out
of conviction and partly out of a need to satisfy their supporters, Congress ministers looked to the Congress institutions as the only representatives of genuine political interests. Thus even the opponents of the
ministries could best maximise their influence from inside the Congress. Only in exceptional circumstances did attempts to mobilise outside the Congress make any sense.

The only major group for whom circumstances were exceptional in
this sense was the Muslim politicians of the Congress-majority provinces who in this period joined the Muslim League to convert it into a
mass-based, agitational, militant communal movement, mobilising not
against the British but against the Congress. During the 1920s the
Muslim political establishment had generally tried to use influence
with the British to compensate for their numerical disadvantage in
most provinces.[206] Ensured of some electoral support by their separate

electorates, many Muslim leaders in minority provinces played on their loyalty to the *Raj* to secure enough government patronage in education and the services to keep their influence alive.[207] At the national level as well, especially when constitutional reforms were being discussed, Muslim leaders were anxious that influence in the Executive should counteract their disadvantage in electoral politics; but the 1935 Government of India Act removed the influence of the British executive . from provincial politics and weakened it in the internal aspects of national government. Although the Communal Award assured Muslim leaders of the support of their own community, it also underlined the weakness of their position in electoral politics in most provinces and at the centre. These changes in the governance of India required a major change in the tactics of Muslim political leaders – the rise of the All-India Muslim League from 1937 was the direct result.

In 1935 Mohammed Ali Jinnah had tried to resuscitate the moribund Muslim League to fight the Provincial Legislative Assembly elections. His tactic was to persuade autonomous provincial leaders to contest the elections on the League ticket; but he had no programme nor any concrete political advantages to offer them. Negotiations with a number of provincial Muslim parties in the Punjab, Bihar, Bengal, Sindh and the United Provinces were started but broke down.[208] In 1936 Jinnah was still a leader without a following; in his election speeches he offered to ally with any 'progressive' elements in the country, even with the Congress. Of the 482 Muslim seats in the provincial legislatures, the League won only 109 in 1936–7[209] – it could not yet be said to represent the majority of India's Muslims.

Between 1937 and 1939, Jinnah was able to impose his leadership on the provincial Muslim politicians in most of the provinces where Muslims were in a minority. The rise of the League was, largely, a reaction to the increasing dominance of the Congress in provincial and national politics. The relationship between the Congress governments and the Muslim politicians has given rise to two myths about the period – that the Congress made an alliance with the League before the elections in some provinces and then refused to keep their side of the bargain and allow a coalition ministry, and that, by the 'Muslim Mass Contacts Campaign', the Congress leaders tried to use their electoral advantage to undercut the League by appealing directly to Muslims and weaning them away from their community leaders.

The story of a Congress agreement with the Muslim League in the United Provinces in 1936 to contest the elections jointly, and the subsequent refusal of the Congress to honour its promise of two ministries for League leaders, has become an integral part of the mythology of Partition. Standard British and Pakistani accounts of the episode[210] claim that a formal electoral alliance was concluded and that, once the election results were known and the Congress had a clear majority, the

Working Committee negotiator (A. K. Azad) offered the League a coalition only if it would disband itself.[211] In fact contemporary evidence, as supplied both by Nehru and by Donaldson (who was Secretary to the U.P. Government in 1937), indicates that this supposed alliance was nothing more than casual co-operation between local Congressmen and Leaguers in a few constituencies where both saw the National Agriculturalist Party as their main opponent.[212] An official of the Government of India Reforms Office later recorded his impression of the affair as that 'these stories had no currency (or very little) until a long time had passed and *until the manufacture of Muslim League grievances had been organised'.*[213]

In any case, the accusations and counter-accusations of propagandists become irrelevant if one looks at the men involved. The League leader anxious for a deal was Ch. Khaliquzzaman, who had been a Congress politician until 1935 and who was now the head of one faction in the Muslim League Provincial Parliamentary Board. On the Congress side, the main advocates of an alliance were M. L. Saxena and, after the elections, Pant and Kidwai. The main Congress opponents were Dr Ashraf, Sardar Narbada Prasad Singh, Narendra Dev and P. D. Tandon.[214] There were obvious empirical motives for these alignments. Despite his defection in the 1935 District Board elections, Khaliquzzaman still had close ties with the Saxena/Srivastava faction in Lucknow;[215] Pant welcomed the prospect of extra support against his socialist rivals in the P.C.C.; Kidwai had only managed to get elected to the P.L.A. with the help of Khaliquzzaman.[216] Narendra Dev, Sardar Narbada Singh and Dr Ashraf were all suspicious of the Ministry's intentions, especially over tenancy legislation, and were loath to see anything that would increase its dominance in provincial politics; P. D. Tandon also had connections with the kisan movement and with associations to advance the use of Hindi, which made him, if not anti-Muslim, at least anti-Urdu. In a recent work S. R. Mehrotra has shown that in fact the terms offered to the League for coalition were not severe, and that negotiations broke down over personalities.[217] Khaliquzzaman was losing ground in the provincial League to the faction led by the Raja of Salempore (who eventually joined the interim ministry)[218] and to secure his own position had to insist on Nawab Ismail Khan being given a place in the ministry. But Pant was unable to accept Ismail Khan, as that would have meant that there were three ex-League members in the ministry of six of seven.[219]

After the Congress ministries had taken office, the chief grievance of the provincial Muslim politicians was that they had 'no part in the Government'.[220] During the dyarchy period, Muslim politicians had tried to use the powers of government to redress their numerical disadvantages in electoral politics; now, with the Government equated with the Congress, they had either to join the Congress or to find new tactics. It was hard for Muslim politicians to join the Congress – their way into the organisation was blocked by the rivalries and ambitions of the Muslim politicians already established there. The Congress Muslims were determined to exploit their new strength to the full. The Muslim Mass Contacts Campaign had been started by Nehru as an attempt to remove communalism from politics by appealing to the economic interests of the Muslim peasant,[221] but in practice it was dominated by attempts by Congress Muslim politicians to increase their standing in the Muslim community at large. Thus the bulk of the U.P. Congress Mass Contacts campaign involved an attempt by certain Congress Muslims to get their candidate elected to the Vice-Chancellorship of Aligarh University and to improve the position of their friends in local Congress organisations;[222] in Bihar the campaign degenerated into a rivalry between several provincial leaders for the power to pack local Congress committees with their own followers.[223] As the network of these provincial leaders spread downwards into the localities, the labels 'Congress' and 'League' became stuck on to existing factional rivalries; they helped to mark these tensions but they did not create them.

The P.L.A. elections showed the Muslim provincial politicians that they could no longer rely on the influence of the British executive to redress their electoral disadvantages; they now had to find a new source of support. The All India Muslim League offered provincial leaders a programme to use against their exclusion from provincial government – mass agitations against supposedly communal discrimination by the Congress governments – plus a voice at the centre to appeal to the British for redress. Thus agitational campaigns were launched against the indoctrination of Muslim children in schools (by the singing of *Bande Matram*, the use of *namaste* as a greeting and the daily salute of Gandhi's portrait), the supposed suppression of Urdu in the services and law courts and the absence of separate electorates to local bodies in Congress provinces. Reports and enquiries were set up by the League to expose the communal nature of the Congress administrations.[224] All this propaganda led to the situation described by the Collector of Patna District (Bihar) in August 1938:

. . . [the] harping on imaginary grievances and the frequent reiteration of the cry that Muslims are being suppressed by the Congress ministry is making Muslims everywhere believe that this is really so.[225]

Provincial League leaders also made use of the local board election campaigns. In Bihar, where these were held on joint electorates in 1939, provincial Congress leaders tried to ensure that an adequate number of Muslims were given Congress tickets.[226] But many D.C.C. leaders, needing all available patronage for their personal use, ignored these instructions,[227] and even where Muslims were given tickets factional struggles between local Congress Muslim rivals often resulted.[228] By organising a boycott of the elections unless separate electorates were created, the League leaders were able to pick up the support of all Muslims who felt themselves hard done by.[229] In a revealing speech on the relationship between his League, the Congress and the Government in Bihar S. A. Aziz declared:

> The Muslim League is no more an enemy or opponent of the Congress than the Kisan Sabha is.[230]

Like the Kisan Sabha leaders in Bihar and the U.P., the Muslim League provincial leaders saw agitation as their only redress against a Congress government from which their influence had been excluded.

The facility with which internal Congress politics during the ministry period stirred up the hornet's nest of factional rivalry – sapping unity, driving erstwhile colleagues into opposition and even giving impetus to wholly new forms of anti-Congress protest – did not pass unnoticed at the time. After the unprecedented rowdyness and violence at the Haripura delegate elections the Bihar P.C.C. set up a committee of enquiry. Searching for the cause of 'this sudden out-burst of the worst passions of the people', the committee asked:

> How is it that people were suddenly seized with a desire to capture power at all costs? . . . So long as the Congress was a fighting machine, it was functioning on a high moral plane. It was, as Mahatma Gandhi put it, like an army following a strict moral discipline. . . . Because . . . there were no material temptations before them . . . only such people sought election as were devoted to the cause of freedom and to the cherished principles of the Congress. . . . Since the acceptance of office by the Congress, great temptations come on the way. Those who had advocated it had thought that it would open vast opportunities for service and sacrifice, would consolidate the position gained so far and intensify the struggle for freedom. It no doubt did bring some reliefs to the people. But it also started attracting opportunists and political adventurers. It demoralised even old Congressmen who felt that now was the time for the reward for the sacrifices made by them in the past. They also claimed a share in the spoils and there was heart-burning if in the distribution of spoils some went without their share.
>
> Khadi, which was the symbol of non-violent revolt against British Imperialism and a badge of service and which represented truth and non-violence, became a qualification for its wearer to secure jobs. The various Congress Committees, instead of becoming organs of the struggle for independence, became a platform for addressing petitions to the Ministry. There was a widespread desire to capture

Congress organisations by all kinds of people so that the position of advantage might be used for securing patronage for themselves their friends and relations and for capturing local bodies.[231]

The ideal of the Congress, the 'fighting machine' operating on a 'high moral plane', was to unite Indians in a national movement to purify the nation and win *Swaraj*; and before 1937 the Congress could claim to be a national movement, to pick up the support of anyone and everyone who did not like government in general or in particular. This was the Congress's strength in opposition – the ability to draw together all manner of groups, however little they understood nationalism and however little they knew each other. When the Congress became both government and opposition its potential strength was greatly increased, but the strains put upon Congress members and institutions was sufficient to seriously impair its ability to exploit this new strength in any effective way.

During the ministry period, the internal power and influence of the provincial Congress leaders grew, especially that of the provincial parliamentary leaders. They now had control of ministerial patronage, of nominations to the local boards and of the provincial programme of the Congress. Although it was still possible for determined Congressmen to oppose the ministers from a firm alternative base – as the U.P. P.C.C. Executive and some district level leaders in other areas could – the ministers and their allies in the provincial-level organisation acquired greater control over the provincial Congress as a whole. Local disputes now tended to be channelled up to the provincial level; we have seen how, in Bihar, the district level conflicts over both the D.C.C. elections in 1938 and the district board elections in 1939 escalated to the provincial level due to the involvement of provincial leaders in local affairs.

There was also a new link between the local and provincial levels in the ministry period – the Congress M.L.A.s. These men were, on the whole, determined to convert their successes at the elections into solid control of both Congress and government institutions in their home areas. They were the links between the localities and the ministries; they had to be consulted over most important matters, including the distribution of Congress tickets for local board elections and the nomination of members of the boards. They also strenuously resisted all attempts to limit their influence within the Congress institutions or keep them out of local politics.

The all-India leaders did make an effort to contain the increasing tensions within the Congress institutions. In 1938 and 1939 they ordered that a system of mediating institutions – election tribunals, appeal committees and the like – be set up to reduce the influence of local bosses in the Congress elections. In several provinces similar arrangements were made to manage the elections to local boards and to supervise the Congress parties in the boards. This did help to reduce visible friction within the Congress, but it did so at a cost. Far from sharing out power among the many, it helped to concentrate it still more firmly in the hands of the few. In Bihar, the effect of establishing Divisional Committees to run the district board elections of 1939 was to bring local disputes to the provincial level where they were settled in accordance with the needs of the provincial bosses. In Gujerat, the appointment of a four-man sub-committee to control all matters concerning the local boards in the province also resulted in the growth of 'bossism'. The committee never met formally, each member dealt on his own initiative within his own territory. The A.I.C.C. Inspector for Gujerat reported in 1940:

> I must admit that the P.C.C. on the whole is working efficiently and smoothly. What I have tried to point out is that the work carried on now is more on individual initiative than on Constitutional principle and should be regularised. The formal sanction of the P.C.C. and its Executive should be obtained and where the sub-committees have been appointed they should be allowed to meet and record their proceedings formally.[232]

The same process went on with the elections to Congress committees. Early in 1938, for example, L. B. Shastri and Nehru went to great pains to arrange the lists of nominations for executive posts in the Allahabad City and District Congress Committees to secure the return of 'good and sincere' men to the district leadership.[233] They may have been in favour of the sincere and good, but the point was that it was men at the top who were deciding who was good and who was bad in the politics of Allahabad.

According to contemporary and to most subsequent accounts,[234] the Working Committee also had complete control over the Congress ministries. But in fact the national leaders had as little control over the provincial parliamentarians as they had had over the 1937 election campaign. Soon after the elections, the Working Committee and important representatives from the provinces met to decide the basic Congress strategy in the legislatures. The policy of the Congress legislature parties was set out, in accordance with a Working Committee resolution, as non-alliance with other parties, preparing for a Constituent Assembly, and the enactment of various agrarian reforms.[235] All Congress M.L.A.s and M.L.C.s were also required to take an oath promising their willingness 'to work under the discipline of the Congress for the furtherance of Congress ideals and objectives'.[236] Both right- and left-wing members of the Working Committee wanted the centre to control the ministries – the right were concerned to prevent internal rivalries splitting the Congress Assembly parties,[237] the left needed to make certain that the ministers did not have it all their own way in the politics of the provinces.[238] In March 1937 the Working Committee set up a Parliamentary Sub-Committee to 'keep in close and constant touch' with the Congress parties in the legislatures.[239] This Sub-Committee consisted of Vallabhbhai Patel, Rajendra Prasad and A. K. Azad; later the provinces were split up between the triumvirate – Patel taking charge of Bombay, Madras, Central Provinces and Sindh; Azad of Bengal, United Provinces, Punjab and the N.W.F.P.; and Prasad of Bihar, Orissa and Assam.[240]

The task of the Parliamentary Sub-Committee was two-fold. It had to help preserve discipline and unity within the parliamentary wings in the provinces and to keep the noses of the Congress ministers firmly to the programme of legislation laid down in March 1937. Neither of these jobs was easy: we have seen that provincial Congressmen were driven by the powerful motive of internal factional struggle in most of their activities during the ministry period. Although the national leaders could chide ministers for their lack of progress in implementing necessary reforms,[241] they could do little to force their hands. Similarly, although concerned to keep the ministries and provincial parliamentarians free of corruption and the divisive effects of factional strife, the Parliamentary Sub-Committee's first priority was to maintain continuity of Congress rule, not to ensure an angelic purity.

The Parliamentary Sub-Committee had the same relationship to the ministries as the A.I.C.C. office had to the provincial organisations – that is, it settled disputes that were otherwise insoluble but did not meddle with everyday affairs.[242] As we saw in the case of the 'Khare Affair' in the Central Provinces, the High Command tried constantly to get a compromise between the disputants and only acted against Khare when it was clear that a united Congress ministry under his leadership was impossible. Apart from arbitrating disputes and listening to grievances, the Parliamentary Sub-Committee also helped the ministries in other ways – for example by offering to negotiate with the large zamindars in the U.P. over the provisions of the Congress Tenancy Bill. The ability of the High Command to impose a general policy on the ministries was very small. Occasionally it got ministers from the different provinces together to discuss common problems; it insisted on superintending any proposals by Congress parties in minority provinces to form coalition ministries. But, apart from this, the High Command did little to initiate and co-ordinate policy. The diversity of situations faced by Congress ministers in the different provinces and the fierce desire for independence at the provincial level prevented the High Command from commanding. As the Central Provinces minister, D. P. Misra, wrote to Dr Khare in November 1937: 'the Members of the Working Committee do not possess, and in the very nature of things cannot possess, an intimate knowledge of our problems and difficulties'.[243]

Although attempts by the all-India leaders to mitigate the rivalries

among their subordinates and to control and direct the activities of the
Congress ministries were not very effective, the ministry period did see
a significant change in the relationship between the national leaders
and their provincial followers. Between 1934 and 1937 the all-India
leaders, both Gandhi and his followers and Nehru and his allies, had
been out on a limb. Their formal control over the activities of the
Congress as a whole was minimal and their rival programmes had little
appeal, or relevance, to the majority of Congressmen. In 1936–7 the
'Gandhians' had been forced to accept a programme of contesting the
elections and taking ministerial office in response to direct pressure
from the provinces and to the need to secure allies against the socialist
challenge to their control at the centre. But, once provincial Congressmen had taken office, the initiative did slowly pass from them back to
the centre.

Between 1937 and 1939 the tensions and struggles within the various
provincial Congress organisations were forced up to the all-India level
and the battles between the ministers and their critics became the
major issues in the all-India struggle for power and initiative. The
ministers looked to the 'Gandhians' for support against their local
opponents while the provincial dissidents relied on the all-India opposition to defend their right to criticise the ministries and to work to
minimise the role of parliamentary activity in the Congress programme. Thus contact between the provincial and the all-India levels was
restored and the leadership vacuum at the top of the Congress hierarchy was filled as national, provincial and local leaders joined forces at
the Congress sessions at Haripura in March 1938 and Tripuri in
March 1939 to do battle on such issues as the relationship between
Congressmen and Kisan Sabhas and the States' Peoples' movement,
the role of parliamentary activity in the long-term strategy of the Congress against the continuance of British rule and the sanctions to be
employed against any attempt to impose the federal scheme of the 1935
Government of India Act. The continuing discussion about constitutional reform also increased the standing of the all-India leadership.
The negotiations initiated by Lord Linlithgow (Viceroy 1936–43) with
the leaders of various sections of Indian political opinion to bring about
all-India federation helped to concentrate Congress concern about
future reform at the national level. Now that the prize of some share in
national political control seemed to be within their grasp, Congressmen
needed above all to retain the image of their movement as a united,
homogenous nation-wide organisation led by a compact and powerful
set of leaders. As the provincial Muslim League leaders in the Muslim
minority provinces had discovered after 1937, a voice at the all-India
level was essential in influencing the next stage of constitutional reform.

It was over the issue of constitutional arrangements at the centre that
the Congress provincial ministers resigned in October 1939, a month

after the outbreak of war had seemed to open up once again the whole question of how the Government of India was to be run. The resignation of the Congress ministers cannot simply be regarded, as it has in the past, as a powerful example of the dictatorial powers exercised by the Congress High Command over their subordinates. As we have seen, the all-India leaders simply were not able to exert this sort of constant, day-to-day control, and any explanation of the resignation of the ministries must be made consistent with this fact. Although in 1937 the provincial Congress leaders had been eager to enjoy the fruits of ministerial office, by 1939 these were beginning to go rotten. Many provincial Congressmen had begun to realise the destructive effects of ministerial power on the unity and homogeneity of the Congress: the impact of personal rivalries and factional strivings was taking its toll.

The year 1939 had seen a series of shocks administered to the Congress ministers – the re-election of Subhas Chandra Bose as Congress President in January was as much a censure of them as of the 'Gandhian' leaders and the increasingly violent protests of the Muslim League were beginning to cause them concern. In addition, the outbreak of war brought with it the likelihood that Congress ministers would have to use emergency powers against dissident Congressmen agitating against the use of Indian resources in an imperial war and the ministers' much-vaunted independence of the Governors would be compromised. Even before they received instructions to quit the ministers had reported that their position would be untenable in this situation.[244] At the same time, all the events of 1939 – the crushing of the Bose revolt, the need to counteract the influence of the All India Muslim League and the opportunity to put pressure on the British at the centre – had switched the initiative from the provincial to the all-India leaders. It should also be remembered that in October 1939 there was no general expectation that the Congress would be excluded from office for the next five years; the resignations were simply a tactic to support Gandhi in his negotiations with the Viceroy, and Linlithgow's action in simply suspending the constitution in the Congress provinces and ordering the Governors to assume full executive powers without attempting to attract alternative ministries minimised the extent of the sacrifice. The actual decision to pull the provincial ministries out is very poorly documented, but one cannot escape the conclusion, from a study of the internal logic of the situation, that had the war, and the accompanying constitutional crisis, not existed then it would have been necessary for the Congress to have invented it.

This survey of events and developments within the local and provincial Congress organisations between 1934 and 1939 has indicated that the existence of an interconnected institutional structure, running from the highest to the lowest level, was the real basis of the strength of the nationalist movement during this period. For several reasons – the economic dislocations of the slump, the wider contacts made during agitational campaigns and the considerable enlarging of the P.L.A. electorates – the politically-aware section of Indian society was expanding rapidly during this period. Because of the ease of access to them and because of their links with other areas and other levels of politics, the Congress institutions attracted a large measure of this increased politicisation. At the same time, the pressures of factional rivalry within the Congress caused established Congressmen to look continually outside the boundaries of the movement to draw in new supporters from the wider political world. It was this process, which had resulted by 1937 in the internal political struggles within Congress institutions becoming the chief dynamic of political development in the provinces and localities of most of India, that was the major contribution made by the lower echelons of the Congress organisations to the political development of the sub-continent. But the dominance of Congressmen in local and provincial politics did not necessarily guarantee the dominance of the all-India Congress leaders at the national level, nor the dominance of any one set of national leaders within the Congress organisation as a whole. In 1936 the power and position of the central leadership as a whole *vis-à-vis* their followers in the provinces and localities had been at a low ebb, while the position of the established leadership within the all-India institutions was extremely precarious. To understand how this situation developed and was eventually resolved we must now look at the impact wrought by the changes in provincial Congress politics between 1937 and 1939 at the national level.

4 Central Congress Politics 1937–9

The election victories in 1937 appeared to confirm the Congress claim to be the most powerful political institution in India. In theory, as their election manifesto had stated, the Congress had only fought the P.L.A. elections in order to destroy the 1935 constitutional settlement from the inside. The new strength of the Congress now seemed to put new weapons into the hands of the all-India leaders in their struggle against the British. The central Congress leaders were committed to preventing the federal scheme of 1935 being brought in and to obstructing its working if it were imposed. But in practice, the all-India leaders lost the ability, if not the will, to carry out these threats.

Between September 1937 and September 1939 there were a number of official and unofficial contacts between the Congress leaders and the British policy-makers. At various times Lord Linlithgow, the Viceroy, had discussions with G. D. Birla, Bhulabhai Desai and Gandhi himself about the Congress attitude to federation. Lord Lothian, a Liberal peer and ex-Under Secretary of State, also sounded out Congress opinion during a tour in December 1937. Nehru, and the left wing of the Congress generally, objected to federation because under it Indians would still have no control over defence, external affairs and the army – which together took over half the budget of the Government of India.[1] Gandhi seemed readier to accept a compromise on these matters (that the Viceroy would discuss them with his Council but retain control of them himself).[2] Right-wing Congressmen's objections to federation had a simpler explanation – the federal legislatures, as the British had planned them, would not allow Congressmen to dominate all-India politics as they could provincial politics. Since the States' representatives were to be nominated by the Princes, British Indian politicians would not be able to dominate the centre without Princely support: Gandhi and his colleagues did not think their chances of obtaining such support were very good.[3] At the Haripura Congress session of March 1938 a Working Committee resolution was passed stressing that the nomination of the States' representatives was the only objection to the federal scheme and amendments from the left pointing up the problems of the reservation of defence, the army, foreign affairs, some aspects of finance and the unlimited powers of the Viceroy, and calling for a mass campaign to oppose federation were all roundly defeated.[4] The initial Congress terms for compromise on a federal constitution were not harsh – they were ready to accept a British India federation, or one with elected representatives from a few 'enlightened' states, such as Mysore.[5] Linlithgow was also eager that the constitution of the States should be made more democratic but, as we will see, the attitude of the Princes and of the British Government to any changes in the terms of the 1935 Act tied his hands,while the Congress leaders found their freedom of action limited by pressures from within their own organisation.

Despite the Working Committee's tentative plans for a compromise on the issue of the States' representatives, the major role which the threat of federation played in high Congress politics between 1937 and 1939 was in the internal struggle for control between the 'Gandhians' and their critics, not in a tactical battle between the Congress leaders and the *Raj*. The new tensions which the acceptance of office in the provinces had caused in the subordinate institutions now spread upwards to dominate the all-India level also. By supporting the ministries and cracking down on dissidents within the provincial Congress organisations, the 'right-wing' leaders hoped to reassert their own leadership at the national level; by supporting those excluded from the ministries, the socialists hoped to regain the initiative that had been so nearly in their grasp in 1936. The issue of federation, with its associated questions of the role of parliamentary and agitational activity in the future programme of the Congress, played a major part in this struggle.

In many ways the 'left-wing' Congress leaders, especially the leaders of the Congress Socialist Party, were initially in a weaker position than before the P.L.A. election campaign. Since the Faizpur Congress session of December 1936 they had steadily lost ground. Their position in the all-India institutions was now precarious; an unsigned note (probably written by M. R. Masani, Secretary of the A.I.C.S.P.) circulated in late 1937 pointed out that the socialists could only find a place on the A.I.C.C. by courtesy of the proportional representation rules – if a distributive voting system were introduced, 'the Socialists would be wiped out'.[6] The C.S.P. leaders saw their role as that of offering 'critical co-operation' to the ministries and of trying to 'develop the Congress into a more effective weapon of the Indian masses in their struggle for . . . National Independence'.[7] But in practice they found that there was 'a very restricted scope for extra-parliamentary activity',[8] they could do little except 'lament for our miseries . . . and wait for better luck next time'.[9]

At the same time, the position of the C.S.P. leadership was being weakened by splits and divisions within the ranks of their party. Since 1936 members of the Communist Party of India had been invited to join the C.S.P. on an individual basis. By this alliance, the C.S.P. leaders had hoped to gain influence in the trades union movement in return for allowing members of the C.P.I. a legal front for their activities. But the communists did much better out of the alliance than the socialists; by 1937–8 members of the C.P.I. held high positions in the C.S.P. Sajjad Zaheer and E. M. S. Namboodripad were the Joint Secretaries of the A.I.C.S.P., two other communists were on the executive committee and a number of provincial organisations had come under their influence. In August 1937, as a result of the discovery of plans for the C.P.I. to either take over or destroy the C.S.P., the socialist leaders tried to ban any new communist enrolments. But they allowed C.P.I. members already in the party to stay and, by 1939, had lost control over a large section of their followers.[10]

The C.S.P. leaders were also weakened by the defection of the Royists. After Roy's release from jail in late 1936, he began a campaign attacking the C.S.P. programme and calling for the P.L.A. election successes to be used as a 'prelude to systematic, well-planned mass action with the object of carrying out the resolution of the Faizpur Congress [on an Agrarian Programme]'.[11] In March 1937, Roy told his followers to leave the C.S.P., timing their resignations to make it look as if the party were collapsing.[12] By April, 40 prominent C.S.P. men in Maharastra, 17 in Karnatak and six in Bombay City had answered his call.[13]

The position of the C.S.P. leaders was further weakened because, as two of them were members of Nehru's Working Committee, they were forced to lend their authority to resolutions that undercut the basis of their party's programme.[14] In these circumstances both they and Nehru were on the lookout for some issue to support to reassert their leadership over the left as well as their standing in the Congress. Although Nehru could see that '[our] general attitude to these [Congress] Ministries cannot be agitational in the old sense; we cannot agitate against ourselves',[15] his search for an alternative policy to the parliamentary programme did mean supporting Congress critics of the ministries. Nehru, just as much as M. N. Roy, wanted to turn the Congress machine that had won the elections into an organisation for a mass campaign,[16] the vital problem was to harness the 'tremendous awakening and ferment' among the peasantry (demonstrated by the growing kisan movements in such provinces as the U.P. and Bihar); unless it allied with 'the new forces that are growing everywhere' the Congress would cease to lead India.[17] In the U.P. and Bihar these 'new forces', as we have seen, took the form of attacks by the leaders of the Kisan Sabhas, who were also Congressmen, on the Congress ministries. But Nehru felt that purging the Congress of these critics would be fatal since 'the left . . . represents a vital part of the movement without which it would lose much of its flair and become increasingly wedded to petty reformist activities'.[18]

Nehru and the C.S.P. leaders had hoped to give peasants a voice in the Congress by encouraging the All-India Kisan Sabha to demand 'functional representation' in the Congress. As the chance of getting this receded,[19] they encouraged the Kisan Sabha organisers to enrol members and take over Congress Committees directly; they suggested that Congressmen opposed to the ministry in their province should set up Kisan Sabhas distinct from the Congress from which they could launch agitations against the ministers.[20] All this seemed a deliberate sabotage of the ministries. This tension had, by the time of the Haripura Congress, helped to make the Bihar P.C.C.s instructions to Congressmen to have nothing to do with kisan organisations an important test-case for the whole movement.

The C.S.P. leaders also joined critics of the Congress ministers for their handling of law and order; they wanted in particular the release of political prisoners jailed by previous Governments for terrorist crimes. The issue was delicate since, by releasing terrorists and legalising banned institutions, the Ministers were likely to invite intervention by the Governors, who would use their special powers. Such use of the special powers would force the Congress ministers to resign. But whatever Gandhi's views on special powers may have been,[21] his wing of the Congress did not want a constitutional crisis over law and order. This matter was first discussed at a Working Committee meeting in August 1937. G. B. Kher, Premier of Bombay, asked the Committee what he should do about five communist labour organisations banned during Civil Disobedience. Nehru was for removing the ban; Gandhi was not, unless the organisations promised to be good while the Congress was in office. A very vague statement that the Congress was against all 'oppressive legislation' was all the help Kher could get, and he was told to ask the advice of the Governor and the Secretariat. Most of the Committee was adamant that the Congress ministries should not fall out with the Governors on this matter.[22] By October 1937 both Kher and G. B. Pant, the Premier of U.P., had been forced to crack down with the full power of the law on agitations in which Congressmen were involved; yet still the Working Committee gave no lead.[23]

Attacks on 'oppressive legislation', and on keeping political prisoners in jail, grew in the provinces. At the A.I.C.C. meeting at Calcutta at the end of October, Masani introduced a resolution criticising the Congress Ministries along these lines. Although it was defeated (by an amendment that the whole matter should be passed over to the Working Committee),[24] Gandhi was indignant that the matter should have been raised at all.[25] As the Haripura Congress session approached, the 'right-wing' leaders, and Nehru as well, became more and more convinced that law and order was not an issue on which a constitutional crisis should be forced.[26] But in Bihar and the U.P., the ministries were being pressured so hard by the Provincial Congress Committees and by provincial opinion generally that they had to order the release of all political prisoners, against the wishes of the Governors. When the Governors refused to sanction these releases, the ministers had to resign. This led to a crisis which dominated the Haripura Congress.

Of course, the Gandhian leaders tried to meet these challenges to their control over the Congress. Kisan and labour movements were outside their control and were usually opposed to the Congress ministries. So they tried to take action against them. Even before the ministries had taken office some all-India leaders had seen the dangers. Prafulla Chandra Ghosh, the 'Gandhian' leader of Bengal, wanted the Working Committee to curb the peasant organisations by ordering Congressmen to work in the countryside through the Congress, not through the Kisan Sabhas.[27] Vallabhbhai Patel agreed with Ghosh that Congress dissidents in the Kisan Sabhas were a real threat.[28] 'Elements who believe in indiscipline and violence' were also at work in labour agitation,[29] and A. K. Azad feared that the time would soon come when differences between left and right over the programme and attitude of the Congress would become 'irreconcilable.[30]

As a long-term measure, the 'Gandhian' leaders turned to the Gandhi Seva Sangh,[31] a completely non-political organisation until 1937. In April 1937 the Sangh had allowed its members to participate in parliamentary work. By the end of 1937, the 'Gandhians' saw that the well-organised and financially well-endowed Sangh might be useful to them in their political battles. Now that the struggle for leadership within the Congress was expressed in terms of an ideological clash between 'Socialist' ideas and 'Gandhian' ideals, the 'Socialists' could gain ground only because 'those of us who still believe with Bapu have not cared to organise the undoubted majority in the nation that his ideas and ideals still command'.[32] So Gandhi's non-political supporters had to be wheeled in. At the annual Conference of the Sangh in March 1938, its members were actively encouraged to canvass and stand for the Congress elections and 'to combat Leftist forces in the parliamentary and political fields generally'.[33] The influence of the Sangh was mainly in rural areas so, in November 1937, the Executive of the Sangh had established a 'Labour Sub-Committee', with Patel, Prasad, Jamnalal Bajaj, Jairamdas Doulatram and J. B. Kripalani as its Executive, to challenge the left wing dominance of the Trade Union movement. With its associate the Hindustan Mazdur Sabha (founded in 1938) the Sub-Committee sought to provide facilities for arbitration, organisation and aid for non-violent agitation to take the Trade Unions and labour organisers away from the influence of the left.[34]

All this was not enough to put down the challenge at the Haripura Congress. Since the whole experiment of office acceptance was at stake, its defenders now used the powers of office to defeat any threat to it. For the first time, the 'Gandhian' leaders wrote to their associates in the ministries and the Provincial Congress Committees asking them to ensure that dissident Congressmen were excluded as far as possible from election as delegates to the General Session and to the A.I.C.C. Rajendra Prasad, for example, wrote to the Bihar leaders listing the problem districts, and urging them to see that the left-wing Congressmen were kept out.[35] He asked that the Provincial and District Congress Committee Executives should not indulge in unconstitutional activity to secure the exclusion of the left, merely that right-wingers should settle their disputes and close their ranks to present a united front against the left wing challenge. But it is difficult not to connect Prasad's injunctions to Bihar leaders with the anti Kisan Sabha resolutions passed by some D.C.C.s and by the Bihar P.C.C. at the end of 1937.

The all-India Congress leaders were not only worried about agitational campaigns in British India; they were also concerned about the relationship between Congressmen in British India and political movements in the Native States. The attitude of the Congress to the States Peoples Movement had never been very clear. Despite a concerted campaign by the leaders of the States Peoples Conference in 1934, the Bombay Congress declared that Congress committees could not be formed in the States, but that States subjects could join British Indian committees.[36] In December 1934, the Working Committee resolved that Congressmen should give sympathy and support to the States subjects in 'legitimate and peaceful struggle', but failed to define what this meant in practical terms.[37] This vagueness did not satisfy some of the Working Committee's critics: in 1935 and 1936 consistent attempts were made by members of the C.S.P. and Congressmen with an interest in the States to clarify the position.

The dissenters wanted to make the point that the struggles in British India and in the States were both part of a wider whole – the fight for democracy and freedom. But, despite a determined effort by the leaders of the States Peoples Conference and Yusuf Meherally and Kamaladevi Chattophadaya of the C.S.P., the Madras A.I.C.C. meeting of October 1935 passed the Working Committee resolution that 'the responsibility and the burden of carrying on that struggle [in the States] must necessarily fall on the States Peoples themselves. ... In the heat of controversy the limitation of the Congress is often forgotten ...' without amendment.[38] At the Lucknow and Faizpur sessions, even with the added support of Nehru, all attempts to change this attitude again failed.[39]

When Nehru became President of the Congress he gave more latitude to Congressmen who were trying to build up an agitational base outside British India than the strict terms of these resolutions allowed. In practice he encouraged the use of the Congress name in State politics and the formation of Congress committees; as he wrote to one inquirer:

It is entirely wrong to say that the Congress or its leaders are not interested in the future of the Indian States Subjects. . . . Therefore it is desirable and necessary that Congress work should be carried on in the Indian States and Congress Committees organised there.[40]

The only limitation he imposed on such activity was a request that the Working Committee should be notified before a civil disobedience campaign was started in any State.[41]

By 1937, affairs in the States were coming to a head. The All India States Peoples Conference had recently been taken over by Pattabhai Sitaramayya, the Andhra Congress leader who had been born in Mysore State,[42] and its earlier concentration on small Marathi States rectified. Activity in the States was also spurred on by the thought that the imposition of Federation would guarantee the autocratic rule of the Princes and exclude the States subjects from any say in local or national government. To prevent this they had to force the Rulers to concede democratic reforms before they accepted the terms of the Federation. By February 1938, the All India States Peoples Conference was considering launching *satyagraha* campaigns in 21 States – including Hyderabad, Kashmir, Jaipur, Bikaner, Patiala, Indore, Bhopal, Cochin, Travencore and Mysore.[43]

Of these putative and actual campaigns, the one in Mysore was the most important, and it was this one which caused the crisis in the Congress over the States Peoples Movement at Haripura. The course of the Mysore agitation revealed clearly the very features that the majority of the Working Committee feared would result from direct Congress involvement in such campaigns. The effect of a widespread agitation in Mysore on the internal politics of the Congress was two-fold. In the first place, the relationship between the Mysore District Congress Committee and the Karnatak Provincial Congress Committee (to which it was technically subordinate) was neither clear nor stable enough to stand the strain to which it was subject. Secondly, the agitation in Mysore attracted and encouraged dissident Congressmen from Karnatak and outside. Both the local C.S.P. leader, Kamaladevi Chattophadaya, and the Karnatak P.C.C. Secretary, N. S. Hardikar, tried to exploit the Mysore agitation to build up their position inside British India. Rebel Congressmen from Bombay City, notably K. F. Nariman and Yusuf Meherally, were also quick to lend the weight of their names to the campaign for increased representative government.[44]

The disruptive effects of the Mysore agitation were not confined to the local level. Riding the wave of feeling against the State authorities' use of repression, the Congress left used the issue against the right-wing leaders. At the A.I.C.C. meeting of October 1937 the C.S.P. leaders, with Nehru's help, managed to get a resolution passed urging all Congressmen to give moral and material support to the campaigns in the

States. This resolution was passed despite strong opposition from a majority of the Working Committee.[45] Nehru could not see what all the fuss was about; he claimed that the resolution had merely continued the *de facto* policy that he had established of 'every sympathy and help but no deliberate law-breaking on our [Congress] part'.[46] But Gandhi now decided that it was time to make a stand. Worried by the tone of the speeches at the A.I.C.C. meeting and concerned that the resolution would lead to demands for a *satyagraha* campaign in British India in support of the Mysore agitation, he thought it was 'imperative to cry a halt'.[47] He publically criticised the A.I.C.C. resolution as *ultra vires* since an A.I.C.C. session could not overrule the policy laid down at the Lucknow General Session and the Working Committee supported this judgement by passing a resolution that the Calcutta decision was to remain ineffective until the whole situation had been reviewed at Haripura.[48]

The opponents of the Working Committee hoped to use the Haripura Congress to press home their advantage, gained at the Calcutta A.I.C.C., over the Congress attitude to the Native Rulers and to reverse the precedent established by the Bihar P.C.C. resolution banning Congressmen from membership of the Kisan Sabhas. Both dissatisfied Congressmen and the States Peoples leaders hoped that the Haripura Congress would give a clear commitment of support for *satyagraha* movements in the States and would allow the All India States Peoples Conference to become the wing of the Congress operating in the States.[49] The Working Committee's resolution had the opposite intention – it declared that all Congress committees in the States should – disbanded and that no work should be carried on in the States by Congressmen, or in the Congress name, without prior Working Committee consent.[50] At the Subjects Committee meeting at Haripura, both left-wing Congressmen and Sitaramayya attacked this resolution; by a series of hurried consultations between A. K. Azad, Sitaramayya, Vallabhbhai Patel, Nehru and Subhas Chandra Bose (the President-elect of the Congress) the Working Committee leaders managed to split the opposition by taking up a suggestion of Sitaramayya's that existing Congress committees in the States should be allowed to continue in existence but should not do any work without Working Committee authorisation.[51] The amended resolution was passed by the Subjects Committee and later by the open session too.[52]

The Working Committee resolution before Haripura on the Congress and Kisan Sabhas sought to support the resolution of the Bihar P.C.C. on the same subject. While it recognised the right of the peasantry to organise into Kisan Sabhas and the valuable role that these Sabhas could play in the struggle for independence, this resolution warned that:

. . . the Congress cannot associate itself with any activities which are incompatible with the basic Principles of the Congress and will not countenance any of the activities of those Congressmen who, as members of the Kisan Sabhas, help in creating an atmosphere hostile to Congress principle and policies.[53]

Kisans were told that the only way they could hope to influence the Congress was by joining it, while Congressmen who took part in campaigns arranged by the Kisan Sabhas against the Congress ministries were threatened with disciplinary action. In the Subjects Committee, both Azad, the Working Committee spokesman, and Bose urged that this resolution should be passed without opposition because of the tension between the Congress ministers and the Governors of the U.P. and Bihar.[54] To the disgust of small minority of delegates, this advice was followed in the Subjects Committee and the open session.[55]

The Haripura Session was dominated by the resignations of the U.P. and Bihar Ministries over the question of the release of political prisoners. In both these provinces the ministers had been under increasing pressure from within the Congress to secure the release of a tiny number of prisoners – 14 in the U.P. and 16 in Bihar. In December 1937, neither the right-wing leaders nor Nehru had thought this issue one on which the Congress should force a constitutional crisis,[56] but by February 1938 the pressure on the Ministries had become so great that the Working Committee ordered them to offer their resignations if the Governors refused to sanction release.[57] Just before the Haripura Session, the U.P. and Bihar Ministries did resign.[58] The Working Committee were careful to keep this 'crisis' under control – they refused to allow all the Congress Ministries to resign in sympathy[59] – but they exploited it to the full. Both the Congress Socialist leaders and Bose were mollified by the resignations – the C.S.P. leaders thought that they heralded a more uncompromising attitude to the new constitution, Bose was anxious to support any move that would place more pressure on the Bengal Government to release the 600 political prisoners it still held. Only ten days after their resignations, the Ministries reached an agreement with the Governors (by which the case for the release of each prisoner was to be reviewed individually) and the Congress went back into office. But, by this time, the ministerial crisis had served its purpose for Gandhi and his colleagues – most of their critics over the Kisan Sabha resolution had been silenced by the need for unity in the face of a direct confrontation with the British.[60]

On paper, the Haripura resolutions represented a substantial victory for the Congress establishment. But in practice the terms of the resolutions were largely ignored. Congress and All India States Peoples Conference leaders even differed over what the Haripura resolution on the

States meant. Vallabhbhai Patel, as President of the Gujerat P.C.C., forbade the establishment of any new Congress Committees in the States on the authority of the Haripura resolution; but the A.I.S.P.C. leaders interpreted the resolution as only a restriction on the programme of Congress Committees in the States, not on the formation of new ones, and encouraged their followers to set up new Congress organisations.[61] The resolution at Haripura clearly banned the use of the Congress name in any parliamentary campaign, but the leaders in several States circumvented this ban by transferring parliamentary activity to a State Congress organisation. Thus the Mysore and Cochin State Congress organisation made full use of the Congress name while remaining technically within the terms of the Haripura resolution.[62] In 1939, the Congress leaders found that they could only control activities in the States by direct, personal supervision. Thus Nehru became the President of the A.I.S.P.C., while Gandhi and Patel led a model agitation in Rajkot and Bajaj led one in his home state of Jaipur.

It is worth pointing out that there is little evidence in all this to support the view of many British officials at the time, and of several historians since, that the Congress leadership saw their involvement with the States Peoples movement as a way of forcing democratic constitutions on the Native Rulers and so ensuring a majority in an elected Federal Assembly. The Haripura resolution on Federation made it clear that the main Congress objection to the 1935 Act scheme was the nomination of States' representatives, but the relationship of the Congress to the States Peoples movement was one governed by internal Congress politicking, not by a grand strategy to acquire power at the Federal centre. The Congress leaders, in their public statements, looked to a change of heart by the Princes, rather than a large-scale agitation, to achieve the election of the States' representatives.[63] In his long series of articles in *Harijan* on the problem, Gandhi attacked the British Residents and Political Officers, rather than the Princes or their administrations, as true authors of repression.[64] Gandhi was not alone in distrusting the influence of British officials in the States: Colonel Haskar, Dewan of Gwalior, had commented during the constitutional discussions on the policy of the Viceroy and the Political Department of making certain that there were enough British Prime Ministers and Political Officers at work in the States to ensure that 'the future representatives of the States in the Federal Legislatures will be completely under British influence'.[65]

The enforcement of the Haripura resolution banning Congressmen from membership of Kisan Sabhas was left up to the provincial Congress organisations. Thus the effect of it varied from place to place, depending on the political situation within each P.C.C. As we have seen, in the U.P. Congress leaders continued to enjoy close contact with the Kisan movement despite the resolution; even in Bihar the link between dissident Congressmen and the Kisan Sabhas was not completely broken.

After the drama of Haripura, the opposition within the Congress at all-India level lacked a clear leader to spearhead an attack on the 'Gandhian' Working Committee members. Jawaharlal Nehru, the leader of 1936, was now unwilling and unable to play this part,[66] and in any case he was out of India for much of 1938. But in October Subhas Chandra Bose, the Congress President, defied Gandhi's wishes by standing for re-election. In the next few months he was able to ally temporarily with all the dissidents within the provincial and all-India Congress and win the presidential election against a candidate officially endorsed by the Working Committee and by Gandhi.

The 'Bose revolt' has often been interpreted as a struggle between 'left' and 'right', between the Organisation and the Ministries, between those who wanted a composite Working Committee and those who wanted to establish a Gandhian dictatorship. It was true that as the dispute developed both sides turned to ideological abstractions to strengthen their case, but it was personal differences that were at the heart of the matter. This was recognised at the time – A. K. Azad wrote after the Tripuri Congress that:

> I consider the affair of Subhas Babu to be neither a struggle between the right and the left, nor the question of composite or homogenous Working Committee. It is only a matter of Subhas and some of his supporters.[67]

In many ways, both Nehru and the 'Gandhians' represented one style of leadership — both were prepared to subsume their provincial ambitions in the needs of the Congress as a nation-wide whole, both looked on Gandhi as a political father-figure, a beneficial as well as a necessary influence on India's development. In this respect Bose was an outsider – he regarded his provincial interest in Bengal as all-important and saw the Mahatma's influence as only a useful political tool. For health reasons (he suffered from tuberculosis) he had been in Europe for some time; his previous links with the all-India leaders had been based more on political expediency than on any identity of interest. This independence of outlook and action was the real source of Bose's challenge to the established leaders.

Even Bose's financial resources were independent of those of the 'Gandhians'. The main sources of funds open to the 'right-wing' leaders were donations from Indian businessmen negotiated by Patel, Desai, Bajaj and G. D. Birla. There was also the capital and interest on certain special appeal funds and the loans that could be raised on them. Nehru had no independent resources; he was completely dependent on the 'Gandhians' for money. Bose's sources of income were smaller, but they were genuinely his own. He could rely on payments for favours shown to Bengali businessmen by the Bengal P.C.C. and the Calcutta

Corporation (as long as he controlled these bodies) and on 'protection money' from large industrial magnates in Bengal, Bihar, Assam and Orissa, given in return for good labour relations. He also had support from a group of non-Bengali businessmen, headed by the Delhi mill-owner Shankar Lal, and could use the funds of the Tropical Insurance Company (of which he and his brothers were directors and Shankar Lal Managing Director) to stabilise his finances. From these sources Bose managed to raise Rs 50,000 simply for the expenses of his delegates and canvassers at Tripuri.[68]

Between the Haripura Congress and the A.I.C.C. meeting in September 1938, there was no formal conflict between Bose and the established leaders.[69] Unlike Nehru, Bose did not force the issue on any general matter of policy or programme. But there were a number of straws in the wind, underlying tensions based on Bose's conception of his own distinctive role as Congress President. After the Haripura session, Bose had tried to get the A.I.C.C. office (the only permanent Congress institution) transfered from Allahabad to Calcutta so that he could 'supervise its work properly'.[70] He failed to achieve this, but even so the unaccustomed interference of the President in routine office matters almost caused J. B. Kripalani, General Secretary since 1934, to resign.[71] Unlike previous Presidents, Bose tried to make use of all the resources of his office to further his provincial ambitions. Nehru later pointed out that the fact that Bose was 'largely occupied with local and provincial affairs in Calcutta' during his first term as President was one reason for the decline in the efficiency of the A.I.C.C. office during 1938.[72]

Another source of tension between Bose and the established leaders was over the question of forming a coalition ministry in Bengal. In 1937 the Parliamentary Sub-Committee had issued clear instructions to the Congress P.L.A. parties in provinces in which they could not assume the ministry, forbidding them to attempt to form coalition ministries.[73] The original plan was for Congress parties in opposition in the P.L.A.s to try independently to get the ministries to accept as much of the Congress programme as possible. But the Working Committee members soon realised that this policy was short-sighted – in practice the Congress M.L.A.s frequently united with other opposition groups against the ministers and the possibility of a future coalition ministry would make these attacks more effective.[74] In 1938 coalition ministries were allowed in Assam and Sindh.[75] Bose regarded Assam as part of his personal sphere of influence and it was his insistence, combined with the advice of Patel and Gandhi, which removed the initial opposition of Azad and Prasad to the formation of a Congress coalition ministry in that province.[76]

Bose now turned his attention to Bengal. In Ocober 1938, at the time that the Assam coalition ministry was set up, Gandhi and Patel had supported his plans for a similar ministry in Bengal.[77] But by December Gandhi had been warned by Birla that a Bengal ministry that included Bose's supporters would lead to the disintegration of the Bengal Congress, and by Azad that the Muslim League would make a powerful propaganda issue out of the fall of a Muslim ministry in a politically sensitive Muslim majority province.[78] Following this advice, Gandhi now refused his consent to Bose's plan. Bose masked his disappointment with threats – he warned Gandhi:

> I shall have to very carefully consider my position. Obviously I cannot be a party to a policy which I am convinced is wholly wrong. . . . If you still adhere to your policy I shall resign.[79]

There was one other bone of contention between Bose and the established leaders, specifically between Bose and Patel. By the terms of the will of Vallabhbhai Patel's elder brother, Vithalbhai, Bose was to be left Rs 100,000 to establish a network of pro-India propaganda in Europe and America. Unwilling to see so substantial a sum of his brother's money go to increase Bose's powers of patronage, Vallabhbhai took advantage of an ambiguous wording to contest the bequest. The case dragged on in the Bombay High Court from July 1938 to March 1939, eventually being decided against Bose.[80]

For most of his first term as President, Bose made little attempt to seek support from other dissident Congressmen against the established leaders. But his insistence on a militantly anti-Federation programme for the Congress did secure him the sympathy of the Congress Socialists and other left-wingers. His exclusion from the inner circle of the Congress national leaders clustered around Gandhi, the basis of his support in Bengal and the situation of Bengal as a province in which the Congress P.L.A. party was in opposition, made him anxious that the presence of Congress ministries in other provinces should not be allowed to dominate the future tactics and programme of the all-India Congress. He was anxious to prevent a Congress 'sell-out' over Federation since even a federal centre under Congress control could not benefit his followers in Bengal very much. In July 1938 Bose issued an unexpected statement warning that even if a majority of Congressmen accepted some sort of compromise over Federation it would mean civil war inside the Congress.[81] This unauthorised statement annoyed the other members of the Working Committee[82] but they did not issue any rejoinder. At the Working Committee meeting in August Bose's colleagues contented themselves with a repetition of their earlier pronouncements on Federation, denying that the Congress would ever support Federation but stressing the resignations of the Congress ministries as the only sanction against its introduction.[83] Because of illness, Bose had not been at the Working Committee meeting when this resolution was discussed; arriving the next day, he categorically contradicted it by declaring that the Congress would start civil disobedience if Federation was imposed.[84] These differences were temporarily glossed over, but at the A.I.C.C. meeting in September they flared up again. Here amendments were brought in against the Working Committee resolution on Federation, demanding preparations for a mass campaign. When these amendments were defeated by large majorities, the dissidents, led by the Congress Socialists, walked out of the meeting.[85]

The right-wing leaders were shocked and annoyed by this demonstration of divisions within the all-India Congress. Gandhi, certainly, saw the walk-out as representing something of a crisis; he wrote that, with the presence of a dissenting group within the central Congress institutions, 'the Congress must cease to be a compact fighting organisation engaged in a life and death struggle with the most experienced and organised corporation in the world'. Warning the dissidents that if they did not believe in the Congress programme then they should leave the Congress, he added:

If chaos is to be prevented, proper measures must be taken in time.[86]

Bose played no direct part in the walk-out but it was his attitude at this meeting, rather than his subsequent anti-Federation campaign, that convinced the 'Gandhians' that they would have to break him to maintained their own control.[87]

The first indication that Bose would definitely run for the Presidentship for a second term was a press statement issued by eight Congress Socialist Party leaders in October calling for his re-election.[88] This move was followed by declarations of support from all sections of Bengali Congress opinion. By this time the basis of Bose's campaign was clear – he was attacking the 'Gandhians' on the Federation issue and calling for preparations for a Congress mass action campaign against Federation in almost every speech he made.[89] The 'Gandhians' were not happy over this state of affairs, they thought that Bose was jeopardising the unity of the Congress and disliked being libelled over their attitude to Federation,[90] but they could not find a strong candidate to oppose him. Gandhi's first thought had been to nominate A. K. Azad who, as a Bengali, might have been able to challenge Bose in his home province and who, as a Muslim, could call for support to prove to the British and the Muslim League that the Congress was not a party to Hindu communalism. But Azad refused to stand, as did Gandhi's second choice, Nehru, so the Mahatma had to fall back on the less well-known Pattabhai Sitaramayya.[91] Azad was in fact nominated for the Presidentship,[92] but Gandhi allowed him to stand down in return for a statement calling on all delegates to vote for Sitaramayya.[93] Bose answered this challenge with a statement pointing out how much support he had received for his campaign.[94] Gandhi now took charge of the 'right-wing' – he saw that Sitaramayya was the weaker candidate, and despite the misgivings of his disciples, ordered them to issue a statement condemning Bose's stand in the name of the Working Committee.[95]

From now on there was no going back. Gandhi had made it clear that there could be no compromise even if Bose won the election,[96] Bose attacked the organised Working Committee campaign against him as unfair.[97] All over India the delegate elections and the Presidential election was fought out in ideological terms – 'right' versus 'left', 'pro-Federation' versus 'anti-Federation', 'pro-Ministry' versus 'anti-Ministry'. By the time of the Presidential election on January 29th, almost every national, provincial and local Congress leader had taken a public stand one way or the other; the only prominent Congressmen who had not declared his interest was Jawaharlal Nehru.[98] Although even Bose admitted that the 'right wing are in a decided majority in the Congress',[99] many political commentators thought that he would win[100] and when the election result was announced it was found that Bose had won – by 1580 votes to 1377.

A study of the voting, province by province,[101] reveals several interesting points. The first is that Bose's majority was, relatively speaking, a small one (203 out of almost 3000) and that it was the vote in Bengal that ensured his victory. Had Azad been Bose's opponent, it is quite likely that the result would have been reversed. Gandhi's allies in Bengal had pointed out earlier that if Azad did not stand then they would have difficulty in breaking down Bose's support there.[102] It is important to remember who the delegates who elected the President were. They had been elected at the local level, in sub-district constituencies, and they formed the Taluka, District and Provincial Congress Committees as well as occupying the delegates' seats at Tripuri. In some areas the delegate elections had been fought out in terms of ideology,[103] but in general it is fair to say that the vote of each province's delegates in the Presidential election reflected the state of internal faction rather than any wider ideological alignment. Bose, who had promised to reduce the role of the Congress ministries in the future programme, gained support in the two important provinces in which there was no ministry – Bengal and the Punjab. In his other main areas of support – the U.P., Tamil Nad and Karnatak – there were ministries, but a vote for Bose could still represent opposition to these ministries or to the previously dominant faction within the provincial Congress. In the U.P., Bose had the support of the large section of the P.C.C. which was opposed to the ministry and its tenancy legislation, of the provincial C.S.P. and even of one of the ministers – R. A. Kidwai.[104] In the Karnatak, N. S. Hardikar, who had lost control of the P.C.C. the year before, backed Bose;[105] here, too, tenancy legislation was causing dissention in the provincial Congress.[106] Sitaramayya's

main support came from Bihar, Gujerat and Andhra. In Andhra he
was on home ground: although he was not the best-known or the
best-loved of the Andhra leaders, he was supported as part of the
campaign for a separate Andhra Province.[107] Gujerat was dominated
by Patel and Bihar by Prasad; even so, in Gaya and Patna Districts in
Bihar, the Kisan Sabha and Congress Socialist leaders surprised even
themselves with the volume of support that they were able to mobilise
for Bose.[108]

The 1939 Presidential election was impossible to control – it brought
too much grass-roots discontent to the surface. The election result in
Mahakoshal is one of the most interesting and one that clearly shows
the anarchy prevailing in the lower reaches of the Congress. In this
province, despite the clever manipulation of executive power by the
ruling P.C.C. faction under R. S. Shukla's ally Thakur Chhedilal to
control even the district level organisations, the result was almost a tie
– 67 for Bose, 68 for Sitaramayya. What had happened was that Bose's
campaign had at last given a common cause to the anti-Chhedilal
district level leaders, G. da Silva, Makhanlal Chaturvedi and Captain
Awadesh Pratap Singh, who had nothing in common except their hostility to the dominant provincial faction. These men had first supported
Khare against Shukla and now voted for Bose to strengthen their own
local challenge in the delegate election.[109] Much of this support for
Bose was of a similarly negative character, as Gandhi later hinted when
he wrote to Subhas that 'your election was . . . [a] censure of the old
horses, especially the Sardar [Patel]'.[110]

Bose's victory came as a shock to the 'Old Guard' (as Gandhi and his
colleagues were called during the crisis). According to Bose, Gandhi
and his lieutenants had thought that he would get only 25 to 30 per cent
of the votes and the result frightened them into thinking that they had
lost control of the national movement.[111] Whether it was making a
virtue of necessity or not, the 'Old Guard' claimed, both in private and
in public, that they were relieved that the tensions within the all-India
Congress had now come into the open and that they could force a
show-down. Patel was particularly keen to force the issue – he wrote to
both Prasad and Nehru expressing his relief that at last there could be a
straight fight between the old leaders and their critics.[112] Gandhi also
looked forward to a clearing of the air; immediately after the election
result was known he made his famous statement ensuring that all
Congressmen knew what was at stake:

> I rejoice in this defeat. . . . I am glad of his [Bose's] victory. . . . Since
> I was instrumental in inducing Dr Pattabhai [Sitaramayya] not to
> withdraw his name as a candidate . . . the defeat is more mine than
> his.[113]

The 'Old Guard' forced the crisis to its logical conclusion. Before the election they had realised that there could be no co-operation with Bose if he won; now twelve members of the Working Committee (Patel, Prasad, Azad, Bajaj, Desai, Mrs Naidu, Kripalani, S. R. Deo, H. K. Mehtab, P. Sitaramayya, Khan Abdul Gaffar Khan and J. D. Doulatram) sent in their resignations.[114] Gandhi's tactic was now to give Bose enough rope to hang himself by forcing him to form a Working Committee made up entirely of his own supporters and to put his programme before the Congress. If the worst came to the worst, Gandhi argued, the parliamentary programme might suffer but the real work of the Congress, the constructive programme, could go on whoever was in charge.[115] Bose, on the other hand, did not want to force a split in the Congress or see its division into two parties pushing forward rival programmes. All that he wanted was a new alliance with the 'Old Guard' on rather more equal terms than before.[116]

Again Nehru was the only Working Committee member to take no clear stand on this issue. Although the 'Old Guard' felt sure of Nehru's eventual support against Bose,[117] he did not resign from the Working Committee with them, pointing out that since twelve members·of the fifteen-man Committee had already resigned it would be impossible to find a quorum to hold any meetings anyway.[118] Bose later blamed Nehru's hostility for his defeat at Tripuri,[119] but in fact Nehru thought that a split in the Congress was neither advisable nor necessary. Although critical of Bose's activities as President and of his use of ideological issues in his re-election campaign, Nehru thought that there were more important matters for the Tripuri Congress to consider than the differences between the *soi-disant* left and right in the Congress.[120] The roots of Nehru's vague and unrealistic attitude to this whole affair lay not in any deep Machiavellian plot but rather in his temperamental unsuitability for, and instinctive shrinking from, the cut and thrust of power politics. He himself gave a hint of this at the time, when he wrote to Bose of the growing lack of principle and trust in Congress politics:

> I cannot stomach this kind of politics and I have kept absolutely aloof from them these many years. I function individually without any group or second person to support me, although I am happy enough to possess the confidence of many.[121]

Between the end of January and the Tripuri Congress in mid-March 1939, neither the 'Old Guard' nor Bose had decided on a clear course of action. Both had had distractions – Gandhi and Patel had become involved in the internal affairs of Rajkot State, culminating in a 'fast to death' by the Mahatma in early March;[122] Bose fell seriously ill in mid-February.[123] In the event, Gandhi was unable to advise his colleagues on any clear strategy to adopt at Tripuri[124] and Bose got no further in any attempt to draw up a suitable programme than a proposal for giving a six-month ultimatum to the British to withdraw the federal plan, to be followed by a civil disobedience movement if they did not do so.

Two important resolutions were put to the A.I.C.C. on the eve of the Tripuri session. One, moved by Sarat Chandra Bose, contained his brother's plans for combating Federation; the other, moved by a group of U.P. and Bihari 'moderates' headed by G. B. Pant, attacked Bose over the allegations that he had made during the election campaign that the 'Gandhians' were preparing to sell out over Federation, called on him to prove these charges and proposed a vote of no-confidence in him if he failed to do so.[125] On 8 March Bose was well enough to take the chair at the meeting. The Pant resolution was then introduced in a slightly modified form. There was no mention of no-confidence and the overtly critical sections of the resolution were watered down,[126] but a clause was inserted calling on Bose to follow Gandhi's wishes in appointing a new Working Committee.[127] This resolution was passed by 218 votes to 135; Sarat Chandra Bose's resolution was never moved.[128] At the Subjects Committee meeting, held shortly afterwards, Nehru introduced the other Working Committee resolution for the Congress.[129] In the open session, amid uproarious scenes, these and the Pant resolution were passed comfortably; only the Bengali delegates and some members of the Communist Party of India defended Bose.[130]

After the event, Bose gave three reasons for his defeat at Tripuri: the opposition of Nehru, the 'betrayal' of the Congress Socialists[131] and Gandhi's tactics in making the leadership issue one of a direct confrontation between himself and Bose.[132] What Bose failed to point out was that he had won the election on a disjointed wave of disaffection and frustration with the establishment, not because of any positive support for himself or his policies. Bose did not have enough committed allies to take charge of the Congress on his own. If the result of the Presidential election campaign had shown the weakness of the 'Old Guard's' control over the lower levels of the Congress organisation, the sequel to the election was to demonstrate the strength of their hold over central Congress politics.

The position of Gandhi and his lieutenants, that had looked so weak in February, was now extremely strong. Between the Tripuri Congress and the A.I.C.C. session at Calcutta in April, Gandhi and Bose were in constant correspondence.[133] Gandhi refused any compromise; he was determined that Bose should either form his own Working Committee and put a definite programme before the A.I.C.C. or else admit his weakness and resign.[134] Gandhi was not even prepared to accept the terms of the Pant resolution because of an ambiguity in its wording. Stating that the Working Committee should be formed in accordance with Gandhi's wishes could mean either that none of the 'Old Guard' should be included in it (as Gandhi had insisted in February), or that

Bose should be the President of a Committee nominated by Gandhi. Because of this second interpretation, Gandhi disowned the Pant resolution entirely and told Bose that it did not offer a viable solution to the problem.[135]

Bose, on the other hand, knew that he had to arrange a compromise or go under. He had no chance at all of forming a viable Working Committee without Gandhi's help. The support of his potential allies, whether from provincial politics or the all-India opposition groups, was too fragmented and mutually contradictory. As B. P. Sinha, the Congress leader from Bihar, pointed out when Bose attempted to form a Committee:

> [He has made] inconvenient commitments to a large number of not very desirable people, making the formulation of a Working Committee utterly difficult

and an alliance with the C.S.P. impossible.[136] Bose's first suggestion for a compromise was a fourteen-man Working Committee with seven members nominated by himself and seven by Gandhi. This idea got nowhere but, under Nehru's influence,[137] talks between Bose and the 'Old Guard' (excluding Gandhi) did start up just before the Calcutta meeting. However they were not fruitful – the 'Old Guard' were prepared to offer Bose two seats but he wanted four (one for Swami Sahajanand Saraswati, one for N. S. Hardikar, one for Sardar Sardul Singh Caveeshar and one for an Assamese politician no-one had ever heard of) and the right to choose the A.I.C.C. General Secretary.[138] At the Calcutta A.I.C.C. meeting Bose announced that he had just received another letter from Gandhi refusing any support or co-operation in forming a new Working Committee and that, as he could not form a new Committee on his own, he was compelled to resign.[139] After a last-minute attempt by Nehru to patch up a compromise had failed,[140] the A.I.C.C. accepted Bose's resignation and elected Rajendra Prasad as the new Congress President.[141]

After the Calcutta meeting, Prasad appointed his new Working Committee. This was composed of the twelve who had resigned in February plus Dr B. C. Roy and P. C. Ghosh – two Bengali Congress leaders opposed to Bose.[142] A place was also kept for Nehru, although he did not accept it immediately.[143] Bose's response to this was to try to set up the sort of national 'left wing' organisation that might have ensured his success at Tripuri, had it existed then. Bose founded both the 'Forward Bloc' (a pressure group within the Congress) and the 'Left Co-ordination Committee' (made up of four members of the 'Forward Bloc', three of the C.S.P., three of the C.P.I. and two Royists) to unite all groups of left-wingers to fight the Congress elections.[144] But neither of these groups lived up to expectations. The 'Left Co-ordination Committee' never managed to produce any co-ordinated action at all, while the 'Forward Bloc' attracted only those who were so excluded from the Congress politics of their home areas as to need desperate measures. Men like Swami Sahajanand in Bihar, K. F. Nariman in Bombay, G. da Silva in Mahakoshal and T. J. Kedar (a Khare supporter) in Nagpur became provincial leaders of the Bloc.[145] Such men, many of whom had had little contact with left-wing ideology, did not make good raw material for a united and dynamic pressure group. The inherent weaknesses in the 'Forward Bloc' were clearly exposed at its Conference held before the Bombay A.I.C.C. meeting of June 1939. Even M. N. Roy, who had been working hard for unity here, admitted that little could be achieved,[146] while the *Times of India* correspondent noted that:

> Nothing has come out of this so far. Numerous difficulties were encountered. Apart from personal rivalries, ideological conflicts became apparent. No two groups belonging to the left agree on what should be done, except to pull down the present leadership. An attempt was made to coalesce on the basis of a minimum of radicalism, but no useful agreement seems to have been reached.[147]

The forcing of the issues at Tripuri had resulted in greater divisiveness – not greater unity – among the ideologists of the left. As J. P. Narain later put it:

> The basic difficulty in the path of unity was the ridiculous idea held by every miserable little party that it alone was the real Marxist Party, and that every other party had therefore to be exploited captured or destroyed.[148]

Gandhi had never regarded the Bose revolt as anything more than a symptom of a still more dangerous disease – the growing corruption in the Congress. For some months Gandhi had been attacking, in a series of speeches, articles and statements, the growth of bogus membership, impersonation at elections, factional rivalry and decline of authority in the Congress. He blamed both Bose's re-election and the growth of opposition to the ministries on this. With their control re-established by the Calcutta A.I.C.C. and Bose's resignation, the Old Guard now turned to an attempt to reform the Congress constitution to remove manipulation, bogus membership and factional disunity from it. At the Haripura Congress the old 'Congress and Mass Contacts Committee' had been merged into a new Working Committee Constitution Sub-Committee[149] to consider ways to reform the Congress constitution. This followed the suggestion of the 'Congress and Mass Contacts Committee', which had recommended that such a committee should be established to consider ways of ensuring 'genuine' membership enrolment, the suitability of 'territorial representation' on the A.I.C.C.[150] and the feasibility of electing the Congress delegates indirectly.[151] Following a constitutional amendment moved by Kripalani at the Haripura Congress, the question of establishing fixed constituencies for the delegate elections was also handed over to this Constitution Sub-Committee.[152]

In fact, the Constitution Sub-Committee only ever considered the questions of indirect elections and genuine membership. They decided in favour of direct election and formulated several proposals to discourage bogus enrolment.[153] These suggestions were approved by the Provincial Congress Committees,[154] but, when the Sub-Committee formally submitted its proposals to the Working Committee in November 1938, these included several new recommendations which seemed designed to antagonise the 'left-wing' – particularly indirect elections and the abolition of proportional representation on the A.I.C.C.[155] On the basis of this report, the Working Committee framed a resolution calling for the creation of fixed electoral rolls under the supervision of the District Congress Committees, indirect election to the Provincial Congress Committees from the districts, a spinning or manual labour qualification for session delegates and the abolition of proportional representation on the A.I.C.C.[156] This resolution was passed by the Committee in December 1938 but it was never published and, because of more important matters, was not introduced at Tripuri.

At Tripuri a resolution was passed on the 'Congress Machinery' which called on the A.I.C.C. to take steps to revise the constitution and to stamp out 'abuses in the enrolment of members, elections and otherwise' within the Congress.[157] Nothing was done about this until the Calcutta A.I.C.C., when a committee of Prasad, Nehru, Sitaramayya, Narendra Dev and Kripalani was appointed to consult provincial opinion and frame recommendations for the A.I.C.C. meeting in June.[158] During May the Committee received 157 suggestions from Provincial and District Congress Committees, from informal groups of Congressmen and from individual members. These suggestions, which were supposed to form the basis of the Committee's recommendations, fell into two main groups. There were proposals from the 'left' to ban Congress M.L.A.s and members of the local boards from membership of Congress Committees and to make the Congress more accessible for workers and peasants. Even more numerous than these proposals were those of Congressmen of all parties who called for increased supervision of membership enrolment and elections, and the establishment of Boards of Management and election tribunals to supervise the holding of elections and to control the actions of the Executive Committees.[159]

When the Constitution Sub-Committee met at the beginning of June, its meetings were overshadowed by the prospect of a renewed clash between Bose, and his supporters, and the 'Old Guard' at the A.I.C.C. meeting later in the month. In these circumstances it is not surprising that the recommendations of this Committee[160] show a desire to suppress Bose as much as a wish to clean up the Congress. The Committee recommended a number of administrative changes designed to remove abuses in the organisation[161] and also two new constitutional clauses which seemed to be aimed directly at suppressing their opponents – the establishment of territorial constituencies without proportional representation for the A.I.C.C. and the provision of powers for the Working Committee to ban from Congress executive committees the members of *any* organisation of which it disapproved (not just the members of a communal organisation as before).[162]

At the Bombay A.I.C.C. meeting later in June the Working Committee submitted these proposals for ratification. Most of them were passed without opposition[163] but the ones specifically attacking the 'left' were never brought in. The proposal to give the Working Committee the power to ban the members of any organisation from executive office was seen to be a threat by most members of the 'left wing'. Both Narendra Dev and Nehru had written minutes dissenting from it in the Sub-Committee's report,[164] while Bose promised the Old Guard a full-scale crisis if they tried to push it through.[165] Gandhi was also opposed to any measure that would needlessly inflame sectarian conflict within the Congress[166] and so this clause was dropped by the Working Committee.[167] The proposal to do away with the principle of proportional representation for two-thirds of the seats on the A.I.C.C. was also resented by the left.[168] Bhulabhai Desai, the Working Committee spokesman on the amendments to the Constitution, did introduce this into the meeting but, after many amendments had been tabled against it and after discussions on the platform between Desai, Nehru and Bose, it was also withdrawn.[169]

To compensate for the loss of these two clauses, the Working Committee brought in two amendments which were aimed at limiting the influence of agitational leaders within the Congress. First Kripalani proposed an amendment to the Constitution that no Congress member should be allowed to vote in the delegate elections until he had been a member for three months; during the debate on this a group of moderate Congressmen led by Satyamurthi and Mohanlal Saxena introduced an amendment extending this probationary period to twelve months. This was passed by 119 votes to 87.[170] Then Desai introduced a proposal concerning the election of delegates. Fixed constituencies were to be provided in each district to elect one delegate for every 100,000 population, provided that there were at least five hundred Congress members for each delegate. Indian States within each province were to be allowed no delegates of their own, but one delegate per 100,000 States Subjects was to be allotted by the P.C.C. concerned for election in British Indian districts where surplus five-hundred member constituencies could be created.[171] Despite vigorous opposition from Bose and his followers (who objected that their influence in the Native States would be negated),[172] this proposal was passed.[173] This amendment had the effect of limiting the influence at a provincial and national level of an enrolment campaign based on a small number of districts. Under the previous constitution, the one delegate per 100,000 population ratio was allotted on a provincial basis, so a district with a high number of Congress members could elect more delegates than its population warranted. The new clause, limiting the population ratio to the district level, prevented this.

In view of subsequent events, it is difficult to estimate how much these constitutional amendments affected the power of the left within the Congress. What is certain is that they did little to halt corruption. For one thing, several of the amendments had been drafted so hastily that their meaning was not clear. The clause relating to the number of delegates to be allotted to each district on the basis of its population and membership figures was especially ambiguous; even Rajendra Prasad failed to interpret it correctly.[174] In 1940 constituencies were still fixed to please the ruling Executives, election tribunals did not adequately contain factional disputes and the P.C.C.s simply ignored any provisions of the new constitution that they did not like.[175]

The 'Old Guard' did not rely on these constitutional amendments to re-establish their dominance. They also introduced a resolution banning any individual or group of Congressmen from starting a *satyagraha* or civil disobedience campaign in the name of the Congress without prior permission from their Provincial Congress Committee. This resolution was clearly intended to limit the activities of Kisan and Labour leaders against the Congress ministries and was attacked by all sections of the left as imposing an intolerable burden on their activities. But in spite of their all-out opposition, the resolution was passed by a 2:1 majority.[176]

To demonstrate the extent of his support after the failure of his campaign at the Bombay A.I.C.C. meeting, Bose organised an all-India Protest Day against the resolutions passed at Bombay.[177] This Protest Day, called for 9 July, was arranged by the Left Co-ordination Committee. But before it took place, both the Congress Socialists and M. N. Roy dissociated themselves from it.[178] In the event, it was a flop. To the Working Committee this move looked like a last, desperate attempt to launch a new challenge at the forthcoming Congress elections, and they were convinced of the need to remain firm and punish Bose for such a blatant breach of discipline.[179] But the members of the Committee were undecided on how harsh their action should be and it was Gandhi who finally drafted the resolution removing Bose from his positions in the Congress and banning him from holding executive office for three years.[180] This resolution affected only Bose himself; action against his confederates was left up to the P.C.C.s. Thus although the Bombay P.C.C. took disciplinary action against Nariman and the Bihar P.C.C. took action against Swami Sahajanand, the U.P.P.C.C. decided 'in the general interests of the Congress' not to penalise any of its members.[181] The Working Committee had no time to consider the matter further; only a month after the formal end of the Bose revolt, the outbreak of the Second World War pitched them into another, much more serious, crisis.

By August 1939 the 'right-wing' Congress leaders had established a tenuous control over the all-India arena, a control underlined shortly afterwards when the provincial ministries answered their call to resign. But this control had been hard-won and the enjoyment of it entailed limitations on future policy. The outbreak of war in September 1939 seemed to throw the whole question of the future constitution of India into the melting-pot once more, but the attitude of the 'Gandhian' leadership to fresh overtures from the British was still to be determined by the primary need of retaining their own control over their followers. As Linlithgow commented after his meetings with Gandhi at the end of September:

> I felt very strongly how thin is the authority of the Right Wing in some respects . . . I suspect that he [Gandhi] no longer feels strong enough to hold this machine [the Congress] and I suspect too that the pressure from the left is becoming more and more marked. I feel considerable doubt as to whether the Right are satisfied that they are in a position to deliver the goods, if any agreement is in fact reached between them and us . . .[182]

5 British Policy and Indian Response 1939–42

By the autumn of 1939 the Congress leadership had managed to secure at least partial control over the enlarged and diversified nationalist organisation that had emerged from the 1937 elections and the ministry period. In the struggle for the initiative between the established central Congress leaders and their provincial subordinates and radical critics, the goal of putting pressure on the British position in India had been somewhat lost to view. Threatened and actual confrontations with the *Raj* had proved useful devices in internal Congress politics, they had served to secure unity and to silence criticism early in 1937 and at the Haripura session, and to add a veneer of ideology to the Bose revolt. But between 1937 and 1939 the all-India Congress leaders had been fully occupied by internal problems and had had neither the opportunity nor the power to further the struggle against the British for freedom and independence directly. The manner in which the Congress had succeeded in seizing the initiative in the provinces in 1936–7 and in filling the vacuum in provincial government created by the 1935 Act disturbed and alarmed the British bureaucrats in India, but did not fundamentally affect the new imperial strategy of abandoning the provinces and retreating to entrenched positions in central government. When the British position in India was subjected to the first strains of a fresh attack in 1939 this came, not from any major accession of strength to its Indian opponents, but by the impact of the unprecedented imperial crisis of the Second World War.

The 1935 Government of India Act had been a response to the still reverberating political consequences of India's sacrifices in the Great War and to the imperial crisis caused by the world depression of the early 1930s. As we have seen, the all-India constitutional solution that it proposed was never a practical proposition, having been designed to solve the problems of the government in London, not the Government of India. But the fact of this vital shortcoming was no reason to expect any automatic rethinking of British policy in the years that followed. There was no major domestic, let alone imperial, crisis in India between 1935 and 1939, while even when a new imperial crisis did occur, in September 1939, it took a year before the flaws in the federal scheme were fully realised in Delhi and London. From the British point of view, the federal solution of the 1935 Government of India Act had been dearly bought in terms of parliamentary time and domestic political disruption and could not be abandoned lightly. Lord Linlithgow, who came to India as Viceroy in 1936, was concerned to make the federal scheme work.[1] To accomplish this he had to secure the co-operation of the Princes, the Congress and the Muslim League, while his ability to manoeuvre was limited by the British Cabinet's disinclination to jeopardise the compromise in British politics that the Act represented. Linlithgow was not the most imaginative nor the most politically astute of men, but even if he had had the vision and skills of Ripon, Irwin and Mountbatten his options were too limited and his hands were tied too tightly to have allowed him to solve the problem of constitutional advance at the centre.

The 1935 Act had laid down that the federation could not come into being until enough Princely States to fill half the seats in the upper house of the legislature and to represent over half the total population of the States had acceded. The Princes were to come into the federation by signing an 'Instrument of Accession' which would supersede the treaties between the ruler and the Crown and would lay down the terms on which each joined up. Thus Linlithgow's immediate problem was that of getting enough signatures on princely 'Instruments of Accession' to enable the federal centre to be established. In 1936 Linlithgow drew up a timetable for the inauguration of federation. After informal discussions with the Political Department, all the Princes were to submit their claims by March 1937 and on the basis of these Delhi would draft individual 'Instruments of Accession' by December 1937. The Princes would then have four months to consider, so that federation could begin in April 1938. Unfortunately, the plan soon ran into difficulties. None of the Princes had been completely happy with the federal constitution as it had eventually emerged from London and they now seized their chance to bargain for better terms. The rulers of several important States – notably Mysore, Hyderabad, Gwalior, Baroda, Bhopal, Kashmir and the Kathiawad States of North Gujerat – began to negotiate about the financial privileges and fiscal rights that they would have to surrender to the federal centre, while the rulers of the smaller States petitioned against their under-representation on the federal legislatures.[2] Because of fears in London about the domestic political consequences of tampering with the Act, Linlithgow was unable to make any concessions on these matters until 1938, when he succeeded in getting agreement from the Secretary of State for some modification of the federal rules about the fiscal autonomy of participating States. But by now the Princes were becoming increasingly worried that participation in a democratic all-India government would add fuel to the growing agitations within their States for representative institutions. In early 1939 the Chamber of Princes rejected Linlithgow's new offer and demanded further assurances that the British would, if necessary, support their autocratic rule against any new demands by their subjects. Linlithgow, who was prepared to welcome some democratisation of the Princes' internal administrations,[3] tried to persuade them, but his hands were again tied by London, where the Conservative 'die-hards' were determined that no Prince should be compelled to join the federation against his will.

Although in strict constitutional terms only the consent of the Princes was necessary to establish federation, the attitude of British Indian politicians was also important. The Princes had demonstrated that the federal scheme could be modified by hard bargaining; the Congress had always maintained an attitude of hostility towards the all-India provisions of the 1935 Act and now the Muslim League leadership began to move towards a similar position. Between 1937 and 1940 the All India Muslim League concentrated on strengthening its claim to speak for all Indian Muslims – under the domination of one man, Mohammed Ali Jinnah. Jinnah's main tactic was to wage a total propaganda war against government – both the actual Congress governments in the provinces and the proposed federation at the centre – in defence of Muslim interests. The 1935 Act envisaged a unitary, strong federal centre, with most of the British Indian representatives being elected by the Provincial Legislative Assemblies. This did not suit the League at all. In all but four British Indian Provinces (Bengal, Punjab, N.W.F.P. and Sindh) Muslims would have a minority of representatives, and the 1936–37 elections to Provincial Legislative Assemblies suggested that only a very few of these Muslims would be Leaguers. Jinnah had to do two things – to win the provinces to the League, and attack the federal plan for the centre. What he wanted was decentralisation, a weaker centre with less control over the affairs of the provinces. He built up alliances with Muslim native rulers against the federation and against the demand that States' representatives at the federal centre be elected by their subjects.[4] Few Muslim politicians were happy with the federal scheme and, once Jinnah had made an attack on Federation, the main plank of the League programme, non-League Muslim leaders could only counter this by proposing their own modifications to the plan. Thus Sir Sikander Hyat Khan, Muslim Premier of a communally mixed party in a Muslim majority province, the Punjab, sought to get British and Congress support for a scheme of federation based on a weak federal centre and a system of 'blocs' of provinces that would free the Muslim majority provinces from the fear of dominance by a predominately Hindu centre.[5] During the negotiations with the Viceroy in 1939 Jinnah consistently asked for more than he knew he could get, linking his provincial and all-India campaigns together by claiming to represent Muslim fears that they would be submerged by the Congress. It was only after the outbreak of war, when the federal plan of the 1935 Act had been suspended, that Jinnah offered his support to the Government of India in return for recognition that the Muslim League alone spoke for India's Muslims.

With the benefit of hindsight, we can see that the first three years of Linlithgow's viceroyalty ought to have demonstrated the unsuitability of the federal scheme of the 1935 Act as a viable solution to the problem of securing Indian co-operation in central government. But in 1939 neither the Viceroy nor the Secretary of State saw any reason to be downhearted, much less to revise their long-term strategy. The success of the Congress in seizing the initiative in provincial government and inserting its own institutional structure as the arbiter of political destiny in the localities between 1936 and 1939, which we can now recognise as a real turning-point in the British struggle to maintain their position in India, made only a small dent in the optimism of Linlithgow and Lord Zetland. The advent of Congress ministries had made the task of individual Governors more delicate, and the attempts of the Congress leaders to use this new power to wring further concessions at the all-India level in early 1937 and early 1938 had caused a fluttering in the dovecotes in New Delhi and Whitehall but, after all, the whole point of the 1935 Act had been to engineer the British retreat from the provincial sphere of government and, as Zetland pointed out in January 1939, '[a]part from this tiresome campaign by Congress against the Princes the Congress Ministers in the Provinces seem to be behaving reasonably'.[6] Trouble was only expected from the Congress if some crisis at the all-India level resulted in the High Command calling on their followers to resign and, with various self-appointed go-betweens (notably G. D. Birla), assuring Linlithgow that Gandhi was considering a compromise on some modified form of federation, no such hiatus seemed likely.[7] The renewed activity of the Muslim League was seen to be a problem, Zetland fearing that Muslim opposition to federation might eventually prove more embarrassing than the Congress opposition,[8] but as late as July 1939 Linlithgow, supported by his provincial Governors, still thought that the Muslims would work federation if it were forced upon them.[9] The pressures on the Princes for some democratisation of their domestic administrations, which would limit their effectiveness as a conservative bastion in the federal legislatures, seemed inexorable, but even this did not greatly concern Linlithgow, who claimed that he had never envisaged the Princes managing to play the role laid down for them in 1935 for more than a very short period.[10]

In 1939 the *Raj* had only eight more years to run, but the illusion of permanence was as strong as ever in Whitehall and Delhi. In the summer of 1938 Linlithgow had been in London for consultations with the British government and on his return he found Bengal, and especially Calcutta, full of rumours that the British intended to quit India within five years. He could find no reason at all for this; as he wrote to Zetland:

> No one, of course, can say what, in some remote period of time or in the event of international convulsions of a particular character, may be the ultimate relations of India and Great Britain. But that there should be any general impression (if in fact it exists) that we are without a policy or that public opinion at Home, or His Majesty's Government seriously contemplate evacuation in any measurable period of time, . . . seems to me astonishing. . . . [O]ur policy in India is envisaged in the terms of the Act; . . . we have every hope of a satisfactory development on constitutional lines of the relations between the two countries on the basis set out in the Act, and of the maintenance for as far ahead as any of us can see today, of relations between India and Great Britain, who have so many points of contact and so many common interests. . . .[11]

Reviewing the British position in India in reply to this letter, Zetland was careful to point out the more dynamic aspects of the situation, notably the rise of the Congress in the provinces and the threatened collapse of the Princes which might open the way for the Congress to dominate the centre also, but he admitted that the inability of India to defend herself without British troops and the growing domestic problem of the division between the Congress and the Muslim League would brake any rapid progress by India towards the full Dominion Status envisaged by the 1935 Act.[12]

This discussion took place in January 1939: not surprisingly, the issue of defence was in the front of the minds of both men. To Linlithgow, 'the acute problem of defence' and 'the steps which we are taking further east in Singapore and the like to maintain our position in the East as a whole' seemed cogent reasons for the British staying in India;[13] for Zetland, Britain's chief bargaining counter was her unique ability to defend India in an increasingly hostile world with 'so many highly-charged Dictators . . . knocking about the planet.'[14] However, in practice, the issue of defence was to prove a weakness of the British position in India rather than a strength. British defence planners needed India as a base, a recruiting ground, a supplier of munitions and war materials and a creditor more than the Indians could be persuaded to admit that they needed British troops to defend them in a war not of their making.

From September 1939 until 1945 the need to obtain the greatest possible support from India for the imperial war effort became the underlying purpose of British policy. But this single aim did not make that policy any easier to evolve – rather it produced an underlying network of delicately balanced interlocking political calculations, against which the more obvious factors of Indian distrust and political ambition, personality clashes and defects among the British policy-makers and the brooding presence of Churchill's anachronistic imperial ideas must be set. Baldly stated, the problem facing the British policy-makers was that only rigorous executive action could ensure maximum efficiency in the Indian war machine, while the growing social and economic impact of the intensifying Indian war-effort led to increasing pressures, from inside and outside India, for political concessions to Indian opinion both in the conduct of the war and in a constitutional settlement after it. At the same time, because of the events and developments of the previous decade, the pressures from within India were increasingly expressed through two strong and incompatible vehicles of political mobilisation – the Congress and the Muslim League – so that any attempt by the British to find a short- or long-term political settlement would result in increased divisiveness and tension within India, which would in turn put the Indian war-effort in jeopardy. In order to maintain their Empire in the short term the British had to go back on the system of substituting informal influence for formal rule which they had been evolving in India for the previous twenty years. The inevitable result of this was that in the long term India was lost to Britain and her Empire.

When Britain declared war on Germany in September 1939 neither the Viceroy nor the Secretary of State thought that their policy would be very much affected. At first Lord Zetland expected Indian opinion to support the British war-effort unconditionally;[15] Lord Linlithgow saw the need to open negotiations with Indian leaders, but also consistently underestimated their determination to exploit the situation for their own ends. Linlithgow had spent the first half of his Viceroyalty stubbornly pursuing the chimera of federation: on the outbreak of war he recognised that the federal scheme should be suspended, but only because the Government of India would find constitutional investigations too 'distracting' in time of war.[16] Although the Secretary of State quickly realised that the federal scheme was now impracticable as an eventual solution to the Indian problem,[17] Linlithgow did not accept this at once. In November 1939 he again asked London to sanction one last effort to get the Princes to accept federation[18] and not until August 1940 did he finally abandon the all-India provisions of the 1935 Act.

Within two weeks of the outbreak of war both the Congress and the Muslim League had passed resolutions offering at best only conditional co-operation. But Linlithgow and the Cabinet in London were not prepared to make many concessions. Both the Congress and the League were demanding promises about India's post-war constitution as the price of their support, yet the British Government and the Viceroy, although prepared to admit privately that India would have to be rewarded for her support during the war by some constitutional advance after it, were adamant that no concessions could be made during the conflict and that nothing should be promised that would limit their freedom of action once the war was over. The British policy-makers had no intention of repeating what they saw as the greatest mistake in India policy of the 1914–18 war – the tactic of buying short-term Indian support by the announcement of definite plans for long-term constitutional advance.[19] Thus the most sweeping statement of intent that Linlithgow was allowed to make was his Declaration of 17 October that, after the war, the British would be:

> very willing to enter into consultations with representatives of the several communities . . . with a view to securing their aid and co-operation in the framing of such modifications [to the 1935 Act] as may seem desirable.[20]

The outbreak of war had found the Congress leaders split over what policy they should follow. The pre-war resolutions on the question had all been drafted by Nehru and had stressed that the Congress should bargain with the British for the promise of large scale constitutional advance in return for support for the war-effort. But these resolutions had not always been passed without protest from Gandhi; in September 1938, for example, he had protested strongly, but unavailingly, that a truly non-violent Congress could not offer support to the war-effort in any circumstances.[21] Gandhi had an interview with the Viceroy in the first week of the war. At this meeting he told Linlithgow of his personal sympathy for Britain and that he would be in favour of unconditional support for the allies.[22] But he also made it clear that this was only an individual viewpoint, not Congress policy. When the Working Committee met, he found himself under attack from all sides. Although Gandhi was supported by four members – Dev, Kripalani, Doulatram and Ghosh – the majority of the Committee, led by Nehru and Azad,[23] insisted on a resolution declaring their willingness to help Britain in a war against Fascism but repeating an earlier demand for Britain to state her war aims in regard to Imperialism and Democracy,[24] warning that the Congress could not long delay condemning Britain's use of India's resources in a war to which she was not a party.[25] Meanwhile, Linlithgow had been interviewing representatives of all Indian opinion: on 17 October he gave his conclusions from these discussions in a reply to the Congress. He declared that while the British Government was not prepared to concede the Congress demand for complete independence it did intend to grant Dominion Status to India eventually and was willing to involve India's leaders in the war effort by 'the establishment of a consultative group, representative of all major political parties in British India and of the Indian Princes'.[26] The Congress leaders could not accept that no constitutional advance in India was possible without the agreement of all sections of British

Indian and Princely opinion, and the Working Committee condemned the Viceroy's statement as 'an unequivocal reiteration of the old imperialist policy' of divide and rule. The Committee also resolved that on these terms the Congress could give no support to the war-effort and as a first step called on the Congress ministries to resign.[27] In fact the Congress leaders were correct in suspecting the intention behind this offer. The Cabinet had only allowed Linlithgow to make the announcement after he had convinced them that a consultative committee would have no power at all and would have no chance to 'entrench itself too deeply in the machinery of Government.'[28] Linlithgow had also assured the Cabinet that the committee would be dissolved the moment it looked like getting out hand.[29]

In the early months of the war British policy was negative; the Cabinet were interested not in a grand gesture that would win Indian support to their cause, but in devising methods to divide and minimise the Indian response to the new situation so that they could carry on as if nothing had happened. They saw the growing rift between the Congress and the Muslim League as their trump card. Although Linlithgow made a genuine attempt to get the two Indian parties to agree to a common programme, both he and the Cabinet looked to the rivalry of the Congress and the League as their most useful weapon against the demands of either. Linlithgow was not prepared to gamble too heavily on the League as a source of loyal support to the *Raj* during the war – he thought that the League was too anti-democratic and anti-nationalist to be a stable political force for long – and he was not prepared to grant Jinnah's demand for a veto on any constitutional advance that did not suit him.[30] But he was still eager to cultivate the League's pretensions as the best hope of counteracting the Congress demand for a voice in the conduct of the war.[31] Most members of the Cabinet also looked to the communal divide as the most effective trap for the forces of nationalism. Churchill was not much more extreme than most when, early in 1940, he condemned the Viceroy's attempts to get an agreement between the Congress and the League as suicidal and pointed to the Hindu/Muslim tension as the bulwark of British rule in India.[32]

In the short term it was indeed the problem of the Muslim League that divided the Congress leaders from the Viceroy at this point. At the outbreak of the war Jinnah was still trying to get recognition, both from the Muslim community and from the British, of his and the League's right to speak for India's Muslims. In September 1939, the League had passed a resolution condemning the 1935 federal scheme as prejudicial to the rights of minorities and demanding that the League be accepted as the Muslim spokesman in future discussions.[33] Linlithgow was anxious to give the League some say in India's future. After the Congress rejection of his October statement, the Viceroy renewed discussions with Gandhi, Prasad and Jinnah. He offered to throw his Executive Council open to representative Indians but left it up to the Congress and the League to agree terms.[34] Jinnah demanded a coalition with the Congress not only at the centre but in the provinces too.[35] Clearly the Congress leaders could not accept this; in reply they revived the demand for a constituent assembly (an elected Indian body to work out a future constitution) as a device to nullify the advantages that the League could gain by appealing to the British for minority safeguards.[36] The negotiations quickly broke down; the Working Committee met in mid-December and declared that the British were still playing the old game of 'divide and rule' and that no solution to the communal problem was possible so long as the Indians looked to the British as arbitrators.[37]

Linlithgow was now content that nothing could be done to entice the Congress into co-operation with the British. He did little to break the deadlock since he imagined that the Congress leaders had calculated that 'if they can hold out for a little longer . . . we shall be prepared to offer them a better bargain.'[38] But he still went on seeing Jinnah and in January 1940 he received the Muslim League's terms for an agreement with the Congress. Jinnah again demanded a Congress/League coalition government in all the provinces and refused to accept any form of democratically elected central government. Linlithgow put these terms to Gandhi but, not surprisingly, they were totally rejected.[39] From the failure of this last initiative until June 1940, Linlithgow continued his advice to the Secretary of State that Britain should 'refrain from action', 'wait upon events', 'avoid running after the Congress' and 'lie back and not move'.[40]

Most provincial Congress leaders were prepared to wait patiently while their national leaders negotiated with the British and with Jinnah. Although there was some grumbling, the Congress M.L.A.s were prepared to wait for the conclusion of the discussions with the Viceroy. The left wing of the Congress were anxious to see a clear stand by the Congress against the Government of India, but they were in no position to force their demands on the national leaders. The events of March to September 1939 had shattered the unity and limited the appeal of the left-wing organisations.[41] The resolutions of the Bombay A.I.C.C. had severely hampered the Forward Bloc; the Communist Party of India and the Royists remained esoteric and mutually hostile groups and the Congress Socialist Party had fallen apart under the strain imposed by events. The C.S.P. had never recovered from its decision to withdraw support from Bose at Tripuri. The leadership was now split and its control over its followers minimal. The provincial parties in Punjab, Bengal and Bihar had renounced the policy of the all-India leaders; in June 1939 Acchut Patwardhan, Dr Lohia, Ashok Mehta and M. R.

Masani had resigned from the party in protest over the influence of the communists within it. Of the original leadership only Dev and Narain were now left – as Dev himself recognised 'the Party has largely lost its character and become a platform'.[42] In 1940 the Congress Socialists were strong only in the United Provinces, and here they consistently sided with the 'right wing' against other leftist groups.[43]

In the first months of the war the leaders of the left-wing groups and the Forward Bloc spread propaganda in favour of a clear rejection of any offer by the British and an all-out campaign against the *Raj*. But they were unable to attract much support; at the A.I.C.C. meeting in October, their demands for a policy of total opposition to the war were heavily defeated.[44] The Bloc's call for a 'National Struggle Week' and 'War Resistance Day' in September went unheeded and its convening of an 'Anti-Imperialist Conference' in October was ignored.[45] The dissident Congressmen did not feel strong enough to launch an anti-British campaign all on their own;[46] they too waited for the end of the negotiations with the Viceroy.

Although they felt no immediate challenge to their leadership, the Working Committee leaders were aware of the need to retain the initiative within the Congress. The only alternative to an agreement with the Viceroy was an eventual mass campaign, but Gandhi and his colleagues felt that neither the Congress itself nor their control over it was strong enough to make civil disobedience a practicable proposition.[47] In October the Working Committee had hinted at a possible future campaign by warning Congressmen to be ready for a call to action, but it had also reminded them that in the past non-violent action had always been tinged with violence and that this must not be allowed to happen again.[48] In November, the Committee had complimented Congressmen on the eagerness that they were showing for civil disobedience but told them that they were not yet ready for it.[49] Throughout 1939 Gandhi and his colleagues had warned Congressmen that they were not ready for civil disobedience;[50] now the Mahatma declared that it was impossible, since indiscipline and factionalism within the Congress would lead to 'violence' and 'civil war' with the Muslim League.[51] He wrote that Congressmen were now less well prepared for civil disobedience than they had been in 1930[52] and urged attention to the constructive programme as the only suitable programme for the Congress.[53]

By February 1940 it had become clear that the negotiations with the British could go no further. The Congress was due to meet at Ramgarh (in Bihar) in March; the Working Committee could not afford to face this meeting without a definite programme. In early March, the Committee met in Patna and clearly established that a civil disobedience campaign should be the objective of the Congress. But the resolution was worded cautiously – it stressed that the Congress would 'unhesitatingly' begin civil disobedience only when the Congress organisation was ready for it; full powers to begin and control the campaign were given to Gandhi. This resolution was also passed by the Ramgarh Congress and instructions were sent out to the Congress Committees to prepare themselves by converting themselves into 'Satyagraha Committees' and 'War Councils' manned by those who had signed the 'Satyagraha Pledge' (committing them to obedience to Gandhi, non-violence and the constructive programme).[54]

This resolution proved adequate for the Ramgarh Congress, but it did not solve the problem of how the Congress leaders were to handle a situation in which they had been snubbed by the Government of India but felt too insecure to launch a civil disobedience campaign directly. From September 1939 to March 1940 they had been able to keep the initiative within the Congress by skilful manoeuvrings so that:

... the 'leftists' are led to believe that direct action is inevitable while the 'rightists' are warned that in the absence of perfect obedience to Gandhi's dictates such action is bound to end in disaster.[55]

The Ramgarh Congress had laid down an agreed programme; it had not laid down how it was to be carried out.

Civil disobedience was to be the programme of the Congress, but Gandhi was in no hurry to start;[56] after Ramgarh he and the Working Committee took some time to assess the situation. Nehru was keen for an immediate mass movement, taking issue with the 'goading' tactics of the Government of India. But he was in a minority of one within the Working Committee. Gandhi, as well as Azad and other Muslim Congress leaders, feared how the League might react to any civil disobedience movement aimed at forcing the British to concede more influence to the Congress; other members of the Committee (including Patel, Prasad and Rajagopalachari) thought that the Congress was not ready yet for a mass campaign, but were worried about 'demoralisation' within the movement if the leaders did not come up with some clear-cut programme for the rank and file to follow.[57]

In the provinces, Congress life went on much as usual. Although the ministries had resigned and the Congress Committees were supposed to be committed to the Ramgarh resolution of preparing for satyagraha,[58] Congressmen were still heavily involved in local board politics[59] and in the United Provinces even contested by-elections to the Provincial Legislative Council.[60] At the Ramgarh delegate elections:

Many people who, for fear of possible conflict, were keeping themselves in the background, have now pushed themselves in front again when the possibility of enjoying the plums of office and power seem to dangle again in front of them.[61]

These same elections produced the usual crop of disputes as various factions struggled for control of the district and provincial organisa-tions.[62] Lacking leaders and unity, the Congress left did badly in these elections; only 646 delegates out of the 3111 elected to the Ramgarh Congress were members of any of the left-wing organisations, while only 99 of the 376-strong A.I.C.C. elected from the provinces were members of any of the left wing parties. The Intelligence Bureau analysed the Congressmen at Ramgarh thus:

A.I.C.C.

Province	Right-wing	C.S.P.	Forward Bloc	Kisan Sabha	Royists	C.P.I.	Other leftists	Total
Ajmere	5							5
Assam	8							8
Bengal	43				4		4	51
Bihar	34	5	1	1				41
Bombay	3	1			1			5
Gujerat	15							15
Karnatak	8		4				4	16
Maharastra	13	1	1		2	3	2	22
Mahakoshal	16		2					18
Nagpur	5							5
Vidarbha	5							5
Delhi	1	1	2					4
Andhra	20	2	1	3	1			27
Kerala	4	5	1	1			1	12
Tamil Nad	27						2	29
N.W.F.P.	6		1					7
Utkal	7	2		1				10
Punjab	16	3	5			4	1	29
Sindh	4		1					5
U.P.	37	17	1		2	5		62
Total	277	37	20	6	10	12	14	376

Source: I.B. Memo no. 38/Cong/40 of 15.4.40 in G.o.I. Home Department (Political) 4/4/40 N.A.I.

The right-wing leaders in the provinces were not keen on civil dis-obedience, but more from a fear of the reaction of the Muslim League than of the movement getting into the hands of the left wing groups in the Congress.[63]

Before the all-India Congress leaders could decide on a definite prog-ramme, the situation had changed again. The success of the German *Blitzkrieg* in Western Europe forced the Working Committee to define its attitude to the possibility of external aggression by Britain's enemies. Gandhi was insistent that the Congress could only act non-violently in such a situation,[64] but the majority of the Committee thought that this attitude was impractical in the event of the invasion of India or of the disturbances that might follow the fall of Britain to

Session Delegates (and P.C.C. members)

Province	Right-wing	C.S.P.	Forward Bloc	Kisan Sabha	Royists	C.P.I.	Other left	Total left	Total
Ajmere	6								6
Assam	53						7	7	60
Bengal	379				23			23	402
Bihar	288						35	35	323
Bombay	14	5	1		1	3	1	11	25
Gujerat	113	3			1			4	117
Karnatak	45	12	44			1	22	79	124
Maharastra	125	9	2		20	10	7	48	173
Mahakoshal	142		3					3	145
Nagpur	28			3				3	31
Vidarbha	35								35
Delhi	5	2	7	1				10	15
Andhra	198						19	19	217
Kerala	35						60	60	95
Tamil Nad	215						17	17	232
N.W.F.P.	55		7					7	62
Utkal	131	12	2			2		16	147
Punjab	159	5	42			17	7	71	230
Sindh	25		1				1	2	27
U.P.	246	200	9		7	15		231	477
Total	2,297	248	118	4	52	48	176	646	2,943*

*The total number of delegates should have been 3,111 but there were vacancies in various provinces.
I.B. Memo no. 38/Cong/40 of 15.4.40 in G.o.I. Home Department (Political) 4/4/40 N.A.I.

Hitler. Therefore the Working Committee resolved that they could not support Gandhi's pacifism. The issue of how the Congress should react to the use of military force was not only a moral one; if the Working Committee condemned the use of violence for national defence then it would have been very difficult for them to co-operate with the Government of India if an opportunity arose. And such an opportunity again seemed possible.

L. S. Amery, the new Secretary of State for India, was working on a plan to make a new offer to the Indian politicians. With the war in Europe going so badly, Linlithgow had been broadcasting appeals for unity and at the end of June he had talks with Jinnah and Gandhi on the probable reactions of the Congress and the League to a further statement clarifying Britain's intentions in India and an offer to participate on the Viceroy's Executive Council. Neither leader was very helpful; Jinnah refused to accept any statement that might compromise Pakistan (while he was willing to join the executive), Gandhi stuck to the Ramgarh Congress demand for complete independence.[65] But

other members of the Congress Working Committee were more eager
to respond to a British initiative. Early in July Patel and
Rajagopalachari got a resolution through the Committee which
declared the Congress's willingness to help the British if a 'National
Government' was established at the centre which would have the
confidence of the C.L.A. and which would be able to work with the
provincial governments.[66]
Gandhi was never reconciled to this plan; he condemned the resolution as showing that the Congress had lost faith in non-violence and
had succumbed to the 'irresistible temptation' that:

> Congressmen can again become Cabinet Ministers. They will have
> an insight into the war machine . . . They will have to raise crores
> and crores of rupees and dispose of them in the war effort.[67]

Gandhi had realised that the Muslim League's opposition to the Congress had developed because the Congress had become identified with
government; in the ministry period it had become a political party
rather than a national movement representing all interests. He was
now trying to re-establish the Congress claim to speak for all classes
and communities. He asserted that:

> The Congress . . . is derived not from the members on the Congress
> registers but from the millions who have never entered the Congress
> but feel that the Congress represents them[68]

and urged that the Congress should:

> . . . represent even those who are hostile to it and who will crush it if
> they can. Not until we make good that claim shall we be in a position
> to displace the British Government and function as an independent
> nation.[69]

If the Congress was to play this role then its programme must be one
specially tailored to meet the circumstances. Ministries were out of the
question, only the vaguer image of the Congress as opponent of British
rule, as had been projected during the civil disobedience movement of
1930–34, would serve.
Gandhi's colleagues did not think like this; they still saw an agreement with the *Raj* as the best way out of their difficulties. But when the
British offer did come, it proved totally inadequate. The Viceroy's
terms, published on 8 August, included an offer of places on the Executive Council and on the War Advisory Committee to 'representative
Indians'. It stressed the rights of minorities and assured them that their
opinions would be respected in any revisions of the 1935 Act after the
war and hinted at the establishment of a constituent assembly of all
parties of Indian opinion to devise the framework of a new constitution.[70]

Patel, Nehru, Azad and Rajagopalachari, the Congress leaders who had put so much store by co-operation, now realised that this avenue of advance was barred. They quickly agreed to a compromise with Gandhi over the question of the Congress attitude to military violence and gave him their support for a civil disobedience campaign.[71] At the A.I.C.C. meeting on 15 September Gandhi offered his own ultimatum to the Viceroy – either Indians were to be given freedom of speech against the war for pacifist reasons or the Congress would begin *satyagraha*.[72] Linlithgow rejected Gandhi's demand and on 13 October the Working Committee accepted Gandhi's plan of campaign; he was promised 'the fullest co-operation in all that he may require or expect them to do'.[73]

The Civil Disobedience movement of 1940–41 was never a mass campaign. Gandhi had planned it in four stages. First there was *satyagraha* by those specifically and individually selected by the Mahatma himself; this stage opened with the arrest of Vinoba Bhave on 21 October. Then, in November, members of the Working Committee, the A.I.C.C. and the P.C.C.s, again selected by Gandhi himself, were allowed to court arrest. Between five and six hundred Congressmen were arrested in this stage, including the Congress President A. K. Azad and ex-members of the Congress ministries. The campaign was suspended for a Christmas holiday from 23 December 1940 to 4 January 1941; when it was restarted, *satyagrahis* were accepted from lists drawn up by the P.C.C.s. In the first month of 1941, nearly 2000 arrests were made, but after that the numbers declined. Finally, in April 1941 ordinary four-anna members of the Congress were allowed to offer *satyagraha*. By June over 20,000 Congressmen had been convicted but then the campaign quickly lost impetus; in October only about 5,600 *satyagrahis* were in jail, the number of arrests was falling and many Congressmen were beginning to voice demands that the campaign should be called off.[74]

This civil disobedience campaign was essentially a holding operation. Gandhi based his strategy round an assumption that it was better for the Congress not take any positive initiative, but to wait until the British and the other Indian parties produced a scheme and then to capitalise on it by setting itself up as the leader of all the opposition to it.[75] The only difficulty about this plan was that neither the British nor the minority parties seemed to be in a position to act in a positive way. The attitude of the War Cabinet in London, especially of Churchill, hampered attempts by the Secretary of State and the Viceroy to break the deadlock, while Jinnah's strategy was dominated by the need to impose his leadership on the recalcitrant Muslim politicians of the Punjab and Bengal by an uncompromising advocacy of the Pakistan scheme. This was more important to him at this stage than any agreement with the *Raj*. By late 1940 Jinnah had led the Muslim League into a position of 'stalemate' because he had failed to get British approval of the Pakistan plan.[76] Thus he was left exalting the claims of the Muslims against all others, and could not take advantage of the wider support offered to him when other minority leaders proposed that he lead them in a united campaign against the Congress claim to speak for all India.[77]

The limited *satyagraha* campaign also served Gandhi's ends within the Congress. By clearly opposing the British Gandhi could keep the appeal of radical dissidents in check, while at the same time he was careful never to let the movement get out of his own control. Although Gandhi admitted to his friends that 'sometimes I get a little worried about the mentality of our young men. I know they are impatient. They might do something stupid. Communism appeals to youth, unfortunately',[78] he was able to keep the initiative. In January 1941 representatives of the Forward Bloc and the C.S.P. met Kripalani at Lucknow to press for a mass civil disobedience campaign. But the radicals realised their own weakness, stressed that 'they did not wish to antagonise the Congress High Command or weaken the Congress' and, when their demands were ignored, could do nothing about it.[79]

The limited *satyagraha* campaign did not affect the bulk of Congressmen in the provinces and localities. They were still allowed to contest elections to local boards up until October 1941. Even after the national leaders decided that no more official Congress candidates should be put up, the Mahakoshal P.C.C., for one, still endorsed the candidature of various Congressmen standing as individuals.[80] In most provinces Congress members of local boards were never asked to resign; even if a member of a board was selected to offer *satyagraha*, Gandhi advised him not to give up his seat so that 'undesirable people' could not take advantage of his sacrifice.[81] Even the process of the selection of *satyagrahis* by provincial and district Congress Committees was manipulated by some Executives to serve factional ends. After it had been decided in 1941 that only those who had been to prison would be eligible to sit on Congress Committees, it was alleged that the Mahakoshal P.C.C. and some D.C.C. Executives had failed to send forward the names of some of their opponents as *satyagrahis* and so had kept them off the Congress Committees.[82] It is true that during 1940 and 1941 the number of Congressmen on the rolls sank considerably[83] but the lack of enrolment was as much due to the suspension of all Congress elections during this period as to any genuine loss of appeal of the Congress. The P.L.A. elections of 1936–37 had shown that the Congress was a formidable election opponent; many opportunist Congressmen remained in the movement and even went to jail 'for fear of losing prestige with the public as Congress officials'.[84]

Gandhi was prepared to take a long-term view of Congress strategy, concerning himself with preparations for a full-scale civil disobedience campaign once the war was over and the British had formulated definite proposals for Indian constitutional reform.[85] But several Congress leaders were disappointed at the slow pace of this design and, late in 1941, attempted to hurry things along. From September 1941 onwards, a group of Congressmen, led by Rajagopalachari, Bhulabhai Desai and Satyamurthi, began to campaign for a return to the 'parliamentary programme'. The possibility of restarting the Swarajya Party was discussed, but it was realised that Gandhi would never give his consent to this move.[86] These leaders met with Congress members of the Central Legislative Assembly in November to discuss ways of securing the return of the Congress ministries in the provinces and some Congress participation in the central executive.[87] As an immediate step Rajagopalachari proposed the return of the Congress members to the C.L.A. and the toning down of the Congress resolution on 'National Government' (passed at the Poona A.I.C.C. meeting of July 1940) to a demand for a composite central Cabinet in which the Congress was to be given several important portfolios. Rajagopalachari thought that this plan would force Jinnah to negotiate on a realistic basis and that, if the Government of India released all the *satyagrahis* in jail, Gandhi would either support it or abdicate from the Congress.[88] But Gandhi said nothing to encourage these hopes: backed up by Patel and Prasad (and sure of the support of Nehru when he was released) he was prepared to admit that the Congress 'was becoming demoralised by the long uproductive civil disobedience campaign but insisted that a return to the 'parliamentary programme' would lead to a worse demoralisation.[89] On 3 December the Government of India announced the release of all *satyagrahis*, but Gandhi replied that this made no difference to his campaign. However, he did advise A. K. Azad, the Congress President, to call meetings of the Working Committee and the A.I.C.C.[90]

These meetings were arranged for late December 1941 – a period dominated by Pearl Harbour and the Japanese drive through Burma. At the meetings Rajagopalachari's plan was clearly rejected – the Working Committee and the A.I.C.C. repudiated any agreement with the *Raj*. Again Gandhi clashed with a majority of the Working Committee over what action the Congress should take in the event of an invasion of India and, in public at any rate, he stepped down from the leadership of the Congress.[91]

During the next months Rajagopalachari tried, without any success, to reach an agreement with Jinnah over joint Congress/League demands for India's future.[92] The rest of the Congress leaders waited for some sign from heaven. Civil disobedience was not re-started, but neither were any practical plans to end the deadlock put into effect. Like other Indian parties they now looked to the British to make a move.[93] In March 1942 their prayers appeared to have been answered.

On 11 March Churchill announced that Sir Stafford Cripps would be sent out to India by the War Cabinet to investigate conditions on the spot and to explain to the Indian leaders new plans drawn up by the War Cabinet which would 'represent a just and final solution to the Indian problem'.[94] Just as in June 1940, the Congress leaders turned aside to investigate this *deus ex machina* – and just as before they were to be sorely disappointed.

This is not the place to give a detailed account of the Cripps Mission to India, the negotiations of April 1942 and the consequent reaction of the Congress and the Government, the one turning to open rebellion, the other to naked repression. The course of these negotiations, and their drastic results, link with the frantic discussions of 1945 to 1947 rather than to the smoother waters of the 1930s. What follows is no more than a sketch of the main changes in British policy that led to Cripps's sudden dash to India, but even a sketch will reveal that the underlying threads of Britain's attitude towards Indian nationalism had undergone no fundamental change since the great period of constitutional discussions from 1929 to 1934.

By the end of 1941 the Congress had called off its *satyagraha* campaign and the Japanese had made a dramatic entry into the war in the Far East. Yet not the Viceroy, nor the Secretary of State nor the Prime Minister thought that their policy in India should be altered to meet these changed circumstances. Linlithgow and Amery were convinced that there could be no advance on the 'August Offer' of 1940; if the Congress continued to repudiate this, then the stalemate must continue.[95] Linlithgow's chief concern was for the conduct of the war; he was opposed to anything that might impede the ability of his Executive Council to prosecute it and that might import the wider political and communal questions into the straightforward task of fighting the Japanese.[96] Amery, while prepared to give way over peripheral issues such as the amount of control exercised by the India Office over India's representatives at the War Cabinet, was still convinced of the need to keep the 1940 Declaration and conciliate Muslim opinion at the expense of the Congress.[97] Churchill, too, could see no advantages to be gained from altering the constitutional arrangements in India. He thought that neither the state of the Indian war-effort nor that of international opinion would be improved by any gesture that the British could make. Like Linlithgow, his main concern was for the military situation; he saw that:

> The Indian troops are fighting splendidly, but it must be remembered that their allegiance is to the King Emperor, and that the rule of the Congress and the Hindoo [sic] Priesthood machine would never be tolerated by a fighting race.[98]

But, outside this triumvirate, pressures for a fresh policy initiative were building up. In February 1942 Stafford Cripps was made Leader of the House of Commons and Clement Attlee was officially named as Deputy Prime Minister. It was their influence that got a new offer under way. Attlee was now convinced that it was necessary to unite India behind the British war-effort by an imaginative scheme of immediate concessions and extensive advances after the war. Although he had no detailed plans, he urged that a representative be sent from London, with wide powers, to negotiate a radical solution.[99]

To the India Office officials, this proposal seemed like a censure of Linlithgow and a dangerous move that would diminish the Viceroy's status; the best that they would consider was that an investigator, rather than a negotiator, should be sent out.[100] Amery supported this view, arguing in Cabinet that there was nothing to be done except hope that the Indian parties would come together of their own accord.[101] But Attlee insisted on a definite advance[102] and, unexpectedly, got support from Churchill.

Both Amery and Linlithgow now prepared positions from which to fend off any more rash calls for action. The Viceroy offered to try and bring the Indian leaders together again, but only by using membership of his Executive Council as bait. He was also prepared to accept some Indian non-official proposals to relax the control of London over the Indian representatives at the War Cabinet, the Pacific War Council and any peace conferences.[103] Looking forward to the end of the war, Linlithgow proposed that the British Goverment should promise to accept any constitution framed by a representative Indian constituent assembly, relying on separate treaties to solve the problem of outstanding British interests.[104] Amery drew this plan up into a draft declaration for the Cabinet, inserting only the detail that the constitution-making body should be elected by the provincial legislatures; the treaties on British rights and obligations were to cover the position of the States, backward classes, public services etc.[105] Such a course would, in practice, have made the drawing up of a constitution for central government almost impossible but, to Amery, the most important point at stake here was that the Viceroy's declaration of August 1940, which had promised protection to the minorities and the Princes, should not be compromised.[106]

Attlee was not to be fobbed off as easily as this. In early March a Cabinet Committee was set up, headed by Attlee, to find a compromise between Amery's proposals and those that Attlee had put forward in his Memorandum to the War Cabinet of 2 February.[107] The committee framed a new declaration retaining Amery's scheme for a post-war constituent assembly but including, at Attlee's insistence,[108] a mention of the right of an independent India to secede from the Commonwealth. The problem of the 1940 Declaration was circumvented by a provision to allow any province that so wished to opt out of the Indian state and set up on its own. For the present, the declaration urged Indian leaders to thrown their weight behind the war-effort and offered them places on the Viceroy's Executive Council, reserving control only over defence.[109] Attlee also won the point that it should not be the Viceroy who should be deputed to sell these terms to India and, although Amery saw himself as the only man for the job,[110] Cripps was eventually designated.

These, then, were the terms with which Cripps was sent out to India. Whether or not they were, in reality, only 'armistice terms in a fierce Ministerial dispute which had threatened to split the war Cabinet'[111] they certainly contained some strange features. The widespread suspicion (shared by Attlee)[112] that the British Government was using the communal problem and the 1940 Declaration to cover up for their unwillingness to offer any sort of advance at the centre was only countered by the provincial 'opt-out' clause, which threatened to Balkanise the sub-continent. This part of the scheme was attacked continuously by the Viceroy and the Commander-in-Chief in India as likely to cause communal tension among civilians and grave anxieties in the armed forces.[113] Amery, it is true, thought that it was really only a bluff, that only by such shock-tactics could the British get the Congress to negotiate seriously with the Muslim League;[114] but, as it stood, this clause did create the impression that 'the unity of India – the goal of British policy hitherto – must be set aside'.[115] The question of the relationship between Pakistan, or independent small Muslim States, the Princes and a Hindu India was ignored completely. As with the federal scheme of the 1935 Act, the British policy-makers had simply made a wilderness of the field of central government, and called it peace. The most important part of the scheme – the immediate offer to Indian leaders for their co-operation in the war-effort – was never worked out in detail. Cripps, the War Cabinet and the Viceroy were all left with different impressions about how far Cripps could go in offering seats in the Executive Council to the Congess and League leaders.[116] It was on this point that the negotiations eventually foundered.

The terms of the Cripps Mission were put forward so hastily that, with the virtue of hindsight, doubts have even been raised as to whether the War Cabinet ever meant them as a serious offer at all. No final conclusion can yet be reached on this point, but it is interesting to note that – as Amery constantly stressed to Linlithgow – for Churchill, at least, it mattered not so much that something should be done as that some attempt should be seen to be made. As the Secretary of State pointed out to the Viceroy when the Defence of India Council scheme was under discussion, if the offer was rejected by the Indian leaders:

the public here, in America, in China and in a large measure even in India, will realise at last that the real difficulty lies in the unreasonableness of Indian Politicians and the incompatibility of their respective domestic policies.[117]

Like the 1935 Government of India Act, the terms of the Cripps Mission were born in the interplay of long-term notions of imperial strategy and immediate political considerations within the British policy-making process. Like the 1935 Act, these terms embodied an impracticable solution to the Indian problem and, again like the 1935 Act, they were rejected by all important sections of Indian political opinion. Cripps's negotiations foundered on disagreements with the Congress on the question of the power of an Indian Defence Member of the Viceroy's executive and the relationship of the Indian members of the Executive Council to each other and to the Viceroy. The Congress leaders wanted the Executive Countil to act as a Cabinet with joint responsibility, so that a Congress majority could dominate proceedings. Neither the British nor the other Indians consulted would concede this point. Cripps had opened his negotiations with the Congress by offering the full amount of concessions possible under the Cabinet scheme, and thus had no room to manoeuvre later on. After the Cabinet had, at Linlithgow's insistence, refused to allow him to modify the terms of the offer to bargain further with the Congress, Cripps was forced to acknowledge the breakdown of the negotiations and return to London. The Congress reaction was swift: in late April the Working Committee passed the 'War Resolution' declaring that India's defence against Japan should be entrusted to a Congress-led non co-operation campaign and in early July the famous 'Quit India' resolution was published, calling on the British to leave India and announcing a mass campaign to eject them if necessary. This was passed by the A.I.C.C. on 7 August and by the end of that month the top leadership of the Congress were in the jails which they were to inhabit for the rest of the war.

With the failure of the Cripps Mission and the launching of the 'Quit India' movement, the British and the Congress retreated to negative, extreme positions. The Congress tactic of accumulating the merit of self-sacrifice through *satyagraha* while forcing their opponents to make the running in finding a solution to pressing political problems was well-tried, but its results were unpredictable and could only be seen in the long term. By declaring a mass agitational movement and courting imprisonment themselves, the national leadership of the Congress were abdicating their power within the movement. Whoever was responsible for the disturbances of 1942 it was not the top leadership, for their incarceration prevented them from giving any lead except that of example. At the same time the British were now able to use repression to cover up for their inability to solve the problem of devolving power in central government and could ignore wider issues to concentrate on winning the war. The British and the Congress leaders had shelved the Indian problem until 1945; the way was now open for others to take up the running in the final stages of the contest to decide the future of the sub-continent.

Epilogue

The events of 1929 to 1942 had not produced a final result in the confrontation between the forces of imperialism and of nationalism in India. The new policies initiated by both the British and the Congress in 1942 were intended to produce a dead-lock, not a solution to the Indian problem. The end game of the British Empire in India was not begun until 1944–5, and then lasted only until 1947. In these final negotiations the British and the Congress leaders were joined by a third major political grouping – the All India Muslim League led by M. A. Jinnah.

In the tripartite negotiations which settled the independence and the partition of the sub-continent, internal Congress politics played little part. The final battles between the *Raj* and its rival heirs were fought out at the national level and over all-India problems. Between 1934 and 1939 and, to a lesser extent, even between 1940 and 1942, the eyes of the Congress leaders had been turned in to events within their own organisation. The major issues in all-India Congress politics had been largely determined by the pressures and problems pushed up from the lower levels of the organisation. The constraints which their subordinates imposed on the ability of the national leaders to lead had also determined the policies they had adopted. Between 1945 and 1947 the all-India leaders of the Congress could abandon their role of producing consensus, resolving disputes and establishing a fragile and complex system of control over their subordinates on the basis of stimuli thrown up from underneath, and were free to act as national negotiators on national issues. But this was only a temporary phenomenon and, although after 1948 the relationship between the all-India Congress leaders and their subordinates was further complicated by Congress control over central government, the origins of the political system of independent India must be sought in the events of 1934–9, not those of 1945–7.

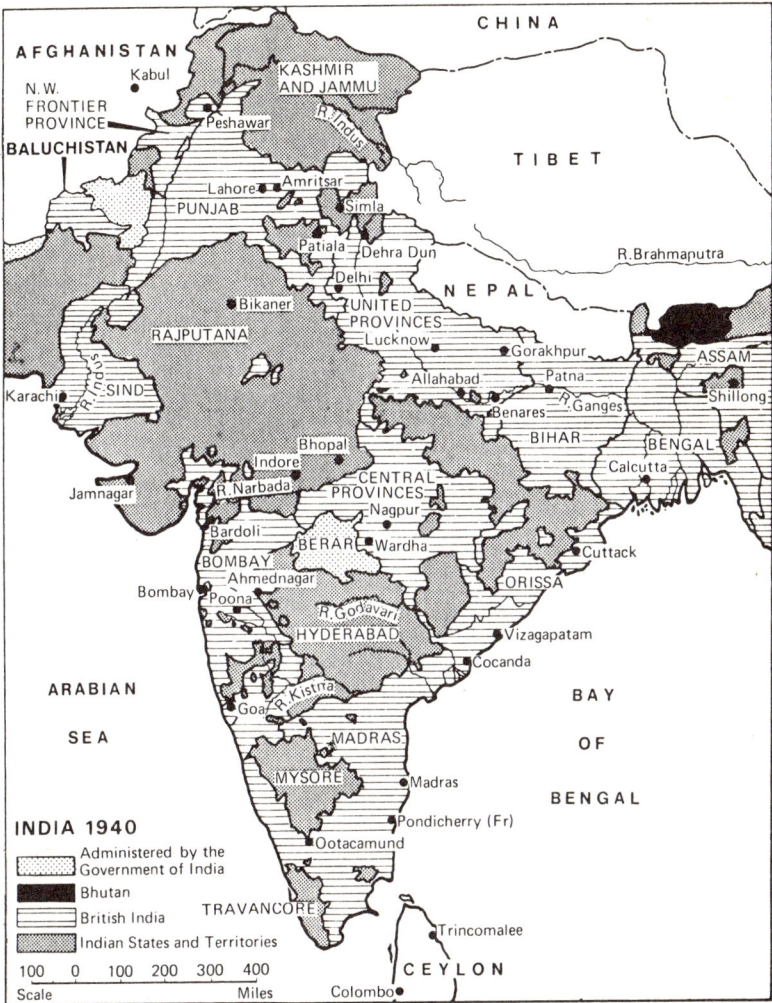

CHINA

AFGHANISTAN

N.W. FRONTIER PROVINCE

BALUCHISTAN

Kabul

KASHMIR AND JAMMU

R.Indus

TIBET

Peshawar

Lahore · Amritsar

PUNJAB · Simla

Patiala · Dehra Dun

Delhi

R.Brahmaputra

NEPAL

Bikaner

UNITED PROVINCES

RAJPUTANA

Lucknow · Gorakhpur

ASSAM

Shillong

Karachi

R.Indus

SIND

Allahabad · Patna

Benares · R.Ganges

BIHAR

BENGAL

Calcutta

Jamnagar

Bhopal

Indore

R.Narbada

CENTRAL PROVINCES

Nagpur

Bardoli

BERAR · Wardha

BOMBAY

Ahmednagar

Cuttack

ORISSA

Bombay · Poona

R.Godavari

HYDERABAD

Vizagapatam

Cocanda

ARABIAN

SEA

R.Kistna

Goa

MADRAS

BAY

OF

BENGAL

MYSORE

Madras

INDIA 1940

Administered by the Government of India

Bhutan

British India

Indian States and Territories

Pondicherry (Fr)

Ootacamund

TRAVANCORE

Trincomalee

100 0 100 200 300 400

Scale   Miles

CEYLON

Colombo

Notes

Chapter 1

1. Between 1870 and 1914 British exports to her traditional markets in Europe and North America were being affected by indigenous industrial development and tariff barriers, while her imports from these countries continued at the same level. India, on the other hand, was exporting much more in the form of raw materials and industrial inputs than she was importing in manufactures from these areas. Only with Britain did India have an adverse balance of trade. Thus Britain's balance of payments deficit with Europe and North America was financed by the triangular relationship between Britain, India and the rest of the industrial world. See S. B. Saul, *Studies in British Overseas Trade 1870–1914* (Liverpool, 1960) Chapters III and VIII.
2. See F. C. R. Robinson, 'Consultation and Control: The United Provinces' Government and its Allies 1860–1906' in *Modern Asian Studies* 5, 4 (1971); A. Seal, *The Emergence of Indian Nationalism* (Cambridge, 1968) p. 153.
3. Quoted in Seal, p. 161.
4. See S. D. Waley, *Edwin Montagu* (London, 1964) pp. 135–6.
5. *Report of the Reforms Enquiry Committee 1924* (Cmd 2360 of 1925).
6. *Report on Indian Constitutional Reforms* (Cmd 9019 of 1918) para 81.
7. CAB 23/6, appendix to War Cabinet no. 428 of 17.6.18, Note by Mr Monatgu 29.5.18.
8. CAB 23/1, War Cabinet no. 24 of 1.1.17, no. 48 of 30.1.17 and appendices.
9. CAB 24/166, CP 299(24) Memorandum on Indian Fiscal Policy by the Secretary of State 13.5.24.
10. CAB 23/22, conclusions of Conference of Ministers 18.6.20; CAB 23/23, conclusions of Conference of Ministers 1.12.20.
11. CAB 6/4, 119-D Telegram 1158ł of 3.9.20 Viceroy (Army Department) to Secretary of State; 117-D Note 'Indian Military Expenditure' by Finance Department, India Office, circulated 7.12.20.
12. Ibid., 115-D 'Report of the Army in India Committee 1919–20 Part 1'.
13. Ibid., 119-D, Telegram 11581 of 3.9.20, Viceroy (Army Department) to Secretary of State.
14. Ibid., 117-D, Note 'Indian Military Expenditure' by Finance Department, India Office, circulated 7.12.20.
15. Ibid., 118-D 'Indian Military Expenditure', memorandum by Secretary of State for India 24.12.20.
16. Ibid., 130-D, 'Report of the Sub-Committee on Indian Military Requirements as amended and approved by His Majesty's Government'.
17. Reading, *Rufus Isaacs 1914–1935* (London, 1945) pp. 294–5.
18. Legislative Assembly Debates 1927 p. 1753.
19. This desideratum was that of the 1926 *Royal Commission on Indian Currency and Finance.*
20. See CAB 23/29, conference of Ministers 20.12.21; Reading, *Rufus Isaacs 1914–1935* (London, 1945) pp. 192–3.
21. Ibid., pp. 295–8; CAB 23/47, 17(24)13 of 28.2.24, 18(24)2 of 13.3.24, 23(24)11 of 27.3.24.
22. Note by B. P. Blackett 22.12.24 in Government of India Home (Public) Department 166-II-1924 N.A.I.

23. 'Report of discussion between Secretary of State and Viceroy 4.6.25', Baldwin MSS E I 93.
24. Quoted in Birkenhead, *Halifax* (London, 1965) p. 222.
25. See ibid., pp. 236–42.
26. Irwin to Baldwin 10.1.29 Baldwin MSS E 5 103.
27. Quoted in S. R. Mehrotra, *Britain, India and the Commonwealth* (London, 1965) p. 141.
28. Note by Irwin, enclosed in Irwin to Baldwin 26.11.29 Baldwin MSS E 5 103.
29. Salisbury to Baldwin 23.10.29, reporting a conversation with Irwin, ibid.
30. Private Secretary to Viceroy to Sapru 27.12.29 Sapru MSS (First Series) I 19.
31. See CAB 23/75, 16(33)1 of 10.3.33 when Hoare makes this point clearly.
32. *Report of Indian Statutory Commission* Vol. II (Cmd 3569 of 1930) p. 290.
33. Ibid.
34. CAB 23/66, 6(31)1 of 14.1.31; see also CAB 27/470, BDG(30)30 of 12.1.31.
35. He told the delegates: 'I have never concealed from you my conviction that this is above all others a problem for you to settle by agreement amongst yourselves.' Quoted in R. Coupland, *The Indian Problem 1833–1935* (Oxford, 1942) p. 127.
36. See CAB 27/521, CI 32(2).
37. Ibid., CI 32(2), (3), (4).
38. CAB 27/520, CI 32(1): CAB 27/521, CI 32(1). In this Hoare again makes the point that to arbitrate on the wider issues would give too much ammunition to Indian critics.
39. See *Communal Decision 1931–2* (Cmd 4147 of 1931–2).
40. See CAB 23/63, 9(30)2 of 7.2.30; CAB 24/219, C.P. 18(31) of 22.2.31, C.P. 35(31) of 2.2.31.
41. CAB 23/68, 58(31)3 of 17.9.31.
42. See Sir Samuel Hoare to Lord Willingdon 2.10.31, 1.4.32 Templewood MSS vol. I.
43. See Viceroy to Secretary of State 26.9.31 ibid. vol. 13; Lord Willingdon to Sir Samuel Hoare 6.10.31 ibid., vol. 5.
44. See Sir Samuel Hoare to Lord Willingdon 28.1.32, 19.1.32 ibid., vol. 1; telegrams between Secretary of State and Viceroy March 1932 ibid., vol. 11.
45. CAB 23/80, 35(34)9 of 17.10.34.
46. See, for example, CAB 27/470, BDG(30)17 'Memorandum on Indian Finance' by the Secretary of State for India 8.12.30.
47. CAB 23/68, 62(31)8 of 22.9.31; Government of India Finance Department 1(36)B of 1931 N.A.I.
48. Lord Willingdon to Sir Samuel Hoare 31.10.33 Templewood MSS vol. 6.
49. CAB 27/470, BDG(30)29 Finance Member, Government of India, to Secretary of State 28.12.30; Viceroy to Secretary of State 1.1.31; 2.1.31.
50. Ibid., BDG(30)17 'Memorandum on Indian Finance' by Secretary of State 8.12.30; BDG(30)29 Viceroy to Secretary of State 1.1.31.
51. See the remarkably smug memorandum by the Secretary of State in CAB 24/247, C.P. 28(34) of 3.2.34.
52. CAB 23/73, 65(32)5 of 7.12.32.
53. See CAB 27/520, CI(32)7 of 4.10.32; 8 of 7.10.32; 9 of 11.10.32; 10 of 12.10.32 and 11 of 13.10.32.
54. Sir Samuel Hoare to Lord Willingdon 20.10.32 Templewood MSS Vol. 2.
55. *Joint Committee on Indian Constitutional Reforms Volume IIB: Minutes of Evidence by the Secretary of State for India and his Advisers* (Parliamentary Papers 1932–3 vol. VII) p. 1026.
56. Proceedings of Executive Council on Indian Statutory Commission Report 24th meeting of 6.9.30 G.o.I. Reforms Office 67/V/30–R N.A.I. Wisely, it was decided not to mention this point to London.
57. See CAB 27/520, CI 32(2) of 12.5.32.
58. Sapru MSS (First Series) M. 6.
59. Lord Willingdon to Sir Samuel Hoare 15.11.31 Templewood MSS vol. 5.

60. CAB 23/79, 17(34)5 of 25.4.34.
61. In a speech to the Commonwealth Labour Conference in July 1928 MacDonald had expressed his hope that 'within a period of months rather than years there will be a new Dominion added to the Commonwealth of our nations, a Dominion of another race. . . . I refer to India.' Quoted in N. Gangulee, *The Making of Federal India* (London, 1936) p. 68.
62. CAB 23/61, 35(29)17 of 25.9.29.
63. CAB 23/64, 46(30)5 of 30.7.30; CAB 27/470, BDG(30)4 Note by Secretary of State dated 29.10.30.
64. CAB 27/470, BDG(30)2 memo by Secretary of State 18.10.30; CAB 23/65, 62(30)15 of 22.10.30.
65. CAB 27/470, BDG(30)8 memo by Prime Minister 19.11.30.
66. The Federal Structure Committee had so far only established the essential powers that the Governor-General must retain. It had not considered the questions of the rights of the Princes, centre/provincial relations, federal finance, the communal problem etc. See CAB 27/470, BDG(31)1 'Points raised in the reports of the sub-committees.'
67. CAB 27/470, BDG(30)8 memo by Prime Minister 19.11.30.
68. See R. J. Moore, 'The Making of India's Paper Federation 1927–35' in C. H. Philips and M. D. Wainwright (eds), *The Partition of India: Policies and Perspectives 1935–1947* (London, 1970) pp. 59–63.
69. Hoare, quoted in N. Gangulee, *The Making of Federal India* (London, 1936) p. 106.
70. Hoare, quoted in R. J. Moore, 'The Making of India's Paper Federation 1927–35', in C. H. Philips and M. D. Wainwright (eds), *The Partition of India: Policies and Perspectives 1935–1947* (London, 1970) p. 62.
71. Sir Samuel Hoare to Lord Willingdon 2.10.31., 19.11.31 Templewood MSS vol. 1; CAB 23/69, 77(31)2 of 13.11.31.
72. Secretary of State to Viceroy 20.11.31 Templewood MSS vol. 13; CAB 23/69, 77(31)2 of 13.11.31.
73. Sir Samuel Hoare to Lord Willingdon 26.11.31 Templewood MSS vol. 1; CAB 23/69, 81(31)2 of 25.11.31.
74. Secretary of State to Viceroy 27.11.31 Templewood MSS vol. 11.
75. See Sir Samuel Hoare to Lord Willingdon 10.12.31 Templewood MSS vol. 1; CAB 27/520, CI 32(2) of 12.5.32.
76. Ibid.
77. Secretary of State to Viceroy 10.1.32, 20.1.32 Templewood MSS vol. 11.
78. CAB 27/521, memo by Secretary of State 9.5.32.
79. CAB 27/521, CI 32(3) of 26.5.32.
80. Sir Samuel Hoare to Lord Willingdon 16.6.32 Templewood MSS vol. 2.
81. See R. J. Moore, 'The Making of India's Paper Federation 1927–35', in C. H. Philips and M. D. Wainwright (eds), *The Partition of India: Policies and Perspectives 1935–1947* (London, 1970) p. 71.
82. For details of this see S. C. Ghosh, 'Decision-Making and Power in the British Conservative Party; a case study of the Indian Problem 1929–34', in *Political Studies* vol. XIII No 2 (1965) pp. 192–212.
83. See Sir Samuel Hoare to Lord Willingdon 27.5.32 Templewood MSS vol. 2.
84. Sir Samuel Hoare to Lord Willingdon 14.9.33 Ibid., vol. 3.
85. Sapru to Colonel Haskar 30.6.33 Sapru MSS (First Series) B 117.

Chapter 2

1. See Gopal Krishna, 'The Development of the Indian National Congress as a Mass Organisation 1918–23' in *Journal of Asian Studies* (1966) p. 420.
2. *Indian Quarterly Register 1925 Vol. II* p. 17.
3. Inspection Report on Maharastra P.C.C. AICC P 28(i) 1929.

4 Report by Secretary Tamil Nadu P.C.C. ibid.
5. Gandhi to J. Nehru 10.1.30 AICC 26 1930.
6. This remark was made at the conference with Irwin in December 1929 and quoted by Sapru in his letter to Cunningham (Private Secretary to Viceroy) of 4.1.30 Sapru MSS (First Series) I 23.
7. Quoted in Birkenhead, *Halifax* (London, 1965) p. 277.
8. See Gandhi to J. Nehru 10.1.30 AICC 26 1930.
9. Report by the Government of the Punjab on the Political Situation 3.1.30 L/P&J/7 373/30 I.O.L.
10. Lord Willingdon to Lord Zetland 13.7.35 Zetland MSS Vol. 6.
11. See M. Desai to C. F. Andrews 20.7.33 Gandhi MSS (Sabamati Series) Sn 21529; Dr Ansari to M. Desai 13.7.33 ibid., Sn 21514.
12. *Indian Annual Register 1933 Vol. I* p. 69.
13. 'Annual Report of the Indian National Congress 1932–3' typescript copy in AICC 6 1933.
14. Gandhi to J. Nehru 14.9.33 AICC (Supplementary Series) 129 1933.
15. *Indian Annual Register 1933 Vol. II* pp. 325–8.
16. Ibid., pp. 331–5.
17. Swami Govindanand to Satyamurthi November 1933 intercepted correspondence in G.o.I. Home Department (Political) 4/19/33 N.A.I. See also other correspondence in this file, the Note of 6.10.33 by Home Member, Government of India, in G.o.I. Home Department (Political) 4/8/33 N.A.I. and K. F. Nariman, *Whither Congress?* (Bombay, 1933) pp. x–xi.
18. The chief correspondents were K. F. Nariman (Bombay), Satyamurthi and Mutharanga Mudaliar (Madras), Swami Govindanand (Sindh), T. A. K. Sherwani (U.P.) and Dr Ansari and Asaf Ali (Delhi).
19. See intercepted correspondence in G.o.I. Home Department (Political) 4/19/33 N.A.I.
20. Satyamurthi to Ansari 11.11.33 ibid.
21. Ansari to K. M. Munshi 23.2.34 in K. M. Munshi, *Indian Constitutional Documents Vol. I* (Bombay, 1967) p. 361.
22. Gandhi to Ansari 18.3.34 intercepted correspondence in G.o.I. Home Department (Political) 3/6/34 N.A.I.
23. *Indian Annual Register 1934 Vol. I.* p. 262.
24. Gandhi to Nehru 14.4.34 Nehru MSS G 11.
25. For one of Gandhi's many statements of this view see *Bombay Chronicle* 17.4.34.
26. See typed list of provincial proposals for Patna A.I.C.C. in AICC 8 1934. For details of events in Bengal see M. L. Setalvad, *Bhulabhai Desai* (New Delhi, 1968) pp. 120–1 and for the U.P. see Fortnightly Reports U.P. Government for April 1934 in G.o.I. Home Department (Political) 18/4/34 N.A.I.
27. The terms 'Gandhi's colleagues', 'associates' and, later in the work, 'Gandhians' are used to mean the hard core of veteran leaders who formed the bulk of all Working Committees from 1930 onwards. These leaders – A. K. Azad, Rajendra Prasad, C. Rajagopalachari, Vallabhbhai Patel, J. B. Kripalani, Jamnalal Bajaj, Mrs Naidu, Khan Abdul Gaffar Khan and Jairamdas Doulatram – did not always necessarily see eye to eye with Gandhi, but they were almost always prepared to follow his lead on matters of long-term policy. Other less regular members of the Working Committee such as Bhulabhai Desai, S. R. Deo and H. K. Mehtab also followed Gandhi's lead when they were appointed. Distinct from the 'Gandhians' were Nehru, the leaders of the Congress Socialist Party and Subhas Chandra Bose.
28. See reports in Government of Bihar and Orissa Political (Special) 96/34 S.C.R.O. Patna.
29. Notably Sir T. B. Sapru. Khaliquzzaman (one of Ansari's lieutenants) wrote to Sapru on 7 April asking him to join the party and lead it in the C.L.A. (Sapru MSS (Second Series) K 45). But Sapru refused.

30. The Ranchi Conference showed the Swarajya Party leaders that some sort of formal relationship with the Congress would be necessary if they were to emerge from the Patna A.I.C.C. with their personal control of the parliamentary programme intact. (See reports in Government of Bihar and Orissa Political (Special) Department 96/34 S.C.R.O. Patna.)
31. See Government of Bihar and Orissa Political (Special) Department 79/34 Part 1 S.C.R.O. Patna.
32. See *Bombay Chronicle* 14.5.34, 18.5.34, 26.5.34, 27.5.34.
33. Ibid. 21.5.34.
34. Ibid. 17.6.34.
35. Ibid.
36. *Bombay Chronicle* 3.8.34.
37. P. D. Tandon, Sarder Narbanda Prasad Singh, Venkash Narain Tiwari, Balkrishna Sharma, Shri Prakash, Sampurnanand, Acharya Narendra Dev and Damodhar Seth Swarup. *Pioneer* 5.5.34.
38. Ibid., 4.8.34.
39. See his press statements in *Pioneer* 7.6.34, 13.6.34.
40. Ibid. 13.9.34.
41. *Pioneer* 20.9.34.
42. *Pioneer* 10.9.34. It is interesting to note that of those who protested Seth Govind Das and D. P. Misra were in the same position (that of a minority faction that feared exclusion) in the Mahakoshal P.C.C. as Kidwai and Tandon in the U.P.P.C.C., while Gidwani feared a dominance of parliamentary considerations in the Congress programme since the Working Committee had also decided that the Congress should not contest the C.L.A. elections in Sindh.
43. *Pioneer* 12.9.34.
44. Rajendra Prasad to Vallabhbhai Patel 13.10.34 AICC G 63 1934.
45. By mid-November Prakash had overdrawn Rs 15,000 and by the end of the month the bank were dunning him for it. Shri Prakash to Ansari 13.11.34, 21.11.34 Ansari MSS.
46. A. N. Sinha to Ansari 12.1.35 AICC G 9 1934–6.
47. Diary Entry 2.3.35 Bhulabhai Desai MSS.
48. The Congress was by far the largest party in the Assembly, but did not command an absolute majority because of the presence of the 39 nominated members.
49. Sapru to Inglis 7.11.34 Sapru MSS (Second Series) I 18.
50. Prasad to Ansari 26.12.34 AICC G 43 (KWI) 1934.
51. Diary Entry 8.2.35 Bhulabhai Desai MSS. The reasons for Bhulabhai's exclusion are not far to seek: to Mahadev Desai, Gandhi's secretary and *confidant*, he was, despite his considerable political skills, a 'lucky dog', a 'consummate cynic . . . woefully lacking in what Matthew Arnold called "mind's brave ardour" and "heroic aims", and . . . even deficient in moral sense'. Mahadev's chief objection seems to have been that Desai, with his legal training, was quite prepared to argue either side of any case. See M. Desai to J. Nehru 19.12.35 J. Nehru MSS D 37.
52. Diary entry 8.2.35 Bhulabhai Desai MSS.
53. Ditto 24.3.36 Ibid.
54. Asaf Ali, writing in *Bombay Chronicle* 7.8.34.
55. K. M. Munshi to Gandhi 6.9.34 K. M. Munshi, *Indian Constitutional Documents* Vol. I (Bombay, 1967) p. 378. See also *Bombay Chronicle* 13.8.34 editorial; article by S. K. Patil in *Bombay Chronicle* 8.8.34.
56. *Bombay Chronicle* 9.9.34.
57. See the article by S. K. Patil, the Bombay Congress leader in *Bombay Chronicle* 29.8.34 in which he states that:
    We are suffering today from utter inactivity and "no work". One must frankly admit that all the quarrels and dissentions which fill the columns after columns of the newspapers today are due, more than anything else, to the absence of any

programme of work which alone could keep our energies harnessed.

58. *Pioneer* 20.9.34. This threat to leave the Congress had been in Gandhi's mind for some time. In July 1934 he and Vallabhbhai Patel had already decided to leave the Congress if they could not reform it satisfactorily (G. D. Birla to Sir P. Thakurdas 3.8.34 Thakurdas MSS 42 (VI)).

59. See statement of Bombay C.S.P. in *Bombay Chronicle* 27.9.34.

60. *Bombay Chronicle* 30.9.34.

61. Ibid. 4.10.34.

62. Ibid. 19.9.34.

63. Ibid. 4.10.34.

64. In practice this did not work however; indeed, the conjunction of the delegate, the P.C.C. and D.C.C. elections under the Bombay Constitution was one of the causes of the vastly increased importance (and hence vastly increased bitterness of contest) of the Congress elections in this period.

65. *Bombay Chronicle* 16.10.34; *Pioneer* 28.10.34.

66. *Bombay Chronicle* 16.10.34; 17.10.34.

67. See his statement in *Bombay Chronicle* 20.7.34.

68. *Bombay Chronicle* 4.10.34; 17.4.34.

69. *Bombay Chronicle* 17.10.34.

70. Patel, especially, had enthusiastically supported the idea from the time of its first mention. On 24 September he had issued a statement to the press (*Bombay Chronicle* 29.9.34) claiming that he hoped Gandhi would not even attend the Bombay session since then the chance to purge all elements who showed a tendency to indiscipline and insubordination (the Congress Socialists) from the Congress might be lost by the Mahatma's obsession with compromise at all costs. Patel was looking for a 'day of reckoning' within the Congress (P. Sitaramayya to Patel 21.9.34 AICC G 43 1934) and feared that Gandhi's presence would inhibit him, as indeed it did.

71. See Kamaladevi Chattophadayya's speech at Bombay 16 October, *Bombay Chronicle* 17.10.34.

72. *Bombay Chronicle* 5.11.34.

73. *Pioneer* 25.10.34. Gandhi had always recognised the need for probable compromise. In early September he had assured Rajagopalachari that he agreed that an insistence on his 'drastic amendments' as a measure of confidence was 'a species of subtle violence' (Gandhi to Rajagopalachari 3.9.34 Prasad MSS VII/35).

74. *Pioneer* 27.10.34; 28.10.34.

75. *Pioneer* 29.10.34; *Bombay Chronicle* 5.11.34.

76. This provision was an attempt by Gandhi to secure what he had seen as one of the most important aims of his proposals published on 16 October – an increased rural orientation for the Congress. However, it seems unlikely that so rigid a distinction between 'rural' and 'urban' areas had much validity. The Delimitation Committee appointed by the British Parliament to lay down constituency boundaries for the proposed P.L.A.s in 1936 pointed out that while defining urban areas as those with over 10,000 in population would suffice to ensure that no urban elements were omitted from the classification, there were many market towns with over that number of population which had no distinctive interests separate from those of the surrounding countryside (*Report of Indian Delimitation Committee 1936 Vol. 1* pp. 6–7). Gandhi, however, was mainly concerned that leaders based in large towns should not, by means of their greater financial resources for recruiting, enrol a disproportionately large number of members and hence secure a disproportionate number of delegates in comparison with areas without the same resources to draw on.

77. During the 1930s the rupee exchange rate was fixed at 1s 6d (7½p); there were 16 annas to the rupee.

78. In fact, despite the pleas of Congressmen who found themselves in conflict with rivals who were also members of the Hindu Mahasabha, this clause was not invoked before 1939.

79. This provision had been specifically included by Gandhi, and was warmly supported by the Congress Socialist Party, because it would help representation for an organised minority. The system worked like this: first of all a 'factor' was established by dividing the number of voters by the number of representatives to be elected. Then a first ballot was taken. All those who received the requisite number of votes were declared elected. Then a second ballot was taken, excluding those already elected, and the votes secured by each candidate added on to those received in the first ballot. Those who had then the required number of votes were declared elected and the process continued until the quota was filled. In a province such as Bombay City, for example, there were (after the constitutional amendments of 1936) 40 members of the P.C.C. and five places on the A.I.C.C. Thus the 'factor' was 8 (40/5 = 8). Under a simple majority system, a C.S.P. faction of, say, nine members would get only one representative elected. Under this system, however, and given the fragmentation of the other voters, they would, by voting as a bloc, secure the return of one representative for each ballot taken and thus obtain at least two delegates – a number out of proportion to their numerical strength on the P.C.C.

80. A convenient copy of the Bombay Constitution is to be found in *Indian Annual Register 1934, Vol. II* pp. 208–15.

81. In several provinces, various provisions of the 1934 Constitution were simply ignored. Karnatak represents an extreme example of this; the P.C.C. decided to make no attempt to enforce the spinning and manual labour clause as this would have left too few qualified members to fill even the P.C.C. executive. They were also unable to collect the required information on membership, as the D.C.C. offices had no full-time workers to collect and send in the membership forms (Secretary Karnatak P.C.C. to Rajendra Prasad 25.8.35 AICC G 68 1934). In almost all provinces the *khaddar*, spinning and manual labour qualifications were enforced more as weapons in interfactional struggles than as devices to ensure a high degree of spirituality in the Congress.

82. Rajendra Prasad to Patel 24.11.34 and to Hasan Iman 13.12.34 intercepted correspondence in G.o.I. Home Department (Political) 145/34 N.A.I.

83. Fortnightly Reports for Bihar and Orissa December 1934 G.o.I. Home Department (Political) 18/12/34 N.A.I.

84. *Bombay Chronicle* 21.1.35.

85. Prasad interview in ibid. 4.11.34.

86. Prasad press statement in ibid. 22.11.34.

87. Ansari interview in ibid. 31.10.34.

88. Report of Government of Bihar and Orissa Political (Special) Department to G.o.I. Home Department No. 2901-C dated 29.4.35 Gvt. B & O Political (Special) 185/35 S.C.R.O. Patna.

89. Fortnightly Report Gvt. Bihar and Orissa for January 1935, G.o.I. Home Department (Political) 18/1/35. N.A.I.

90. A resolution preparing for the use of the A.I.V.I.A. workers in this field was passed by the U.P.P.C.C. executive at its meeting at Cawnpore in April 1934. The only effective A.I.V.I.A. organisations in U.P. were in the districts where it was misused in this way – Allahabad, Muttra, Gorkhpur and Unao. Fortnightly Reports U.P. Government to G.o.I Home Dept. for January, February, March and April 1935 in G.o.I. Home Dept. (Political) 18/1,2,3 & 4/35 N.A.I.

91. M. Desai to Nehru 6.9.35 Nehru MSS S37: 'S.S.' report of 5.1.36 in G.o.I Home Department (Political) 4/20/36 N.A.I.

92. *Searchlight* 13.4.36.

93. Government of Bihar and Orissa Political (Special) Department 185/35 S.C.R.O. Patna.

94. For an account of earlier attempts to found a socialist party see J. P. Haithcox, *Communism and Nationalism in India: M. N. Roy and Comintern Policy 1920–39* (Princeton, 1971) pp. 216–9.

95. This resolution caused immediate dissent in the U.P., where members of the Party had immediate hope of election to the Congress Executives. The resolution was never implemented in practice; eighteen months after it was passed there were three C.S.P. members on the Working Committee.

96. P. L. Lakhanpal, *A History of the Congress Socialist Party* (Lahore, n.d.) p. 37.

97. Ibid., pp. 142–9.

98. J. P. Haithcox, *Communism and Nationalism in India: M. N. Roy and Comintern Policy 1920–39* (Princeton, 1971) p. 219.

99. Ibid., p. 220.

100. 'The Basic Idea of Socialism' by J. P. Narain in *Bombay Chronicle* 13.8.34 p. 12.

101. See 'The significance of the Socialist Conference Resolutions' by P. P. Varma *Searchlight* 13.12.36 p. 5.
'Fight the Menace of War' by 'A Congress Socialist' *Bombay Chronicle* 11.6.34 p. 6. Press statement by Y. Meherally in ibid. 23.3.35 p. 11.

102. Sampurnanand, *Memories and Reflections* (London, 1962) p. 76.

103. Sinha, *The Left Wing in India* (Muzaffapur, 1965) pp. 317–8. The Working Committee intended this resolution to ban any Congressman who 'preaches class war' from membership of an executive committee. J. Bajaj (Acting President I.N.C.) to Uma Nehru 21.6.34 AICC G 29 1934.

104. *Pioneer* 18.7.34; *Bombay Chronicle* 1.10.34. This criticism was a common one – Sitaramayya referred to the Socialists as copying the 'goody goody phraseology of Western Socialists' without any real knowledge of the problems involved (*Bombay Chronicle* 1.10.34).

105. Of these, even Birla later complained that the growth of socialist agitation within the I.N.C was having a deleterious effect on labour relations especially where the employer was a Congress supporter. Birla to Prasad 12.1.36 AICC G 43 (KWI) 1935.

106. P. Sitaramayya to Patel 21.9.34 AICC G 43 1934.

107. Gandhi press statement 17.9.34 in L. C. Sinha, *The Left Wing in India* (Muzaffapur, 1965) p. 371; Gandhi to Masani 29.5.34 Gandhi MSS (Nidhi Series). Gandhi seems to have been offended because the C.S.P. leaders had not followed Jawaharlal Nehru in consulting him before proposing any radical measures. He told representaives of the C.S.P. in June 1934 that if Nehru had been free then their programme would never have been passed as it was. See A. T. Hingorani (ed.), *Jawaharlal Nehru by M. K. Gandhi* (Bombay, 1960) p. 60.

108. Comrade Sampurnanand's Thesis issued February 1935, in AICC G 23 1935.

109. On the latter point see *Bombay Chronicle* 11.8.34; General Secretary C.S.P.'s Circular February 1935 (reprinted in *Pioneer* 5.7.35).

110. The attitude of C.S.P. members to the new constitution was revealed at a party meeting called before the Bombay session to decide policy on this matter. Here a resolution was passed calling for the abolition of the Presidentship, the election of the Working Committee by the A.I.C.C., the refusal to the Working Committee of power to change or initiate policies, the establishment of a 2500 delegate session and the abolition of the four anna membership fee and *khaddar* clause.

111. The best account of these developments is contained in two works by Swami Sahajanand Saraswati (both in Hindi) *Kisan Sabha ka Sansmaren* (Allahabad, 1947) and *Mera Jivan Sangharsa* (Patna, 1952). For all my information on Bihar politics in this period I am most grateful for the help of Mr G. McDonald of the University of Western Australia, whose generosity in giving advice, information and even source material made a great difference to my stay in Patna and my knowledge of this field.

112. Fortnightly Report, Government of U.P., for May 1934 G.o.I. Home Department (Political) 18/5/34 N.A.I.

113. For all-India kisan developments, see N. G. Ranga, *Peasants and Congress* (Madras, 1939); *Revolutionary Peasants* (Delhi, 1949); and *Kisans and Communists* (Bombay, 1949); Sahajanand, *Kisan Sabha ka Sansmaren* (Hindi) (Allahasad, 1947); *Mera Jivan*

Sangharsa (Hindi) (Patna, 1952). At the Faizpur meeting the Congress Socialist leaders were attacked by an alliance of Kisan Sabha leaders and Communists.
114. *Bombay Chronicle* 4.12.34.
115. Ansari to Prasad 8.8.35 AICC G 45 (KWI) 1935; *Leader* 31.7.35.
116. Prasad to Nehru 19.12.35 Prasad MSS VI/36.
117. Diary Entry 24.2.36 Bhulbhai Desai MSS.
118. *Pioneer* 27.10.34.
119. 'S.S.' Report of 29.9.35 in G.o.I. Home Department (Political) 4/7/35 N.A.I.
120. M. Desai to Nehru 6.9.35 J. Nehru MSS D 37.
121. Gandhi to Nehru 22.9.35 ibid. G11.
122. See Ansari to Prasad 8.8.35 AICC G 45 (KWI) 1935; Diary Entry 28.8.35 B. Desai MSS; Satyamurthi to Prasad 30.11.35 Prasad MSS X/35.
123. See Prasad to Ansari 12.8.35 AICC G 45 (KWI) 1935.
124. Rajagopalachari to Prasad 2.2.36 Prasad MSS VIII/36.
125. Ansari to Prasad 28.9.35 Prasad MSS IV/35; Diary Entry 28.8.35 B. Desai MSS.
126. Prasad to Nehru 19.12.35 Prasad MSS VI/36.
127. Diary Entry 26.6.36 B. Desai MSS.
128. *Pioneer* 30.1.36.
129. 'S.S.' Report dated 4.12.35 in G.o.I. Home Department (Political) 4/13/35 N.A.I.
130. Diary Entry 7.2.35 Bhulabhai Desai MSS; Kripalani to Prasad 15.2.36 Prasad MSS III/36.
131. Kripalani to Prasad 15.2.36 Prasad MSS III/36.
132. Diary Entry 26.6.36 B. Desai MSS.
133. The point behind this demand was as follows: the C.S.P. leaders believed, with some justification, that they had good contacts among the various Trades' Unions and Kisan Sabhas – both organisations of workers and peasants outside the Congress. If the principle of direct, or functional representation of these bodies on Congress committees could be established it would give a direct right to these organisations to return representatives to the committees in proportion to their nominal membership strength. Thus the C.S.P. would gain a number of allies and supporters in all levels of the Congress organisation. Also, this arrangement would minimise the influence of the local Congress bosses on labour and kisan leaders which they would obtain if these leaders had to fight their way up the ladder of Congress institutional politics in the normal manner.
134. This committee never met formally at all. Originally supposed to report by July 1936, it was then given until the Faizpur Congress in December. By this time two separate notes by Prasad and Narain were available, but no report. At the Faizpur Congress, the committee was re-established with the addition of Kripalani and Nehru and called on to report by April 1937. A first draft of proposals was available by August 1937, and was circulated to the P.C.C.s. These were then revised and submitted to the Haripura Congress of February 1938. No action was taken, however, the proposals of the Committee being simply included in the terms of reference of the Constitutional Revision Sub-committee appointed at that session. See AICC G 80 (KWI) 1938.
135. *Indian Annual Register 1936 Vol. I* p. 249; *Pioneer* 16.4.36.
136. G.o.I. Home Department (Political) 4/18/36 N.A.I.: *Indian Annual Register 1936 Vol. I* p. 250: *Pioneer* 14.4.36; 15.4.36. The original resolution would have represented a dangerous policy statement for the Congress to fight the P.L.A. elections on, elections in which they needed the support of at least some members of the landed classes.
137. See letter from B. Desai of 2.4.36 in M. L. Setalvad, *Bhulabhai Desai* (Bombay, 1965) pp. 168–70.
138. AICC G 31 1936; 16 1936; 25 1936.
139. *Pioneer* 12.4.36.
140. *Leader* 4.7.36; 9.7.36.

141. The same point was made by Nehru in reply to a letter from a Congressman who complained that, since he had no interest in the P.L.A.s, there was no programme for him to carry out. Nehru stressed that '. . . whether we are interested in the Councils or not we are all interested in strengthening the Congress in the national movement. Therefore we must all work together for the success of the Congress at the elections' (Nehru to G. C. Sondhi 2.11.36 AICC G 5 (KWI) 1935).
142. Gandhi to Agatha Harrison 30.4.36 intercepted correspondence in G.o.I. Home Department (Political) 4/11/36 N.A.I.
143. Minutes of Working Committee meeting 27 and 28.4.36 in AICC G 31 1936.
144. Clarifying this, in a letter to Gandi dated 25 May, Nehru complained that 'the Committee as it took shape was not my child, I could hardly recognise it and to some inclusions . . . I reacted strongly' (intercepted correspondence in G.o.I. Home Department (Political) 32/12/36 N.A.I.).
145. Intercepted correspondence in ibid. What seems to have happened is that Gandhi, who before the Lucknow Congress had promised that he would keep Nehru under control (Birla to Sir P. Thakurdas 20.4.36 Thakurdas MSS III), insisted on the bulk of the 'old guard' being retained on the Working Committee. In his letter to Nehru on 29 May he pointed out that Nehru refused to have a 'right-wing' woman, Mrs Naidu, on the Committee and would not substitute a 'left-wing' woman for one of the C.S.P. members. The only member over whose inclusion Nehru was subjected to any pressure was Bhulabhai Desai. Nehru seems to have accepted this arrangement cheerfully at the time, but to have rebelled when he discovered the intensity of the opposition to him on the Working Committee.
146. See J. Nehru, *Bunch of Old Letters* (Bombay, 1958) pp. 188–98.
147. M. Desai to Nehru 26.8.36 AICC G 85 (i) 1936.
148. Prasad to Patel 14.7.36 Prasad MSS 1/36.
149. Note by Prasad, undated but written December 1936, in Prasad MSS III/36.
150. In a speech in January 1937 Patel admitted that the Congress had 'captured the P.L.A.s because we cannot fight when our own men are stabbing us in the back' *Searchlight* 12.2.37.
151. He gave his reasons as his unwillingness to be the cause of a split with Nehru, various personal and health considerations and, most importantly, that the factionalism of Madras politics made his position so insecure that he could not afford to divert his attention to the national sphere.
152. Rajagopalachari to Nehru 23.11.36. Prasad MSS VIII/36.
153. See Prasad MSS Files no. 1/36, VIII/36; *Bombay Chronicle* 23, 25 and 28.11.36.
154. See *Indian Annual Register 1936 Vol. II* pp. 205–6; 235–6. In both the Subjects Committee and the general session it obtained a 2:1 majority.
155. See Government of Central Provinces and Berar Fortnightly Reports for February and March 1937 in G.o.I. Home Department (Political) 18/2 and 18/3/37 N.A.I.; *Searchlight* 2.3.37; AICC 42 1937.
156. AICC G 39 (i) 1937. The decision of each P.C.C. was based on the votes of the D.C.C.s, an interesting indication of which was the essential unit of the Congress election campaign.
157. Gvt C. P. Fortnightly Reports for March 1937 in G.o.I. Home Department (Political) 18/3/37 N.A.I. One leader from Chhattisgarh Division was reportedly so confident of entering the Ministry on 1 April that he had refused to accept any briefs for after that date.
158. A sub-committee at this meeting laid down the major conditions as that the Governor was not to preside at cabinet meetings, was to consult the Ministers over all executive function, must accept the Ministers' advice on all occasions and must not use his 'discretionary powers' under the Act in relation to the appointment of the Advocate General, the withholding of assent from Acts of the P.L.A. and the exercise of 'safeguards' for the services, minorities and to maintain law and order, except on the advice of the ministers.

159. AICC 42 1937.
160. *Leader* 19.3.37, AICC 42 1937.
161. Nehru to Prasad and Patel 29.3.37 AICC E 1 1936.
162. For an account of the attitudes and actions of the British during this episode, see R. J. Moore 'British Policy and the Indian Problem 1936–40' in C. H. Philips and M. D. Wainwright (eds), *The Partition of India: Policies and Perspectives 1935–47* (London, 1970) pp. 79–95.
163. *Pioneer* 1.4.37.
164. I. N. Gurtu to Sapru 17.6.37 Sapru MSS (Second Series) G. 110.
165. Sapru to Lord Lothian 26.7.37 Sapru MSS (First Series) L. 56.
166. *Leader* 8.7.37. The exception, for reasons which are not clear, was Bihar.
167. AICC 42 1937.
168. J. Nehru, *The Unity of India; Collected Writings 1937–40* (London, 1941) p. 62.
169. *Leader* 25.6.37.
170. 1935 and 1936 were bad years for most of them. For Patel, for example, they were years of 'political depression', years in which he fell out with his closest associates in Gujerat, when he was almost forced to resign as president of the Gujerat P.C.C. and when even his plans for local action (founding a series of ashrams to serve as centres for Congress activities) evoked little enthusiasm. (See N. D. Parikh, *Sardar Vallabhbhai Patel Vol. II* (Ahmedabad, 1956) pp. 192–7; G.o.I. Home Dept. (Political) 3/8/35 N.A.I.

Chapter 3

1. AICC P 31 1935, G 72 1936.
2. See AICC 31 1936.
3. Secretary Maharastra P.C.C. to General Secretary A.I.C.C. 31.1.38 AICC G 80 1938.
4. This account is compiled from the following AICC files:
   P 9 1934; G 5(K.W.1) 1935; P 35 1935;
   G 5(KWII) 1936; P 9 1936.
5. For details of this dispute see press reports in *Pioneer* and *Leader* July to November 1935; AICC P 20 1934; P. D. Tandon MSS Serial Nos 994–999; Prasad MSS III/35.
6. The U.P. Scheme failed because the provincial leaders could not find the Rs. 700 per month needed to keep it going. (See AICC P 20 1934). In Gujerat there was money (the surplus from the fund raised to fight the plague outbreak in Borsad District) but the provincial leaders had other, more directly political, uses for it. (See N. D. Parikh, *Sardar Vallabhbhai Patel* (Ahmedabad, 1956) Vol. II pp 192–7; G.o.I. Home Department (Political) 3/8/35 N.A.I. What caused the collapse of the Bihar plan is uncertain, but it sank quickly and without trace. (See Secretary Bihar P.C.C. circular letter 17.11.34 in AICC P 5 1934–6.)
7. When Anugrah Narain Sinha, one of the top Bihari Congress leaders, was advised to take up All India Village Industries Association work, he replied that he would do so only when his political career was over. Diary Entry 11.1.35 A. N. Sinha MSS.
8. D. O. No. 152–C 25.5.36 Bihar History of the Freedom Movement Series, file no. 84. S.C.R.O. Patna.
9. Fortnightly Report of the Government of Bihar and Orissa for February 1935 in G.o.I. Home Department (Political) 18/2/35. N.A.I.
10. A. N. Sinha, 'Autobiography', typescript copy in Sinha Memorial Library, Patna, p. 171.
11. Congressmen subsequently formed coalition ministries in Assam, Sindh and the N.W.F.P.
12. 'Movement' in F. G. Bailey's sense of a ground organisation in which:
    . . . voluntary workers give their services because they are in the habit of doing so, and in the last resort because they are morally (that is, without calculation of

immediate personal material gain) convinced of the rightness of their party's policies.

See F. G. Bailey, *Politics and Social Change, Orissa in 1959* (Berkeley 1970) p.138.

13. Fortnightly Report of U.P. Government for February 1937. G.o.I. Home Department (Political) 18/2/37 N.A.I.
14. Nawab of Chhatari to Sapru 30.5.37 Sapru MSS (Second Series) K. 84.
15. The full figures were as follows:

| | 1919 Electorate | | | | 1935 Electorate | |
	Total	% of population	Average per seat	Total	% of population	Average per seat
Madras	1,470,900	3·1	15,000	7,224,000	15·5	33,693
Bombay	888,801	4·1	10,335	3,726,000	17·1	18,630
Bengal	1,331,803	2·6	11,682	8,000,000	16·0	32,000
U.P.	1,646,290	3·4	16,463	7,500,000	15·5	32,895
Punjab	745,000	3·1	10,493	2,800,000	11·9	16,000
Bihar & Orissa	418,324	1·1	5,504	3,500,000	9·3	20,000
C.P.	199,500	1·3	3,627	1,950,000	12·5	17,411
Assam	228,832	3·3	7,406	1,040,000	12·1	9,630
N.W.F.P.	119,922	–	4,283	242,000	9·9	48,400
Total	7,049,372	2·75	9,421	35,982,000	13·3	25,406

Source   Note on Franchise Committee Proposals, G.o.I. Reforms Office no. 102/32 R & KW N.A.I.

16. G.o.I. R.O. No. 13 of 1932; G.o.I. Reforms Office 102/32R & KW N.A.I.
17. See *Indian Franchise Committee Report Vol I* pp. 48–78. Most Provincial Governments were not in favour of increasing the electorates to as high a figure as 10 per cent. They claimed that such an increase would present insurmountable administrative problems in compiling the electoral rolls and running the elections (see G.o.I. Reforms Office 38/32R N.A.I.). This concern seems to have been genuine, not simply a respectable excuse for resisting pressure to increase the level of franchise. The India Office officials thought that only in Bihar and Orissa did government concern for administrative practicability mask a desire to manipulate the level of the franchise for political ends (see L/P & J/9/185 I.O.L.).
18. G.o.I. R.O. no. 13 of 1932; G.o.I. Reforms Office 102/32R & KW N.A.I.
19. *Indian Franchise Committee Report Vol. I* pp. 48–78.
20. For a convenient statement of the old P.L.C. electorates see *Indian Franchise Commission Report Vol. I* pp. 281–3; for local board electorates see *Indian Statutory Commission Report Vol. V* pp. 1067, 1071 and 1079. In most provinces hurried legislation was passed after 1937 to bring the local board electorates in line with the new provincial ones. One exception was Madras, where the local board electorates had been lowered in 1930 to the same level as was to be introduced later for the P.L.A.
21. See Congress Parliamentary Board Circular of 8.5.36 Prasad MSS 1/36; *Leader* 14.5.36.
22. But too much should not be made of the efficiency of the Congress canvassing as the turnout of voters was as high in areas and constituencies that the Congress did not win or contest as in those they did. The lowest percentage turnout was in Madras, where the Congress won its highest percentage of seats. In the U.P. and Bihar the turnout was as high in the Muslim seats, which the Congress did not contest, as in the seats which it did. See *Return showing the Results of the Elections in India 1937* (Cmd. 5589 of 1936–7) pp. 5–13.
23. See Fortnightly Reports of U.P. Government for February 1937 in G.o.I. Home

Department (Political) 18/2/37 N.A.I.
24. P. N. Chopra *Rafi Ahmed Kidwai – His Life and Work* (Agra, 1960) pp 44–6.
25. Fortnightly Reports C.P. Government for February 1937. G.o.I. Home Department (Political) 18/2/37 N.A.I.
26. Diaries no. 8 & 9, entries of 29.12.36; 19.2.37 B. S. Moonje MSS.
27. See C. J. Baker 'Political Change in South India 1919–37' Chapter 9, fellowship dissertation, Queens' College, Cambridge, 1972 (unpublished).
28. For events in Madras see ibid. The *Indian Statutory Commission Report Vol II* pp 136–56 contains a good general survey of the weaknesses of the dyarchy ministries.
29. For the early history of the N.A.P. see correspondence in Hailey MSS, Vols. 24, 25, 26 & 27.
30. *Leader* 27.8.36.
31. Ibid. 30.8.36.
32. Election results taken from AICC E 23 1937.
33. For a more detailed account of the N.A.P. and the 1937 elections see P. D. Reeves 'Landlords and Party Politics in the United Provinces' in D. A. Low (ed.) *Soundings in Modern Asian History* (London, 1968) pp. 261–91, especially pp. 268–79.
34. For an idea of the problems caused by this lack of material see D. D. Taylor 'Indian Politics and the elections of 1937', Ph. D. Thesis, University of London, 1972 (unpublished); P. D. Reeves 'Changing Patterns of Political Alignment in the General Elections to the United Provinces Legislative Assembly, 1937 & 1946' in *Modern Asian Studies* Vol. 5 no. 2 (1971) pp 111–142.
35. For an elaboration of these terms see F. G. Bailey, *Politics and Social Change, Orissa in 1959* (Berkeley, 1970) p 138.
36. R. Kothari 'Prospects for Democracy' *Economic Weekly* Vol XIII no. 23 (10.6.61) p. 889.
37. See Gopal Krishna 'One Party Dominance – Development and Trends' in Centre for the Study of Developing Societies, Occasional Papers no. 1 *Party System and Election Studies* (Bombay, 1967) pp. 19–98; F. G. Bailey *Politics and Social Change, Orissa in 1959* (Berkeley, 1970) pp. 59–67.
38. See, for example, Myron Weiner's studies of Guntur District, Andhra Pradesh, in M. Weiner, *Party-Building in a New Nation* (Chicago, 1967) pp. 133–217 and M. Weiner & R. Kothari (eds), *Indian Voting Behaviour* (Calcutta, 1965) pp. 177–202.
39. P. R. Brass 'Political Participation, Institutionalisation and Stability in India' in *Government and Opposition* Vol. 4 no. 1 (1969) pp. 23–53, p. 34.
40. See M. Weiner, *Party Politics in India: The Development of a Multi-Party System* (Princeton, 1957) pp. 12–16, 253; W. H. Morris-Jones 'The Indian Congress Party: A Dilemma of Dominance' in *Modern Asian Studies* Vol. 1 no. 1 (1967) p. 110.
41. R. Kothari 'Prospects for Democracy' in *Economic Weekly* Vol XIII no. 23 (10.6.61) pp. 889–90. Even where the importance of internal factional conflict is noted, it is still seen as subservient to ideology and broad issues of principle in the pre-independence period. (See P. R. Brass, *Factional Politics in an Indian State: The Congress Party in Uttar Pradesh* (Berkeley, 1965) pp. 34–43.)
42. The classic use of this term is in R. Kothari 'Parliamentary Government: Law and Usage' in *Economic Weekly* Vol. XIII no. 20 (20.5.61) p. 785.
43. The percentage of those who voted to the number of electors in contested constituencies varied from 51·6 in Madras to 72·8 in the N.W.F.P. The overall average was 54·55 per cent. See *Return Showing the Results of the Elections in India 1937* (Cmnd 5589 of 1936–7) p. 5.
44. See D. A. Washbrook, 'Country Politics: Madras 1880 to 1930' in J. A. Gallagher *et al* (eds), *Locality Province & Nation* (Cambridge, 1973) pp. 155–211.
45. S. A. Kochanek, *The Congress Party of India: The Dynamics of One Party Democracy* (Princeton, 1968) pp. 370–404.
46. This information has been supplied by Dr C. J. Baker of Queens' College, Cambridge.

47. Diary Entry 29.2.36 Bhulabhai Desai MSS.
48. This information is compiled from press reports in *Leader.*
49. In percentage form, the M.L.A.s formed 25 per cent of the C.P. delegates at Lucknow, 12 per cent at Faizpur, 13 per cent at Haripura, 9 per cent at Tripuri and 9 per cent at Ramgarh. This information is compiled from the brief biographies of the M.L.A.s supplied by Sir Hyde Gowan, Governor of the C.P., in his letter to Lord Linlithgow of 7.3.37 (Linlithgow MSS Vol. 12) and from the lists of delegates in AICC 19 1936; G 58(i) 1936; G 96(a) 1937; 28(I-III) 1938; G 60(KW1) 1939–40.
50. See R. Prasad, *Autobiography* (Bombay, 1957) p. 427.
51. Of the 10 man panel appointed by the P.C.C. in January 1936 to arbitrate election disputes four were members of the Kisan Sabha/C.S.P. alliance. *Searchlight* 29.1.36.
52. See C.O. no. 643-C, Bihar Pradesh History of the Freedom Movement file no. 15, S.C.R.O., Patna.
53. For a manuscript copy of the report see Prasad MSS VII/37.
54. See *Searchlight* 9.8.36; 30.9.36.
55. Fortnightly Report of Government of Bihar and Orissa for October 1936 in G.o.I. Home Department (Political) 18/10/36 N.A.I.
56. See *Searchlight* 7.6.36; 14.6.36; 17.6.36; 24.7.36; 29.7.36; *Indian Nation* 5.6.36; 6.6.36; R. Prasad to V. Patel 17.11.36 Prasad MSS 1/36.
57. R. Prasad to V. Patel 17.11.36 Prasad MSS 1/36.
58. Ibid.
59. *Indian Nation* 19.2.37
60. A. N. Sinha, 'Autobiography', typescript copy in Sinha Memorial Library, Patna, p. 172.
61. Ibid., p. 173.
62. It is not certain how the provincial leaders felt about Sahajanand's resignation. Some of those who had given support to the Kisan Sabha in 1934 and 1935, Shri Krishna Singh for example, may well have been sorry to see such a valuable, if unreliable, ally depart. Rajendra Prasad expended a lot of energy trying to prevent Sahajanand resigning (see ibid., p. 173) but whether this was simply a reflex action by a born mediator, or whether it was a genuine attempt to preserve unity, is unclear.
63. *Indian Annual Register 1936 Vol. I* p. 255 Working Committee Resolution of 24.7.36.
64. Pant to Prasad 11.5.36 Prasad MSS 1/36.
65. See press statement issued by Patel, Nehru, Abdul Gaffar Khan, and Bajaj 17.11.36 AICC E 1(i) 1936.
66. Patel to Prof. Ranga 21.5.37 Prasad MSS II/37.
67. R. Prasad, *Autobiography* (Bombay, 1957) p. 427.
68. Thus although one of Dr Khare's nominees in Nagpur was disallowed in favour of a member of the P.C.C. minority faction, in Mahakoshal one of the Das/Misra faction's nominees was displaced at Shukla's request, even though 33 of the 38 nominations from the province had already gone to members of Shukla's faction. (*Leader* 23.12.36; 30.12.36; Fortnightly Report of Government of Central Provinces and Berar December 1936 in G.o.I. Home Department (Political) 8/12/36 N.A.I.).
69. See Patel/Nehru/Biyani correspondence November–December 1936 in AICC P 7 1936; E 1 1936.
70. See Nehru/Pant correspondence in AICC E 1 1936; P 20 1936.
71. A. Gaffer Khan to D. P. Misra 21.7.36 Mahakoshal P.C.C. MSS Inter-Provincial Congress Committee Correspondence Series, 1936 file.
72. See 'Appeal against disciplinary action of the P.C.C. by six Yeotmal Congressmen 7.4.37' AICC E 22 1937; T. G. Bande (Secretary Yeotmal D.C.C.) to Nehru 10.7.37 AICC P 22 (i) 1937.
73. Prasad to Secretary U.P. Parliamentary Committee 13.7.36 Prasad MSS 1/36.
74. Secretary Berar P.C.C. to General Secretary A.I.C.C. 12.4.37 AICC E 23 1937.
75. Figures taken from list of U.P. election expenses in L/P & J/7/1149 I.O.L.

76. Ibid.
77. Item 14 of minutes of first meeting of the Board on 1.7.36 (marked 'not for publication'). See Prasad MSS I/36.
78. All India Parliamentary Board Circular no. 6 of 8.10.36 AICC P 1 1936.
79. Diary Entry 10.2.36 B. Desai MSS.
80. See correspondence in AICC G 47 1939.
81. Prasad to Secretary U.P. Parliamentary Committee 13.7.36 Prasad MSS I/36.
82. Assistant Secretary U.P.P.C.C. to General Secretary A.I.C.C. 17.5.37 AICC P 20 1937.
83. Fortnightly Reports of Government of Bihar for February 1937 in G.o.I. Home Department (Political) 18.2.37. N.A.I.
84. Prasad to Patel 17.11.36 Prasad MSS I/36.
85. Fortnightly Reports of Government of Bihar for December 1936 in G.o.I. Home Department (Political) 18/12/36 N.A.I.
86. A. N. Sinha, 'Autobiography', typescript copy in Sinha Memorial Library, Patna p. 174.
87. Dalmia to Prasad 15.11.36; 1.12.36 Prasad MSS I/36
88. Mahmud to Prasad undated (late November 1936) Prasad MSS I/36.
89. A. N. Sinha, 'Autobiography', typescript copy in Sinha Memorial Library, Patna p. 173.
90. Ramashray Roy 'Election Studies: Selection of Congress Candidates I–V' in *Economic and Political Weekly Vol. I* no. 20, *Vol. II* nos. 1, 2, 6 & 7 (December 1966–February 1967).
91. Ibid., V – 'Structure of Authority in the Congress' in *Economic and Political Weekly Vol. II* no. 7 (18.2.67) pp. 413–15.
92. 'Report of the Bihar P.C.C. Enquiry Committee into Cases of Violence at the Delegate Elections of December 1937' AICC P 6 1939–40.
93. E. Krishna Iyer to Nehru 21.11.36 AICC G 5(a) 1936.
94. R. M. Sharma Memorandum on the Congress organisation 6.5.38 AICC G 43 1938.
95. General Secretary's Report to Haripura Congress February 1938, typescript in AICC 63 1937.
96. As the P.C.C. President commented, 'the only work of the Congress Committees is the various elections'. See A.I.C.C. inspector's report on Andhra P.C.C. July 1938 to June 1939 AICC G 28 1938.
97. Ditto Karnatak P.C.C., ibid.
98. '[T]he Congress Committee had, for the last four months [March–June 1938], no work before them except these elections to the District Boards.' Ditto Berar P.C.C., ibid.
99. Ditto Bihar P.C.C., ibid.
100. Ditto Berar P.C.C., ibid.
101. Thus in Guntur District the membership figure for 1937–8, when there was a district board election, was 877,980; in 1938–9 it was 27,452. In East Godaveri where the district board election was in 1939 the 1937–8 figure was 39,477 and the 1938–9 figure 61,299. Ditto Andhra P.C.C., ibid.
102. *Indian Nation* 15.5.37.
103. Ibid. 20.5.37
104 *Searchlight* 10.5.38
105. Ibid. 20.12.38.
106. Prasad to Nehru 19.4.39. Prasad MSS 3-C/39.
107. See *Indian Nation* 5.5.39.
108. Mahesh Prasad Narain Singh was a large zamindar who had entered the Congress in 1936 and had acquired the Chairmanship of the District Board in 1937 after the resignation of Chandeshwar Prasad Narain Singh, which had formed part of the deal between the Bihar Government and the zamindars over Tenancy legislation.
109. Ibid. 12.5.39; 17.5.39; 18.5.39; 28.5.39; 10.6.39. The last report claimed that of the

eleven independents returned, all were Congressmen and members of the D.C.C. or a Thana C.C., not just the five 'left-wingers'.
110. See *Indian Nation* 28.3.39; Bihar Government History of Freedom Movement file no. 18 & 63 S.C.R.O. Patna; AICC P 6 1939/40.
111. Assistant Secretary B.P.C.C. to General Secretary A.I.C.C. 20.4.39 AICC P 6 1939.
112. When the P.C.C. considered disciplinary action against Congressmen who had opposed official party nominees in these elections, the *Indian Nation* commented: 'To an impartial observer this appears ludicrous and a contradiction in terms in view of the fact that those who opposed the Congress candidates in the last Assembly elections were adopted as Congress candidates in the District Board elections'. *Indian Nation* 26.5.39
113. The Prasad Papers include a fat file of complaints, petitions and counter-petitions on this subject: file 1-N 1939.
114. *Indian Nation* 1.10.39; General Secretary Bihar Provincial Depressed Castes' League to Prasad 6.4.39; B.B. Das Gupta to Prasad 19.8.39 Prasad MSS 1-B/39
115. Prasad to Mahmud 15.7.39 ibid.
116. Mahmud to Prasad 18.7.38 Prasad MSS 3-B/38.
117. Khare to Patel 5.5.37 ibid. 2-C/38.
118. See Shri Murti Babu to Prasad 12.7.38; Patel to Prasad 14.7.38 Prasad MSS 1-B/39; 1-L/39.
119. See A. N. Sinha to Prasad 6.7.38 ibid. 3-B/38; enclosure in V. Patel to Prasad 19.7.39 ibid. 1-B/39
120. *Leader* 15.3.37; Fortnightly Reports C.P. Government March 1937, G.o.I. Home Department (Political) 18/3/37 N.A.I. R. S. Shukla was leader of the Mahakoshal P.L.A. Party and D. K. Mehta was deputy leader.
121. R. R. Deshmukh to Khare 9.2.38 Prasad MSS 2-C/38
122. Like many politicians with access to executive power but unsure of the security of their position, Khare was building up support by a policy of aiding Moslems in appointments. Misra to Khare 7.5.38 ibid.
123. Patel to Khare 11.7.38 ibid.; see also correspondence in AICC P 13 (2) 1938.
124. Misra to Khare 9.5.38; undated notes by Prasad. Prasad MSS 2-C/38.
125. Misra to Khare 9.5.38 Prasad MSS 2-C/38. Misra claimed in April 1938 that Khare had used the police to destroy the Congress in Jubblepore and Khare had also ordered the C.I.D. to investigate the activities of another of his colleagues – P. V. Gole.
126. See *Central Provinces Ministerial Crisis. Statements issued by Shri Sunhas Chandra Bose, Congress President, Parliamentary Sub-Committee, Acharya J. B. Kripalani General Secretary A.I.C.C. and Mahatma Gandhi.* (Allahabad, no date) pp. 6–10.
127. *Leader* 20.3.38.
128. Ibid. 7.4.38.
129. Ibid. 16.4.38.
130. Ibid. 14.5.38.
131. Ibid.
132. Ibid. 19.5.38.
133. Ibid.
134. Ibid.
135. Ibid. 1.6.38.
136. Ibid.
137. This Board was the body through which the 'High Command' was to supervise the Ministry.
138. Ibid. 13.7.38.
139. Ibid.
140. Ibid. 17.7.38.
141. Ibid.18.7.38.
142. Ibid. 22.7.38.

143. Ibid. 23.7.38.
144. Ibid. 24.7.38.
145. Ibid. 25.7.38.
146. Ibid. 29.7.38.
147. Ibid.
148. Ibid. 4.10.38.
149. Gole to Shukla, Misra and Mehta 8.5.38 Prasad MSS 2-C/38.
150. Sampurnanand and Narendra Dev were both offered Ministries, but both refused because of the C.S.P. ban on accepting office. When Sharma resigned in 1938, Sampurnanand did accept the Education Ministry, but broke with the C.S.P. to do so.
151. H. C. Bajpai to Nehru 13.12.37 AICC P 20 (i) 1937.
152. See *Leader* 11.11.37; 14.11.37; G. N. & H. D. Srivastava to Nehru 9.11.37 AICC P 20 (i) 1937.
153. See AICC P 20 (i) 1937.
154. *Leader* 19.11.37. But the P.C.C. Executive passed a resolution declaring that the President of the Political Conference should not in future be automatically returned as the President of the P.C.C. also. Therefore Saxena had to stand again for the Presidentship of the P.C.C.
155. Nehru to K. D. Malaviya *et al.* November 1937 AICC P 20 (i) 1937.
156. *Leader* 19.1.38. The Governor, Sir Harry Haig, regarded Saxena's position on the P.C.C. as most insecure and felt that Nehru's ideas on the importance of unity represented the only check that existed on the 'left-wing' majority (Haig to Linlithgow 22.1.38 Haig MSS Vol. 7).
157) Haig to Linlithgow 23.8.37 Haig MSS Vol. 17.
158. See *Leader* 3.9.37.
159. Haig to Linlithgow 22.9.37 Haig MSS Vol. 17.
160. *Leader* 31.12.37; 1.1.38; 2.1.38.
161. Fortnightly Reports U.P. Government for April 1937 in G.o.I. Home Department (Political) 18/4/37 N.A.I.
162. *Leader* 19.4.37.
163. Ibid. 26.11.37.
164. The tenancies of all occupancy tenants, the heirs of occupancy tenants and tenants on the landlord's *sir* (demesne) land who had cultivated for the previous five years (if the landlord paid more than Rs 100/- in land revenue or Rs 10/- in income tax) were to be made hereditary.
165. Any tenant on *sir* land who held a lease for five years or over was to have hereditary rights. If the landlord leased his *sir* land for less than five years he had to cultivate it personally for three years after the ending of each lease before he could re-let it.
166. Landlords could no longer get possession of a tenant's lands by court order and tenants could no longer be arrested for non-payment of rent. Landlords were to charge no more than 6¼ per cent per annum simple interest on unpaid rent. Court orders could only be obtained for extracting arrears of more than Rs 10/- and only for arrears in the two previous years' rent.
167. *Leader* 26.3.38.
168. Figures for the whole of the U.P. for the year 1945–6 (excluding the hill tracts of Almora, Garwhal and Naini Tal) reveal that of the 1,898,050 zamindars in the province 1,888,977 paid less than Rs 250/- land revenue. Only 19·2 per cent of the total land of the province was demesne land (*sir* or *khudkhast* holdings) but zamindars paying under Rs 250/- in land revenue held 81·4 per cent of this. 86·5 per cent of the *sir* and *khudkhast* land of the province was cultivated personally by its owner. The vast bulk of the U.P. zamindars were small landholders, mostly cultivating their own lands and letting very little out to tenants. See *Report of United Provinces Zamindari Abolition Enquiry Committee Vol. II* (Allahabad, 1948) pp. 3, 4, 5 and 94.
169. *Leader* 29.6.38; 3.7.38.

170. Ibid. 15.8.38. In their negotiations with the landed magnates in the P.L.C. the Congress ministers were prepared to go even further than this. At one point they were considering removing the clauses in the Bill granting hereditary rights to some tenants of the *sir* lands of landlords paying up to Rs 100 in land revenue. See Ibid. 15.8.38.
171. A memorandum written by the Secretary of the U.P.P.C.C. (who was not a left-winger) pointed out that the Bill would favour the small zamindars and the large tenants. A grant of hereditary rights to occupancy tenants would make their position unassailable, while their sub-tenants would enjoy few rights. See AICC 17 1938.
172. In September 1938 Pant and Katju declared that, with the P.L.C. leaders unwilling to accept any compromise, the only people benefiting from the Tenancy Bill were the left-wing critics of the Ministry. See Haig to Linlithgow 26.9.38 Haig MSS Vol.|7.
173. After September the negotiations were carried on by the Congress Working Committee Parliamentary Sub-Committee – the 'High Command'.
174. *Leader* 14.11.38.
175. Ibid. 3.7.38; 12.7.38; 13.7.38.
176. Ibid. 24.7.38.
177. *Leader* 2.10.28; AICC P 20 (i) 1938
178. Haig to Linlithgow 23.11.38 Haig MSS Vol. 7.
179. *Leader* 4.4.38; 19.6.38; ibid. 7.4.38.
180. Ibid.
181. Ibid. 16.4.38, 23.4.38. Nehru had to hurriedly withdraw his criticisms when he found that Dev had organised the demonstration. Even so his precipitate haste in condemning the meeting was not appreciated by his erstwhile allies on the P.C.C. Damodhar Swarup Seth complained to him that the demonstration had only been intended to strengthen the hand of the Ministry by putting pressure on the magnates in the P.L.A. and complained that Nehru's attack on it 'has given once more a very strong stick to the group in power to beat the poor leftists who were already groaning under various tyrannies of the Rightists in office' (Damodhar Swarup Seth to Nehru 18.4.38 AICC P 20 (ii) 1938).
182. *Leader* 29.4.38.
183. Ibid. 28.5.38. The P.C.C. resolution condemned the trouble-makers as 'some individuals who, being unable to find a place in the district Congress executive, have sought to organise the Kisan Sabhas locally which might give them greater prominence'.
184. *Leader* 30.6.38.
185. Ibid. 20.10.38; 21.10.38; 1.11.38.
186. Ibid. 25.7.38; 18.10.38.
187. Ibid. 31.12.38.
188. Ibid. 3.1.39; *Pioneer* 1.1.39; Haig to Linlithgow 10.1.39 Haig MSS Vol. 2.
189. Haig to Linlithgow 24.1.39 Haig MSS Vol. 2.
190. See the example of Shibben Lal Saxena in Gorukhpur. Haig to Linlithgow 25.3.39; 10.4.39; 26.4.39 Ibid.
191. *Leader* 28.5.39; 26.8.39. Donaldson to Private Secretary to Viceroy 28.8.39 Haig MSS Vol. 2.
192. *Indian Nation* 11.7.37; 13.7.37.
193. The best example of this was the agitation at Barhiya Tal in Monghyr District. See Fortnightly Reports Bihar Government March 1937 in G.o.I. Home Department (Political) 18/3/37 N.A.I.
194. Notes by Rajendra Prasad on Bihar Tenancy proposals in AICC P 6 (ii) 1937.
195. A separate Bakasht Lands Bill was passed in 1938 but its terms were so lax that the zamindars were able to avoid them with ease. See W. Hauser 'The Indian National Congress and Land Policy in the Twentieth Century' in *Indian Economic and Social History Review* 1963–4 Vol. 1 p. 64.

196. *Indian Nation* 12.12.37.
197. *Indian Nation* 4.5.38; 10.5.38; 15.5.38; 24.5.38.
198. Report of the Bihar P.C.C. Enquiry Committee into Cases of Violence at the delegate elections of December 1937. AICC P 6 1939.
199. *Searchlight* 28.12.37; 15.1.38; 19.1.38.
200. Ibid. 20.5.38.
201. *Searchlight* 14.12.37; 19.12.37.
202. The Divisional Officer of Patna wrote of these campaigns:
     [The Kisan Leaders] are not at all interested in bringing about any amicable settlement but are only anxious to retain the leadership of the Kisans, for which it is necessary that the fight about *bakasht* lands should continue and spread over the districts.
     Fortnightly Reports for Patna Division July 1939. Bihar History of the Freedom Movement file 63 S.C.R.O. Patna.
203. *Searchlight* 15.11.37.
204. AICC Inspector's Report on Karnatak P.C.C. July 1938 to June 1939, AICC G 28 1938. See also J. Nehru, *The Unity of India* (London, 1941) pp. 82–3.
205. *Searchlight* 15.12.37.
206. Especially in the U.P. and Bihar. Only in the Punjab, Bengal, Sindh and the N.W.F.P. were the Muslims in a majority.
207. This picture is drastically over-simplified. The Muslim polity was no less bedevilled by factionalism and rivalry than other sections of Indian political society, and those who were in opposition to the established Muslim politicians in several provinces tended to join or at least ally with the Congress to give a wider basis to their opposition. But it is generally true to say that, by the late 1920s, it was becoming increasingly difficult for Muslim politicians in the minority provinces to risk being accused of supporting Hindus against the interests of their co-religionists.
208. See Z. H. Zaidi, 'Aspects of Muslim League Policy 1937–47' in C. H. Philips and M. D. Wainwright (eds) *The Partition of India: Policies and Perspectives 1935–47* (London, 1970) p. 246.
209. The league did not contest all the Muslim seats; Jinnah claimed that his organisation won sixty to seventy per cent of the seats it had contested. See Ibid., p. 253.
210. See R. Coupland, *The Indian Problem: Indian Politics 1936–42* (London, 1943) pp. 110–12; A. W. Khan, *India Wins Freedom – The Other Side* (Karachi, 1961) pp. 79–81.
211. In Azad's own account of the episode he shifts the blame on to Nehru. See A. K. Azad, *India Wins Freedom* (Calcutta, 1960) pp. 160–1.
212. Nehru to Prasad 21.7.37 Nehru MSS R 20; Note by Donaldson dated 14.8.40 in G.o.I. Reforms Office file no. 89/40-R.N.A.I.
213. Note by J. Thorne dated 15.8.40 ibid. (italics in source).
214. Ch. Khaliquzzaman, *Pathway to Pakistan* (Lahore, 1961) p. 167.
215. He refers to some of the Lucknow M.L.A.s in 1937:
     Gopi Nath Srivastava, Mohan Lal Saxena, Jagdamba Narain, Gopal Narain Saxena, Harkanarath Misra, Jai Karan Nath Misra, Pushkar Nath Batt . . . some of whom were as dear to me as my own younger brothers . . . had been my constant companions and co-workers in every field of political or municipal activity. (Ibid. p. 167.)
216. Ibid., p. 158.
217. S. R. Mehrotra, 'The Congress and the Partition of India' in C. H. Philips and M. D. Wainwright (eds), *The Partition of India: Policies and Perspectives 1935–47* (London, 1970) pp. 195–9.
218. Nehru to Prasad 21.7.37 Nehru MSS R 20.
219. One Muslim politician, Mohammed Ibrahim, elected on a League ticket, had already joined the Congress on the promise of a Ministry.
220. Sir Harry Haig to Linlithgow 10.5.39 Haig MSS Vol. 6.
221. Nehru to Members of the Working Committee 24.11.37 Nehru MSS I 14 (i a).

222. See AICC B 11(2) 1938; B 12 1938; P 20 1938; 38 1937; 31 1937; 48 1937.
223. See *Searchlight* 6.5.38; 19.5.38; 25.5.38.
224. See *The Report of the Committee appointed by the Council of the All India Muslim League to Inquire into Muslim Grievances in the Congress-Governed Provinces 1938* [Pirpur Report]. Published in Jamil-ud-Din Ahmad (ed.), *Historic Documents of the Muslim Freedom Movement* (Lahore, 1970) pp. 258–332.
225. Fortnightly Report for Patna District August 1938 in Bihar History of the Freedom Movement file 62 S.C.R.O. Patna.
226. *Indian Nation* 30.5.39.
227. Ibid.
228. In Darbhanga the League boycott of the elections to the Municipality gained support by the exclusion from Congress tickets of one Congress leader's supporters (Abdul Gaffoor's) by another (Prof. Abdul Bari) *Indian Nation* 30.5.39; Binodanand Jha Minute on Darbhanga Municipality 3.9.38 Prasad MSS 3-B/38.
229. *Searchlight* 14.4.38.
230. *Searchlight* 23.6.38.
231. In AICC P 6 1939–40.
232. A.I.C.C. inspector's report on Gujerat P.C.C. July 1939 to June 1940 AICC 14 1939.
233. L. B. Shastri to Nehru 6.3.38 Nehru MSS S 132.
234. See examples quoted in W. H. Morris-Jones, *Parliament in India* (London, 1957) pp. 67–9.
235. *Leader* 1.3.37; 22.3.37.
236. Ibid. 20.3.37.
237. As early as March 1937 Patel was worried about the affairs of the Bombay P.L.A. party and wrote, 'unless stronger control from the Centre is exercised, things will go wrong.' Patel to Nehru 9.3.37 J. Nehru, *A Bunch of Old Letters* (Bombay, 1958) p. 225.
238. Nehru pointed out that ' . . . achieving national independence for India . . . will come, not through Ministries, but through the organized strength of the Indian people acting through the Congress.' J. Nehru, *The Unity of India: Collected Writings 1937-40* (London, 1941) p. 75.
239. *Leader* 23.3.37.
240. Congress Parliamentary Sub-Committee Circular No. 4 of 11.7.37 Prasad MSS II/37.
241. See Prasad's attempts to get the Bihar ministry on to the right track: Prasad to Shri Krishna Singh 4.3.38 Prasad MSS 3-B/38; Patel to Prasad 19.7.39 Ibid. 1-B/39.
242. J. B. Kripalani, General Secretary of the A.I.C.C., described the set-up thus: The only body that controls the legislatures and the ministries is the . . . Parliamentary Sub-Committee. Only in very serious and rare cases is there any interference. Normally the legislature party is an autonomous group. . . . Kripalani to President Cochin Congress Committee 30.6.38 AICC G 35 1938.
243. D. P. Misra to Dr Khare 8.11.37 Prasad MSS 2-C/38.
244. Patel to Prasad 31.8.39 Prasad MSS 1-C/39.

Chapter 4

1. See Linlithgow to Zetland 30.12.37 Linlithgow MSS Vol. 4.
2. 'Note on interview with G. D. Birla' Linlithgow to Zetland 3.12.37 Ibid.
3. See Linlithgow to Zetland 9.9.37, 3.12.37, 30.12.37, 11.2.38 Ibid., Lothian to Sapru 27.12.37 Sapru MSS (First Series) L.63
4. *Bombay Chronicle* 17.2.38.
5. 'Note on Interview with G. D. Birla' Linlithgow to Zetland 3.12.37 Linlithgow MSS Vol. 4.
6. In AICC G 40 1938.
7. Interview with M. R. Masani *Searchlight* 11.4.37.

8. A. Patwardhan to Nehru 10.12.37 Nehru MSS P 56.
9. G. Mazumdar (Secretary Bengal C.S.P.) to Dr K. M. Ashraf 21.5.37 AICC 49 1937.
10. See J. P. Haithcox, *Communism and Nationalism in India: M. N. Roy and Comintern Policy 1920–1939* (Princeton, 1971) pp. 234–6; L. P. Sinha, *The Left Wing in India* (Muzaffarpur, 1965) pp. 456–7.
11. Press statement issued 9.2.37, quoted in Government of Bombay Fortnightly Reports for February 1937 in G.o.I. Home Department (Political) 18/2/37 N.A.I.
12. See J. P. Haithcox, *Communism and Nationalism in India: M. N. Roy and Comintern Policy 1920–1939* (Princeton, 1971) pp. 231– 2.
13. Government of Bombay Fortnightly Reports for April 1937 in G.o.I. Home Department (Political) 18/4/37 N.A.I.
14. At the Working Committee meeting of March 1937 Nehru stressed the invidious position of himself and his two C.S.P. colleagues:

    They felt that though they were in the Committee they were not able to affect its decisions on any major issue and that by remaining in the Committee they were making themselves responsible for the carrying out of policies with which they did not agree.

    Minutes of Working Committee Meeting March 1937 AICC 42 1936.
15. J. Nehru, *The Unity of India – Collected Writings 1937–40* (London, 1941) p. 80.
16 See his speech to the National Convention of March 1937 – appreciation by G.o.I. Home Department in Home Department (Political) 4/10/37 N.A.I.
17. J. Nehru to Members of the Working Committee 24.11.37 J. Nehru MSS I 14 (iia).
18. 'Review of Events' submitted to Subjects Committee Haripura, *Bombay Chronicle* 17.2.38.
19. In August 1937, the 'Mass Contacts Committee' appointed by the Working Committee in 1936 produced a first draft of its recommendations. These included Jai Prakash Narain's idea of 'Associate Membership', which tried to make the primary Congress organisations more accessible to rural agitators. 'Associate Members' were to pay no membership fee, and to have no voting powers, but they were to be allowed to canvass during election campaigns (for the Congress Committees) and to speak and canvass at meetings of the proposed 'Panchayats' (village or ward Committees). However, when these ideas were circulated to the P.C.C.s, opinion was firmly against both 'Associate Membership and 'Panchayats'. Both ideas were dropped in the Mass Contacts Committee's final report to the Haripura Subjects Committee AICC G 80 (KWI) 1938; AICC 36 1936.
20. See Narendra Dev's Presidential speech at the Shahabad District Kisan Conference, *Indian Nation* 9.6.37; Prafulla Chandra Ghosh's objections to Nehru's activities in P. C. Ghosh to R. Prasad 18.6.37 & 2.7.37 Prasad MSS 1/37; G.o.I. Home Department Intelligence Bureau Summary of the Indian National Congress and Kisan Sabhas 8.7.37 in G.o.I. Home Department (Political) 11/1/37. N.A.I.
21. It was over the question of the Governor's use of their special powers that Gandhi had kept the Congress out of office in early 1937.
22. Minutes of Working Committee meeting 14–17.8.37 AICC 42 1936.
23. Minutes of Working Committee meeting 26.10.37 AICC 42 1936.
24. *Leader* 2.11.37.
25. See 'The A.I.C.C.' by M. K. G. *Harijan* 13.11.37.
26. See Vallabhbhai Patel to Rajendra Prasad 12.12.37 Prasad MSS II/37.
27. See Ghosh to Prasad 12.6.37 Prasad MSS XI/37.
28. He wrote to Prasad on 2.10.37: 'They are waiting for a time when they could displace us; that is why I have given them no quarters [sic] and they have always attacked me mercilessly'. Prasad MSS II/37.
29. V. Patel to Prasad 22.9.37 ibid.
30. A. K. Azad to Prasad 26.11.37 ibid. III/37.

31. The Gandhi Seva Sangh had been founded in 1923 to build up support for the constructive programme.
32. J. Doulatram to Prasad 24.11.37 Prasad MSS I-G/37.
33. 'Note on the Gandhi Seva Sangh 12.3.40' in G.o.I. Home Department (Political) 4/18/40. N.A.I.
34. See correspondence and papers in AICC G 56 1938 and Prasad MSS I-G/37.
35. See Prasad to Shri Krishna Singh 2.12.37, Prasad to Ramdayalu Singh 7.12.37 Prasad MSS XV/37; Patel to Prasad 21.11.37 ibid. II/37.
36. AICC G 27 1934. During 1934 the leaders of the States Peoples Conference (which claimed national status but was in fact confined in interest and influence to Maharastra) had had talks with Gandhi. Throughout these negotiations, Gandhi held to the line laid down by the 1928 Calcutta Congress resolution on the subject – that the Congress could sympathise with the activities of the States subjects, but that the Congress could not interfere in the internal affairs of the States. (See AICC G 27 1934; *Bombay Chronicle* 31.7.34.)
37. *Indian Annual Register 1934 Vol. II* p. 220.
38. *Indian Annual Register 1935 Vol. II* p. 276 ff.
39. See AICC G 27 1934; 25 1936; 85 (v) 1936.
40. Nehru to N. S. Hardikar 3.9.36 AICC G 27 1936.
41. Nehru to Secretary Mysore Congress Board 27.8.37; Nehru to Secretary Karnatak P.C.C. 27.8.37 AICC G 88 1937.
42. Sitaramayya had resigned from the Working Committee after supporting Nehru on the office-acceptance issue at the Lucknow Congress in April 1936.
43. *Bombay Chronicle* 16.2.38.
44. See AICC G 27 1937; G 88 1937; P 11 1937.
45. Secretary Karnatak P.C.C. to Nehru 14.11.37 AICC G 88 1937.
46. Nehru to Secretary Karnatak P.C.C. 11.11.37 ibid.
47. Mahadev Desai to Nehru 2.12.37 Nehru MSS D 37.
48. *Bombay Chronicle* 3.1.38.
49. See P. Sitaramayya's press statement in *Bombay Chronicle* 10.2.38 and Presidential speech to the All India States Peoples Conference ibid. 16.2.38. Also see articles by Dr Sumant B. Mehta in ibid. 24.1.38; 2.2.38.
50. Working Committee spokesmen claimed that the reasons for this resolution were that the Congress had to conserve its strength for a struggle against Federation in British India, that because of the diversity of the political situation in each State no general action would be appropriate and that the States Peoples organisations must learn to build up their own strength without leaning on the Congress (see *Bombay Chronicle* 15.2.38; 11.2.38). But the terms of their resolution indicate that a major, if unspoken, consideration was the problem of control.
51. Constructive work was allowed as a matter of course; prior sanction had to be obtained for any agitational or parliamentary activities.
52. *Bombay Chronicle* 19.2.38; 21.2.38. The C.S.P. was not a party to this compromise, but their amendment was heavily defeated in the open session.
53. Quoted in N. G. Ranga, *Peasants and Congress* (Madras, 1939) p. 86.
54. See below.
55. *Leader* 20.2.38; 21.2.38.
56. Vallabhbhai Patel to Prasad 12.12.37 Prasad MSS II/37.
57. Minutes of Working Committee meeting 3/6.2.38 AICC 42 1936.
58. *Leader* 17.2.38.
59. Ibid. 21.2.38.
60. It is interesting that both Mahadev Desai (Gandhi's secretary) and Jai Prakash Narain saw the Haripura Congress as an oasis of unity in a desert of dissention. Desai wrote:
    The Haripura Congress will long be remembered as the Congress which re-solved difficulties to a minimum and which actively promoted co-operation

184

between the different schools of thought in the country based on a spirit of give and take . . . (*Harijan* 26.2.38).

Narain, in a press interview, was more explicit:

There was a spontaneous closing of ranks. Differences were packed into the background and the whole Congress spoke with one voice . . . [It was] a new chapter in the relations of Left and Right wings (*Searchlight* 5.3.38).

61. Balvantry Mehta (General Secretary A.I.S.P.C.) to S.C. Bose 26.3.38 A.I.S.P.C. MSS Second Series No. 7. A.I.S.P.C. Circular Number 4 of 1938 7.3.38 AICC G 35 (i) 1938.
62. All attempts by the Congress leaders to stop this activity were in vain (see correspondence in AICC G 35 1938). What is more, the membership of the Mysore State Congress (involved in parliamentary work) and of the Mysore District Congress Committee (restricted to constructive work) was basically identical. (See A.I.C.C. Inspector's report on Karnatak P.C.C. July 1937 to June 1938 in AICC P 11 1939.)
63. See Patel's speech as President of the Deccan States Peoples Conference May 1938 *Searchlight* 24.5.38 and Gandhi's articles in *Harijan* 7.1.39; 14.1.39; 21.1.39; 4.2.39; 11.2.39; 18.2.39.
64. See ibid.
65. Colonel Hasker to Sapru 19.6.33 Sapru MSS (First Series) H 113.
66. Bose unkindly described Nehru's activities in the Working Committee after Haripura thus:

> Would it be wrong to say that usually you monopolised most of the time of the Working Committee? If the Working Committee had another member as talkative as yourself, I do not think that we would ever have come to the end of our business. . . . To be brutally frank, you sometimes behaved in the Working Committee as a spoilt child and often lost your temper. Now, in spite of all your 'nerviness' and jumpiness, what results did you achieve? You would generally hold forth for hours together and then succumb in the end. Sardar Patel and the others had a clever technique for dealing with you. They would let you talk and talk and they would ultimately finish up by asking you to draft *their* resolution. Once you were allowed to draft the resolution, you would feel happy, no matter whose resolution it was. Rarely have I found you sticking to your point till the last.

S. C. Bose to Nehru 28.3.39 in J. Nehru, *A Bunch of Old Letters* (Bombay, 1958) pp. 339–40.

67. A. K. Azad to Nehru 17.4.39 Nehru MSS A 115. Nehru had the same factors in mind when he wrote to Bose warning him that 'behind the political problems there are psychological problems' and urging him to promote 'faith and understanding between colleagues' (Nehru to Bose 4.2.39 in J. Nehru, *A Bunch of Old Letters* (Bombay, 1958) p. 321).
68. Note by Sir John Ewart, 'Review of Congress Financial Resources' dated 9.3.39 in G.o.I. Home Department (Political) 4/14/40 N.A.I.
69. Bose had to operate with an even less sympathetic Working Committee than Nehru had had in 1936. At Haripura the Congress Socialists had refused to serve under him and his only committed supporter in the Working Committee of 15 was his brother, Sarat Chandra Bose.
70. Bose to Nehru 28.3.39 in J. Nehru, *A Bunch of Old Letters* (Bombay, 1958) p. 340.
71. In March 1938 Kripalani had considered resigning after Bose had criticised him for sending out a routine press statement without showing it to the President first and had insisted on being allowed to vet every public statement before it left the office. (Kripalani to Nehru 14.3.38 Nehru MSS K 103).
72. J. Nehru, *The Unity of India: Collected Works 1937–40* (London, 1941) p. 127.

73. Minutes of Working Committee 5/7.7.37 AICC 42 1937.
74. Prasad to Patel 11.10.38; Patel to Prasad 15.10.38 Prasad MSS 4-A/38.
75. See correspondence in ibid.
76. See ibid.
77. Patel to Prasad 15.10.38 ibid.; Bose to Gandhi 21.12.38 Nehru MSS B 105.
78. Bose to Gandhi 21.12.38 Nehru MSS B 105.
79. Ibid.
80. *Leader* 15.7.38; 21.7.38; 8.2.39; 18.3.39.
81. *Leader* 12.7.38.
82. Kripalani wrote of it to Nehru (who was in England):

    'We did not appreciate the President's statement. . . . First, it was a little hysterical, if I may say so, . . . and then it was needlessly prejudicial to other colleagues who had not expressed themselves'.

    (Kripalani to Nehru 11.8.38 Nehru MSS K 103).
83. *Leader* 26.8.38.
84. Ibid. 27.8.38.
85. Ibid. 18.9.38.
86. *Harijan* 15.10.38.
87. See S. C. Bose to Nehru 28.3.39 in J. Nehru, *A Bunch of Old Letters* (Bombay, 1958) p. 331.
88. *Leader* 23.10.38. These leaders, Z. A. Ahmad, Sajjad Zaheer, E. M. S. Namboodripad, Jeevandan, H. Mukerji, Sardar Sohan Singh Joshi, B. Panigrahi and P. Sundarappa were all members of the Communist Party of India and not in full agreement with the rest of the C.S.P. leadership. Official C.S.P. support for Bose did not come until January 1939.
89. See his speech at Lucknow in November 1939 (*Leader* 23.11.38) and statement issued 17.1.39. (S. C. Bose, *Crossroads* (London, 1962) pp. 85–6).
90. Patel wrote to Prasad:

    No one is anxious to join the Federation, but you cannot prevent him [Bose] from using any argument to suit his own purpose. He is making a mess of Congress politics. But what can we do?

    (Patel to Prasad 19.11.38 Prasad MSS 4-A/38).
91. Gandhi to Nehru 21.12.38 Nehru MSS G 11. On 15 January 1939 Azad did finally consent to stand, but he cried off again two days later (Kripalani to Prasad 7.2.39 Prasad MSS 2-A/39).
92. Two requisitions were submitted for Azad's candidature. One, signed by Satyamurthi and a group of Madrassi Congressmen, was put in before Azad had consented to stand; the other was signed by Patel, Bajaj and Kripalani among others (*Leader* 13.1.39; 20.1.39).
93. Kripalani to Prasad 7.2.39 Prasad MSS 2-A/39.
94. Reprinted in S. C. Bose, *Crossroads* (London, 1962) pp. 87–8.
95. Kripalani to Prasad 7.2.39 Prasad MSS 2-A/39. The statement belittled the office of the President and his role in policy-making and called on Bose to retire in the name of unity. For the full text see S. C. Bose, *Crossroads* (London, 1962) pp. 89–90.
96. Kripalani had pointed out to Gandhi that if the Working Committee issued a statement attacking Bose and Bose won then all the Committee members would have to resign. Gandhi replied:

    'Certainly, how could you be in his cabinet?'.

    (Kripalani to Prasad 7.2.39 Prasad MSS 2-A/39).
97. See 'Second Statement of Subhas Chandra Bose' in S. C. Bose, *Crossroads* (London, 1962) p. 90.

98. Kripalani had written to Prasad that Jawaharlal never made up his mind on anything until the last possible moment, but that they could assume that he was opposed to Bose (Kripalani to Prasad 7.2.39 Prasad MSS 2-A/39). Nehru had issued a remarkably non-committal statement on 26 January deprecating Bose's stand, claiming Federation was not an issue on which the Congress ought to be divided and extolling the virtues that Azad would have brought to the Presidency if he had been a candidate. For the full text of this see S. C. Bose, *Crossroads* (London, 1962) pp. 97–9).
99. Ibid. p. 92.
100. See *Leader* 28.1.39.
101. The votes were as follows:

	Bose	Sitaramayya
Burma	8	6
Ukkal	44	99
Tamil Nad	110	102
Gujerat	5	100
Punjab	182	86
Berar	11	21
Bengal	404	79
Kerala	80	18
Andhra	28	181
U.P.	269	185
Bihar	70	197
Delhi	10	5
Maharastra	77	86
Assam	34	22
Sindh	13	21
Bombay City	14	12
Nagpur	12	17
Ajmere	18	8
Karnatak	106	41
Mahakoshal	67	68
N.W.F.P.	18	23
	1,580	1,377

Leader 1.2.39.

102. Prafulla Chandra Ghosh pointed out that: 'the last-minute withdrawal of Maulana Sahib has made the position here rather difficult' (P. C. Ghosh to Kripalani 21.1.39 AICC G 79 1939). Azad himself had discovered, long before the election, that some of his Bengali Muslim supporters felt that they could only vote for Bose if he himself did not stand (A. K. Azad to Patel October 1938 Prasad MSS 4-A/38).
103. This happened, for example, in Bihar, where provincial factional rivalries had already taken on the language of a struggle between 'left' and 'right' (see *Indian Nation* 25.1.39).
104. *Leader* 27.1.39; 28.1.39; 30.1.39; G. B. Pant to Nehru 21.4.39 Nehru MSS P 26. Kidwai had asked for permission to resign from the U.P. Ministry in November 1938 (Kidwai to Patel 12.11.38 AICC PL 2 1938); his canvassing for Bose was seen as part of a bid for the Premiership. (Sir J. P. Srivastava to Sapru 7.8.39 Sapru MSS (Second Series) S. 553; Sir H. Haig to Linlithgow 8.2.39 Haig MSS Vol. 2).) Pant later admitted to Haig that he and his colleagues did not take Bose's threat seriously enough and did not make enough preparations for the elections (Sir H. Haig to Linlithgow 8.2.39 Haig MSS Vol. 2).
105. Hardikar was one of the few people Bose thought he could count on in a Working Committee. (See Kripalani to Doulatram 12.5.39 AICC G 32 1939.)

106. A.I.C.C. inspector's report on Karnatak P.C.C. July 1938 to June 1939. AICC P 11 1939.
107. See correspondence in AICC G 79 1939.
108. *Indian Nation* 29.1.39; Fortnightly Reports Patna District January 1939 in Bihar Pradesh History of Freedom Movement file no. 63 S.C.R.O. Patna.
109. See AICC P 13 1938; P 13 1939; G 47 1939.
110. Gandhi to Bose 2.4.39 Prasad MSS 2-C/39.
111. See S. C. Bose, *Crossroads* (London, 1962) p. 112.
112. Patel to Prasad 8.2.39 Prasad MSS 1-C/39; Patel to Nehru 8.2.39 in J. Nehru, *A Bunch of Old Letters* (Bombay, 1958) p. 322.
113. *Harijan* 4.2.39.
114. *Leader* 22.2.39.
115. See *Harijan* 4.2.39.
116. See S. C. Bose, *Crossroads* (London, 1962) p. 107.
117. Prasad to Kripalani 5.2.39 Prasad MSS 2-A/39.
118. Nehru to Bose 1.3.39 Nehru MSS B 105.
119. S. C. Bose, *Crossroads* (London, 1962) p. 113.
120. Nehru to Bose 4.2.39 in J. Nehru, *A Bunch of Old Letters* (Bombay, 1958) pp. 317–21.
121. Ibid. p.321.
122. The fast lasted only five days and did not prove fatal.
123. He suffered a long attack of bronchial pneumonia; at the Tripuri Congress his temperature varied between 103° and 105°.
124. Gandhi advised his colleagues to adapt their plans to whatever circumstances they found at Tripuri (Kripalani to Prasad 2.3.39 Prasad MSS 2-A/39).
125. *Leader* 1.3.39; 4.3.39.
126. The resolution now merely 'deplored' Bose's accusations about Federation; during the A.I.C.C. session this clause was further modified to read 'regretted' (*Leader* 10.3.39).
127. Ibid. By this stage, Patel was working closely with Pant (see Bose to Gandhi 10.4.39 in Prasad MSS 2-C/39) and this addition to the resolution was intended to force Bose to form a Working Committee without any of the twelve members who had resigned in February.
128. *Leader* 12.3.39.
129. The most important of these resolutions was the one on the 'National Demand' which called for the purification and unification of the Congress, the rejection of the Federal plan and a campaign to demand a Constituent Assembly for both British India and the States. This resolution was extremely mild – it did not lay down any programme of Congress opposition to Federation, not even calling on the Ministries to resign if Federation was introduced. Another resolution hinted at a possible modification of policy about the States. The rest were concerned with an attack on British foreign policy over the Spanish Civil War, a welcome to an Egyptian delegation to the Tripuri Congress and a statement of solidarity with the people of China. All amendments to these resolutions (including one moved by Congress Socialists to the National Demand resolution calling for a six-month ultimatum) were heavily defeated (*Leader* 13.3.39; 14.3.39).
130. Ibid. 14.3.39.
131. S. C. Bose to A. N. Bose 17.4.39 in S. C. Bose, *Crossroads* (London, 1962) p. 113. After trying to persuade Bose to moderate his stance before Tripuri, the Congress Socialist leaders had supported him in the Subjects Committee, but had remained neutral in the open session.
132. Bose alleged that:
    [Gandhi] came to the rescue of the Old Guard and called their defeat his own defeat. Opinion among the 'centrists' began to veer round. They were inclined to support us – but they were not prepared to kick out Gandhiji – they said (ibid. p. 112).

133. Reprinted in ibid. pp. 126–70.
134. See Gandhi to Bose 2.4.39 ibid. p. 140.
135. Gandhi to Bose 10.4.38 Prasad MSS 2-C/38. For more on this point see S. C. Bose, *Crossroads* (London, 1962) pp. 127–8; 131–2; 136–8; 140–2.
136. *Congress Socialist* 26.3.39.
137. See Nehru to Azad 20.4.39 Nehru MSS A 115.
138. J. B. Kripalani to J. D. Doulatram 12.5.39 AICC G 32 1939.
139. *Leader* 1.5.39.
140. Nehru moved a resolution calling on Bose to withdraw his resignation and co-operate with a Working Committee appointed by Gandhi but Bose refused, claiming that he would then be in an impossible position. It is also unlikely that Gandhi would have accepted this arrangement (*Leader* 1.5.39; 2.5.39).
141. Ibid. 2.5.39.
142. See AICC G 20 (iii) 1939.
143. Kripalani to Doulatram 12.5.39 AICC G 32 1939.
144. Bombay Government Fortnightly Reports for June 1939 in G.o.I. Home Department (Political) 18/6/39 N.A.I.; L. P. Sinha, *The Left Wing in India* (Muzaffarpur, 1965) pp. 468–70.
145. *Leader* 13.7.39.
146. Government of Bombay Fortnightly Reports for June 1939 in G.o.I. Home Department (Political) 18/6/39 N.A.I.
147. *Times of India* 23.6.39.
148. Quoted in J. P. Haithcox, *Communism and Nationalism in India: M. N. Roy and Comintern Policy 1920–39* (Princeton, 1971) p. 237.
149. The membership of this Committee altered during its existence. At its first meeting it consisted of Nehru, Doulatram, Sitaramayya, A. Patwardhan, Kiran Shankar Roy, S. A. Brelvi and Kripalani, but its final report was signed by B. Desai, Brelvi, Sitaramayya, Kripalani and M. A. Iyengar. See AICC G 43(i) 1938; G 31(ii) 1939.
150. Under the Bombay Constitution of 1934, the A.I.C.C. members for each province were elected by the delegates of that province as a whole. It was felt that the election of as many as 40 A.I.C.C. members in a single election led to unwieldy and uncontrollable elections and blind voting by most of the electorate. 'Territorial representation' was a device to break down each province into divisions and to have the delegates from each division elect their A.I.C.C. members separately.
151. Indirect election would have meant that the Taluka Congress Committees were elected by the primary members, the District Congress Committees by the Taluka bodies and the Provincial Congress Committees (and Congress session delegates) by the districts. The proponents of this scheme (of whom Rajagopalachari was the most prominent) thought that it would encourage the development of small, local Congress Committees that did not have enough members to affect the delegate elections under a system of direct election and that it would help to remove the bitterness of the contests at the annual Congress elections. See AICC G 80 (KWI) 1938.
152. *Bombay Chronicle* 22.2.38. Gerrymandering was one of the most common pieces of sharp practice used by Provincial and District Congress Committee executive officers to maintain their control over the Congress institutions of their areas. This practice caused great bitterness. Fixing permanent constituency boundaries would have meant that although the reigning Provincial and District Congress Committee Executives could have drawn favourable boundaries at first, they would have had no chance to alter them later to accommodate changes in the political situation. Kripalani's successful amendment at Haripura established only the principle of fixed constituencies; a great deal of work was still needed on the problem before this reform could be put into effect. The matter was handed over to the Constitution Sub-Committee, but that body did nothing about it (see AICC P 1 1938; AICC G 31(ii) 1938).

153. Including fixed electoral rolls at the sub-taluka level, supervision by the P.C.C.s of all elections, biennial elections and the establishment, in principle, of fixed constituency boundaries. See AICC G 43(i) 1938.
154. See AICC G 42 1938. Of the twelve P.C.C.s that replied, four favoured indirect elections and seven direct elections, all approved stricter controls on membership enrolment in principle, only one mentioned fixed constituencies at all and only four favoured territorial representation on the A.I.C.C.
155. AICC G 31 (ii)1938. S. A. Brelvi, who had links with the Congress Socialists, dissented from these recommendations.
156. Ibid.; *Bombay Chronicle* 16,12.38.
157. See AICC G 31 (ii) 1939.
158. Ibid.
159. See AICC G 31 (i–iv) 1939.
160. The Committee's meetings were also attended by Gandhi, Patel and B. Desai (AICC G 31 (ii) 1939).
161. These included various checks on the activities of Thana and Mandal Committees, stricter rules about membership enrolment (attestation of enrolment by a witness, rolls to be kept by the D.C.C.s, etc.), the establishment of provincial and district election tribunals to hear complaints, the requirement of a certificate of *khaddar*-wearing as a qualification to vote in the delegate elections, a qualification of three years standing as a member before membership of an Executive Committee and fixed, territorial constituencies for the delegate elections. AICC G 31 (ii) 1939.
162. Ibid. While most of these amendments had been suggested by other Congressmen writing into the Committee, these last two had not been. Of the 157 suggestions sent in to the A.I.C.C. office, only one had proposed that members of any non-communal organisation should be banned from holding office in the Congress. No mention at all was made about ending proportional representation. The left-wing press had no doubts about the underlying purpose of the decision to revise the constitution. The *Bombay Sentinel* saw the move to eradicate corruption as a move to eradicate the left (*Bombay Sentinel* 22.6.39), while the *Hindustan Standard* protested:

> This cry of corruption has . . . been raised to strengthen the dominance of one particular group. For after all who is free from corruption?

Hindustan Standard 7.6.39, clipping in AICC (Suppl.) 120 1939–40.
163. The *khaddar* clause was removed, however.
164. AICC G 31 (ii) 1939. Dev wrote:

> . . . it would be highly improper to prevent Congressmen from participating in class organisations whose political objective is the same as that of the Congress but whose economic programme may not for the moment be identical with that of the Congress.

165. *Bombay Sentinel* 22.6.39.
166. Ibid. 23.6.39.
167. Ibid. 26.6.39.
168. Dev wrote a minute of dissent against this clause also in the Sub-Committee report. AICC G 31 (ii) 1939.
169. *Bombay Sentinel* 26.9.39.
170. *Bombay Sentinel* 26.6.39.
171. Thus in a district where there was a population of 100,000 and a Congress membership of 1,000, only one delegate could be returned. But if there were any Indian States in the province with a total population of over 100,000, a second constituency could be created in the district, taking up the surplus Congress members.
172. *Bombay Sentinel* 27.6.39.
173. Ibid.
174. See correspondence between Raj Kumar Chakravarthy, Prasad and Kripalani in

AICC G 43 1939. The disputed clauses, in all their vagueness, ran as follows (Article X (g)):

> (i) Each district shall be entitled to elect not more than one delegate, for each lac [sic] of its population provided that for every delegate to be elected, there are not less than 500 primary members enrolled during the year.
>
> (ii) The number of delegates remaining unallotted to the constituencies on account of the inclusion of the population of the Indian States in any Province, shall be distributed by the Executive of the P.C.C. concerned, in such manner as in its opinion would meet the requirements of the case, subject to the rule of minimum enrolment of 500 primary members for each delegate.

For a convenient copy of the 1939 Congress Constitution see *Indian Annual Register 1939 Vol. I* pp. 358–363.

175. See A.I.C.C. inspectors' reports in AICC 14 1939.
176. *Times of India* 28.6.39; *Leader* 29.6.39.
177. By this stage Bose was desperate for allies. While in Bombay he had had (unsuccessful) talks with Dr Ambedkar and Dr Khare for joint action and had talked with Jinnah to try and get an alliance with the Muslim League in Bengal against Fazl-ul Huq (Prasad to Patel 14.7.39 Prasad MSS 1-C/39).
178. Fortnightly Reports of Bombay Government for July 1939 in G.o.I. Home Department (Political) 18/7/39 N.A.I.; Z. A. Ahmad to Nehru 18.7.39 Nehru MSS A 26.
179. Patel to Prasad 5.7.39; Prasad MSS 1-C/39.
180. *Harijan* 26.8.39. For the text of the resolution see *Leader* 13.8.39. Azad was certainly one member of the Working Committee who thought the action against Bose too harsh (see Azad to Nehru 17.8.39 Nehru MSS A 115).
181. *Leader* 21.8.39.
182. Linlithgow to Zetland 27.9.39 Linlithgow MSS Vol. 8.

Chapter 5

1. In June 1936 he wrote that it was 'vital that the impetus of the new Statute and the consummation of Provincial Autonomy should carry us straight on into Federation.' (Linlithgow to Zetland 15.6.36 quoted in J. Glendevon, *The Viceroy at Bay: Lord Linlithgow in India 1936–43* (London, 1971) p. 30).
2. As Sir Arthur Lothian, one of Linlithgow's three emissaries sent to discuss terms with the Princes in 1936, discovered, 'each State tried to make its own special bargain, which, if conceded, in view of the number of States involved, would have resulted in utter confusion.' Sir A. Lothian, *Kingdoms of Yesteryear* (London, 1951) p. 149.
3. See his remarks to Bhulabhai Desai in September 1937 ('My interview with the Viceroy on 7th September 1937', typescript in Bhulabhai Desai MSS) and his speech to the Chamber of Princes in March 1939 (cited in J. Glendevon, *The Viceroy at Bay: Lord Linlithgow in India 1936–43* (London, 1971) pp. 117–18).
4. Especially with the Nizam of Hyderabad. If the Nizam was allowed to nominate his own representatives, they would all have been Muslims; if they were elected by his subjects, Hindus would predominate.
5. K. M. Munshi's notes on interview with Sir Sikander Hyat Khan 1938 in K. M. Munshi, *Indian Constitutional Documents Vol. I* (Bombay, 1967) p. 386.
6. Zetland to Linlithgow 29.1.39 Linlithgow MSS Vol. 7.
7. Zetland to Linlithgow 15–17.1.39 ibid.
8. Zetland to Linlithgow 24.1.39 ibid.
9. Linlithgow to Zetland 7.7.39 ibid., vol. 8.
10. Linlithgow to Zetland 12.4.39 ibid., vol. 7.
11. Linlithgow to Zetland 3.1.39 ibid.

12. Zetland to Linlithgow 24.1.39 ibid.
13. Linlithgow to Zetland 3.1.39 ibid.
14. Zetland to Linlithgow 24.1.39 ibid.
15. See CAB 67/1, W.P. (G)(39)21, Memorandum by Secretary of State 25.9.39.
16. CAB 67/2, W.P.(G)(39)70, Viceroy to Secretary of State 3.11.39.
17. CAB 67/1, W.P.(G)(39)21, Memorandum by Secretary of State 25.9.39.
18. CAB 67/2, W.P.(G)(39)70, Viceroy to Secretary of State 3.11.39.
19. See CAB 65/1, W.M.29(39)12 of 27.9.39; CAB 65/1, W.M.59(39)8 of 25.10.39; CAB 67/2, W.P.(G)(39)54, Viceroy to Secretary of State 24.10.39; CAB 65/5, W.M.30(40)4 of 2.2.40.
20. CAB 67/1, W.P.(G)(39)21, Memorandum by Secretary of State 15.9.39.
21. *Leader* 28.9.38; 29.9.38; 4.10.38.
22. For a review of Congress policy in the early months of the war see I.B. Memo no 29/Cong/40 of 20.3.40 G.o.I. Home Department (Political) 4/17/40 N.A.I.
23. See *Harijan* 26.8.39; 23.9.39; 14.10.39; 21.10.39; Sapru to Haskar 13.11.39 Sapru MSS (Second Series) H.80; P. Sitaramayya, *History of the Indian National Congress Vol. II* (Bombay, 1947) pp. 130–2. According to Sitaramayya, the Working Committee agreed that Prasad should resign as President to make way for Nehru, the expert on international affairs and anti-fascism, but then found that they did not have the constitutional power to replace the President.
24. By this demand the Congress leaders hoped to embarrass the British by showing them to be using colonial resources to fight a war for freedom.
25. *Indian Annual Register 1939 Vol. II* pp. 226–8.
26. R. Coupland, *Indian Politics 1936–42* (London, 1943) p. 217.
27. Ibid., pp. 217–18. By 15 November all the Congress ministries had resigned and the constitution had been suspended in those provinces.
28. CAB 67/1, W.P.(G)(39)24 Secretary of State to Viceroy 27.9.39.
29. Ibid., Viceroy to Secretary of State 28.9.39.
30. See CAB 67/2, W.P.(G)(39)53 Viceroy to Secretary of State 22.10.39.
31. See CAB 67/1, W.P.(G)(39)24 Viceroy to Secretary of State 28.9.39.
32. CAB 65/5, W.M. 30(40)4 of 2.2.40.
33. R. Coupland, *Indian Politics 1936–42* (London, 1943) p. 216.
34. *Indian Annual Register 1939 Vol. II* pp. 242–3.
35. Ibid., pp. 243–5.
36. Ibid.
37. Ibid., p. 249.
38. Quoted in R. J. Moore, 'British Policy and the Indian Problem 1936–40' in C. H. Philips and M. D. Wainwright (eds), *The Partition of India: Policies and Perspectives 1935–47.* (London, 1970) p. 88.
39. Ibid.; one major obstacle to serious discussions between the League and the Congress was Jinnah's insistence that the Congress and the League should negotiate to solve the communal problem as the representatives of the Hindu and Muslim communities, thus forcing the Congress to tacitly admit itself to be a communal organisation.
40. Quoted in ibid.; see also CAB 65/6, W.M.89(40)10 of 12.4.40.
41. By 'left-wing' we mean those who were dissidents as much as socialists. The Viceroy continually stressed that the Congress was under the influence of 'the left' at this time, but by 'the left' he meant Nehru.
42. *Searchlight* 5.7.39.
43. I.B. Circular Memo No 38/Cong/40 dated 15.5.40 in G.o.I. Home Department (Political) 4/4/40 N.A.I.
44. *Leader* 11.10.39.
45. Bombay Government Fortnightly Reports for September 1939 in G.o.I. Home Department (Political) 18/9/39 N.A.I.; *Leader* 1.10.39; 11.10.39.
46. Professor Ranga, the Kisan Sabha leader, admitted that the Sabha had 'flirted' with

the idea of starting an 'independent anti-war national campaign' but had dropped it as they could not get 'the blessing of Mahatma Gandhi'. N. G. Ranga, *Revolutionary Peasants* (Delhi, 1949) p. 98.

47. One Working Committee member, A. K. Azad, had suggested that direct action was the only solution if the negotiations with the Viceroy failed (see *Leader* 21.9.39), but the Congress leaders refused to commit themselves definitely on this issue.
48. *Indian Annual Register 1939 Vol. II* p. 237.
49. Ibid. p. 239.
50. For example, in May 1939 Vallabhbhai Patel had pointed to the 'dissensions, indiscipline and corruption in the Congress organisation' and had predicted that 'if *Satyagraha* is started there will be anarchy in the country.' *Leader* 12.5.39.
51. *Harijan* 4.11.39; 11.11.39; 13.11.39.
52. Ibid. 2.12.39.
53. Ibid. The Independence Day Pledge (drafted by the Working Committee in mid-December 1939 for Congressmen to swear to in ceremonies on 26 January 1940) also stressed that the Congress could hope to succeed in its objectives only by following the constructive programme (*Indian Annual Register 1939 Vol. II* p. 250).
54. AICC G 28 1940; I.B. Memo no. 29/Cong/40 of 20.3.40 in G.o.I. Home Department (Political) 4/17/40 N.A.I.
55. Ibid.
56. See *Harijan* 9.3.40; 24.4.40.
57. Minutes of Working Committee meeting 16–19.4.40 AICC G 32 1940.
58. By spreading propaganda, training *satyagrahis* and converting the Congress Committees into *Satyagraha* Committees manned only by those who had signed the *satyagraha* pledge (AICC G 1 1940; G 28(ii) 1940).
59. In Madras, Congressmen contested the Kistna and Malabar District Board elections in February 1940. (Government of Madras Fortnightly Reports for February 1940 in G.o.I. Home Department (Political) 18/2/40 N.A.I.) In Bihar, provincial and district Congress politics were still dominated by the after effects of the 1939 district board elections. (Secretary Bihar P.C.C. to General Secretary A.I.C.C. 10.5.40 AICC G 16 1940).
60. Government of United Provinces Fortnightly Reports for February 1940 in G.o.I. Home Department (Political) 18/2/40 N.A.I.
61. J. Nehru to Gandhi 4.2.40 in J. Nehru, *A Bunch of Old Letters* (Bombay, 1958) p. 427.
62. These quarrels were especially bitter in Mahakoshal and Nagpur.
63. See Fortnightly Reports for April, May, June, July and August 1940 from all provincial Governments in G.o.I. Home Department (Political) 18/4,5,6,7,8,/40 N.A.I.
64. Gandhi had appealed to 'every Briton . . . to accept the method of non-violence instead of the method of War'. He urged Britain to fight Nazism without arms, sacrificing the Empire and the whole of the British Isles if necessary (*Harijan* 6.7.40). Gandhi wished to declare the unwillingness of the Congress to accept the idea that 'India should maintain armed forces to maintain her freedom against external aggression or internal disorder' and he was allowed by the rest of the Working Committee to carry on his own independent campaign on this issue (*Indian Annual Register 1940 Vol. II* p. 175).
65. See R. J. Moore, 'British Policy and the Indian Problem 1936–40' in C. H. Philips and M. D. Wainwright (eds), *The Partition of India: Policies and Perspectives 1935–47* (London, 1970) p. 90.
66. *Indian Annual Register 1940 Vol. II* pp. 176–7; *Harijan* 13.7.40.
67. *Harijan* 6.7.40.
68. Ibid. 29.9.40.
69. Ibid. 13.7.40.
70. R. J. Moore, 'British Policy and the Indian Problem 1936–40', in C. H. Philips and M. D. Wainwright (eds), *The Partition of India: Policies and Perspectives 1935–47* (Lon-

don, 1970) p. 91.
71. Bombay Government Fortnightly Reports for September 1940 in G.o.I. Home Department (Political) 18/9/40 N.A.I.
72. R. Coupland, *Indian Politics 1936–42* (London, 1943) pp. 247–8.
73. Ibid., p. 248.
74. Ibid., pp. 248–50.
75. The Central Intelligence Officer, Nagpur, assessed Gandhi's plans thus:

> a . . . continuation of the stalemate during the period of the War or a temporary agreement, if any, arrived at between the non-Congress political parties and the British Government is not likely to harm the country's or the Congress cause. On the contrary, he [Gandhi] expects to benefit from either situation.

Review of Political Situation April 1941 by C.I.O. Nagpur in G.o.I. Home Department (Political) 4/8/41 N.A.I.

76. D.O. no. 125 of 30.11.40 G.o.I Home Department (Political) 31/1/40 N.A.I.
77. D.I.B. u.o. no. 127/Cong/41 G.o.I. Home Department (Political) 17/4/41 N.A.I.
78. Quoted in G. D. Birla to Sir P. Thakurdas 18–19.12.40 Thakurdas MSS 177.
79. D.I.B. u.o. no. 1/C.S./41 G.o.I. Home Department (Political) 3/33/40 N.A.I.
80. See Beohar Rajendra Singh to Prasad 26.10.41 AICC P 12 1940.
81. See Note of Interview of President Maharastra P.C.C. with Gandhi enclosed in D.I.B. u.o. no. 55/Cong/40 of 24.12.40 G.o.I. Home Department (Political) 3/33/40 N.A.I.
82. See correspondence in AICC P 12(i) 1941; P 12 1942–6.
83. In 1938–39 Congress membership had been 4,511,858; in 1939–40 it was 2,973,452; in 1940–1, 1,481,616. I.B. Circular Memo no. 37/Cong/40 of 24.5.41 G.o.I. Home Department (Political) 4/6/41 N.A.I.
84. D.I.B. u.o. no. 55/Cong/41 of 15.1.41 in G.o.I. Home Department (Political) 3/33/40 N.A.I.
85. Intercepted letter K. Rangaswami to K. Srinivasan 13.10.41 in G.o.I. Home Department (Political) 4/8/41 N.A.I.
86. See G.o.I. Home Department (Political) 4/8/41 N.A.I.
87. Ibid.
88. Ibid.
89. Ibid.
90. R. Coupland, *Indian Politics 1936–42* (London, 1943) p. 264.
91. Ibid., pp. 265–6.
92. Ibid., pp. 269–70.
93. In January 1942 Sapru had cabled Churchill, urging him to break the deadlock by proposing some new terms on which the Indian leaders could co-operate with the *Raj*.
94. R. Coupland, *Indian Politics 1936–42* (London, 1943) p. 271.
95. See Linlithgow to Amery 21.1.42. N. Mansergh and E. Lumby (eds), *India The Transfer of Power 1942–7 Vol. I* (London, 1970) no. 23; Amery to Churchill 22.1.42 ibid. no. 27.
96. See Wavell's record of a conversation with Linlithgow in October 1943 in P. Moon (ed.), *Wavell The Viceroy's Journal* (Oxford, 1973) p. 33.
97. See Amery to Linlithgow 10.1.42 N. Mansergh and E. Lumby (eds), *India The Transfer of Power 1942–7 Vol. I* (London, 1970) no. 9.
98. Churchill to Attlee 7.1.42 ibid. no. 6.
99. Attlee to Amery 27.1.42, memorandum by Attlee for War Cabinet ibid. nos. 42 and 60.
100. Minute by Sir D. Monteath 4.2.42 ibid. no. 64.
101. Amery to Linlithgow 9.2.42 ibid. no. 89.
102. Ibid.

103. Earlier, Linlithgow had ridiculed the notion of 'Home Rule for the Viceroy'. See Linlithgow to Amery 21.1.42 ibid. no. 23.
104. See H. V. Hodson, *The Great Divide Britain-India-Pakistan* (London, 1969) pp. 93–4.
105. Draft Declaration, circulated by the Secretary of State for India 28.2.42 in N. Mansergh and E. Lumby (eds), *India The Transfer of Power 1942–7 Vol. I* (London, 1970) no. 193.
106. See Amery to Churchill 25.2.42 ibid. no. 181.
107. Ibid. no. 60.
108. See Amery to Linlithgow 2.3.42 ibid. no. 218.
109. See annex to War Cabinet Committee on India I(42) 3rd meeting ibid. no. 194.
110. Amery to Churchill 5.3.42 ibid. no. 240.
111. H. V. Hodson, *The Great Divide Britain-India-Pakistan* (London, 1969) p. 94.
112. See Amery to Churchill 15.2.42 N. Mansergh and E. Lumby (eds), *India The Transfer of Power 1942–7 Vol. I* (London, 1970) no. 126.
113. See Linlithgow to Amery 9.3.42 ibid. nos. 284, 285.
114. See Amery to Linlithgow 10.3.42 ibid. no. 304.
115. Enclosure in Butler to Amery 6.3.42 ibid. no. 255.
116. See H. V. Hodson, *The Great Divide Britain-India-Pakistan* (London, 1969) pp. 97–103.
117. Amery to Linlithgow 13.2.42 N. Mansergh and E. Lumby (eds), *India The Transfer of Power 1942–7 Vol. I* (London, 1970) no. 112.

Bibliography

1 GOVERNMENT RECORDS

Cabinet Office Papers, Public Records Office, London
Premier's Office Papers, Public Records Office, London
Proceedings of the Secretary of State for India in Public and Judicial Department Series, India Office Library, London
Proceedings of the Government of India in Home Department (Political Branch) Finance Department and Reforms Office, National Archives of India, New Delhi
Proceedings of the Government of Bihar and Orissa (later Government of Bihar) in Political Department (Special Series) and in Bihar Pradesh History of the Freedom Movement Series, State Central Record Office, Patna

2 OFFICIAL PUBLICATIONS

Communal Decision (Cmd 4147 of 1931–2)
Despatches of Provincial Governments in India Containing Proposals for Constitutional Reform (Cmd 3712 of 1930–1)
Final Report of the Royal Commission on the Administration of the Expenditure of India (Cmd 131 of 1900)
Government of India Despatch on Proposals for Constitutional Reform (Cmd 3700 of 1930–1)
Moral and Material Progress and Condition of India (annual)
Proposals for Indian Constitutional Reform (Cmd 4268 of 1932–2)
Report of the Committee appointed by the Secretary of State for India to advise on the question of the Financial Relations between the Central and Provincial Governments in India (Cmd 724 of 1920)
Report of the Committee appointed in connection with the Delimitation of Constituencies and connected matters Vols. 1 and II (Cmd 5099–10 of 1935–6)
Report of the Conditions and Prospects of British Trade in India (Cmd 442 of 1919)
Report of Financial Enquiry Committee by Sir O. Niemeyer (Cmd 5163 of 1935–6)
Report of Indian Franchise Committee Vol. 1 (Cmd 4086 of 1931–2)
Report of Indian Statutory Commission Vols. 1–III (Cmd 3568–70 of 1929–30)
Report of Joint Committee on Indian Constitutional Reforms
Report on Indian Constitutional Reforms (Cmd 9109 of 1918)
Resignations of the Ministries in Bihar and the United Provinces 1938 (Cmd 5589 of 1937–8)
Return Showing the Result of the General Election to the Legislative Assembly in India in 1934 (Cmd 4939 of 1934–5)
Return Showing the Results of Elections in India 1937 (Cmd 5589 of 1937–8)
Royal Commission on Indian Currency and Finance 1926 (Cmd 2687 of 1926)
Statistical Abstract of British India (annual)
Statistical Abstract for United Kingdom (annual)
Views of Indian States on the Government of India Bill (Cmd 4843 of 1934–5)

Constitutional Relations between Britain and India: The Transfer of Power 1942-7 Editor-in-Chief, Nicholas Mansergh
Government of India (Provincial Legislative Assembly) Order 1936
Indian Franchise Committee Vols. 2–5 1932
Indian Statutory Commission Vols IV–XVII 1930

Report of the Committee appointed in connection with the Delimitation of Constituencies and connected matters Vol. 3 1936

Annual Statement of Sea-borne Trade of British India
Census of India 1931
Committee on Indian Exchange and Currency 1919
Indian Central Banking Enquiry Committee 1931
Legislative Assembly Debates

3 NEWSPAPERS
Bombay Chronicle
Bombay Sentinal
Indian Nation
Leader
Pioneer
Searchlight
Times of India

Congress Socialist
Harijan
Modern Review

4 ORGANISATIONS
Papers of the All India Congress Committee, Nehru Memorial Museum, New Delhi
Papers of the Mahakoshal Provincial Congress Committee, Nehru Memorial Museum, Newdelhi
Papers of the All India States Peoples Conference, Nehru Memoiral Museum, New Delhi

5 PRIVATE PAPERS
Dr Ansari MSS, Nehru Memorial Museum, New Delhi
B. Desai MSS, Nehru Memorial Museum, New Delhi
M. K. Gandhi MSS, Gandhi Smarak Nidhi, Delhi
M. R. Masani MSS, Nehru Memorial Museum, New Delhi
Syed Mahmud MSS, Nehru Memorial Museum, New Delhi
Dr B. Moonje MSS, Nehru Memorial Museum, New Delhi
J. Nehru MSS, Nehru Memorial Museum, New Delhi
R. Prasad MSS, National Archives of India, New Delhi
Sir T. B. Sapru MSS, microfilm copy in the possession of Dr A. Seal, Trinity College, Cambridge
A. N. Sinha MSS, A. N. Sinha Institute of the Social Sciences, Patna
P. D. Tandon MSS, National Archives of India, New Delhi
Sir P. Thakurdas MSS, Nehru Memorial Museum, New Delhi

Baldwin MSS, University Library, Cambridge
Brabourne MSS, India Office Library, London
Haig MSS, India Office Library, London
Hailey MSS, India Office Library, London
Halifax (Irwin) MSS, India Office Library, London
A. P. Hume MSS, India Office Library, London
Linlithgow MSS, India Office Library, London
Templewood (Hoare) MSS, India Office Library, London
Zetland MSS, India Office Library, London

6 UNPUBLISHED AND MANUSCRIPT SOURCES
C. J. Baker, 'Political Change in South India 1919–1937', fellowship dissertation, Queens' College, Cambridge, 1972

R. A. Gordon, 'Aspects of the History of the Indian National Congress with Special Reference to the Swarajya Party 1919 to 1927', D.Phil. thesis, Oxford, 1970

W. Hauser, 'The Bihar Provincial Kisan Sabha 1929–42: A Study of an Indian peasant movement', Ph.D. thesis, Chicago, 1961

T. D. Rider, 'The Tariff Policy of the Government of India and its Development Strategy 1894–1924', Ph.D. thesis, Minnesota, 1971

R. Roy, 'Study of Bihar Pradesh Congress Committee', Ph.D. thesis, Berkeley, 1966

T. A. Rusch, 'The role of the Congress Socialist Party in the Indian National Congress 1931–42', Ph.D. thesis, Chicago, 1955

A. N. Sinha, 'Autobiography', typescript copy in Sinha Memorial Library, Patna

D. D. Taylor, 'Indian Politics and the elections of 1937', Ph.D. thesis, London, 1972

D.A. Washbrook, 'Politics and Social Change in Madras Presidency 1880–1920', fellowship dissertation, Trinity College, Cambridge, 1971

7 PUBLISHED SOURCES – JOURNALS

P. R. Brass, 'Political Participation, Institutionalisation and Stability in India' in *Government and Opposition* Vol. *4, no. 1 (1969) pp. 23–52*

M. F. Franda, 'The Organisational Development of India's Congress Party' in *Pacific Affairs* xxv, no. 3 (1962) pp. 248–60

S. C. Ghosh, 'Decision-Making and power in the British Conservative Party: a Case Study of the Indian Problem 1929–34' in *Political Studies* Vol. XIII, no. 2 (1965) pp. 192–212

P. Harnetty, 'The Indian Cotton Duties Controversy 1894–96' in *English Historical Review* (1962) pp. 684–702

W. Hauser, 'The Indian National Congress and Land Policy in the Twentieth Century' in *Indian Economic and Social History Review* (1963–4) no. 1 pp. 57–67

R. Kothari, 'Parliamentary Government: Law and Usage' in *Economic Weekly* Vol. XIII, no. 20 pp. 783–90

——, 'Prospects for Democracy' in *Economic Weekly* Vol. XIII, no. 23 pp. 885–92

Gopal, Krishna, 'The Development of the Indian National Congress as a Mass Organisation 1918–23' in *Journal of Asian Studies* Vol. XXV, no. 3 pp. 413–30

W. H. Morris-Jones, 'From Monopoly to Competition in Indian Politics' in *Asian Review* Vol. 1, no. 1 (1967) pp. 1–12

——, 'The Indian Congress Party: A Dilemma of Dominance' in *Modern Asian Studies* Vol. 1, no. 1 (1967) pp. 109–32

P. D. Reeves, 'Changing Patterns of Political Alignment in the General Elections to the United Provinces Legislative AssemY ⅛ & ⅜⅞ AND ⅛ & ½¾' IN *Modern Asian Studies* Vol. 5, no. 2 (1971) pp. 111–42

F. C. R. Robinson, 'Consultation and Control The United Provinces' government and its allies 1860–1906' in *Modern Asian Studies* Vol. 5, no. 4 (1971) pp. 313–36

D. Rothermund, 'Constitutional Reform versus National Agitation in India 1900–50' in *Journal of Asian Studies* xxi, no. 4 pp. 505–522

R. Roy, 'Election Studies: selection of Congress Candidates I–V in *Economic and Political Weekly* Vol. 1, no. 20 and Vol. 2, nos 1, 2, 6 & 7 (Dec 1966–Jan 1967)

E. T. Stokes, 'Cripps in India' review article in *The Historical Journal* Vol. XIV (1971) no. 2 pp. 427–34

8 PUBLISHED SOURCES – BOOKS

D. H. Aldcroft and H. W. Richardson, *The British Economy 1870–1939* (London, 1969)

A. K. Azad, *India Wins Freedom: An Autobiographical Narrative* (Calcutta, 1959)

A. K. Bagchi, *Private Investment in India 1900–1939* (Cambridge, 1972)

F. G. Bailey, *Politics and Social Change, Orissa in 1959* (Berkeley, 1970)

A. K. Banerji, *India's Balance of Payments* (London, 1963)

Birkenhead, Lord, *Halifax* (London, 1965)
G. D. Birla, *In the Shadow of the Mahatma* (Calcutta, 1953)
S. C. Bose, *Crossroads* (London, 1962)
——, *The Indian Struggle 1920–42* (London, 1964)
P. R. Brass, *Factional Politics in an Indian State: The Congress Party in Uttar Pradesh* (Berkeley, 1965)
M. Brecher, *Nehru–A Political Biography* (London, 1959)
A. K. Cairncross, *Home and Foreign Investment 1870–1913* (Cambridge, 1953)
P. N. Chopra, *Rafi Ahmed Kidwai – His Life and work* (Agra, 1960)
Central Provinces Ministerial Crisis. Statements issued by Shri Subhas Chandra Bose, Congress President, Parliamentary Sub-Committee, Acharya J. B. Kripalani, General Secretary A.I.C.C., and Mahatma Gandhi (Allahabad, n.d.)
Centre for the Study of Developing Societies, Occasional Papers No 1: *Party System and Election Studies* (Bombay, 1967)
R. Coupland, *Indian Politics 1936–42* (London, 1943)
——, *The Indian Problem 1833–1935* (Oxford, 1942)
H. Dalton, *High Tide and After* (London, 1962)
S. T. Das, *Indian Military – Its History and Development* (New Delhi, 1968)
I. M. DrummBritish Economic Policy and the Empire 1919—1939 (London, 1972)
J. A. Gallagher, G. Johnson and A. Seal (eds), *Locality, Province and Nation. Essays on Indian Politics 1870–1940* (Cambridge, 1973)
N. Gangulee, *The Making of Federal India* (London, 1936)
J. Glendevon, *The Viceroy at Bay. Lord Linlithgow in India 1936–43* (London, 1971)
S. Gopal, *The Viceroyalty of Lord Ripon 1880–1885* (Oxford, 1953)
——, *The Viceroyalty of Lord Irwin 1926–31* (Oxford, 1957)
Sir M. Gwyer and A. Appadori, *Speeches and Documents on the Indian Constitution 1927–47 Vol. I* (Oxford, 1957)
J. P. Haithcox, *Communism and Nationalism in India: M. N. Roy and Comintern Policy 1920–1939* (Princeton, 1971)
A. T. Hingorani (ed), *Jawaharlal Nehru by Mahatma Gandhi* (Bombay, 1960)
E. J. Hobsbawm, *Industry and Empire* (London, 1968)
H. V. Hodson, *The Great Divide: Britain-India-Pakistan* (London, 1969)
M. Howard, *The Continental Commitment* (London, 1972)
Indian Annual Register (Calcutta)
Indian Quarterly Register (Calcutta)
Indian Year-Book and Who's Who (Bombay 1934–5)
Jamil-ud-din, *Historic Documents of the Muslim Freedom Movement* (Lahore, 1970)
——, *Some Recent Speeches and Writings of Mr. Jinnah* (Lahore, 1942)
Journal of the Parliaments of the Empire (London)
Ch. Khaliquzzaman, *Pathway to Pakistan* (Lahore, 1961)
A. W. Khan, *India Wins Freedom – The Other Side* (Karachi, 1961)
Dr. N. B. Khare, *My Political Memoirs or Autobiography* (Nagpur, n.d.)
S. A. Kochanek, *The Congress Party of India; The Dynamics of One-Party Democracy* (Princeton, 1968)
K. M. Kurian, *The Impact of Foreign Capital on the Indian Economy* (New Delhi, 1966)
P. L. Lakhanpal, *A History of the Congress Socialist Party* (Lahore, n.d.)
Sir A. Lothian, *Kingdoms of Yesteryear* (London, 1951)
D. A. Low (ed.), *Soundings in Modern South Asian History* (London, 1968)
S. R. Mehrotra, *Britain, India and the Commonwealth* (London, 1965)
V. P. Menon, *The Story of the Integration of the Indian States* (Calcutta, 1956)
——, *The Transfer of Power in India* (Calcutta, 1957)
K. Middlemass and J. Barnes, *Baldwin: A Biography* (London, 1968)
B. R. Mitchell and P. Deane, *Abstract of British Historical Statistics* (Cambridge, 1960)
D. E. Moggridge, *British Monetary Policy 1924–31* (Cambridge, 1972)
P. Moon (ed.), *Wavell – The Viceroy's Journal* (Oxford, 1973)

W. H. Morris-Jones, *Parliament in India* (London, 1967)
——, *The Government and Politics of India* (London, 1964)
R. Mukerjee and H. L. Dey, *Economic Problems of Modern India* (London, 1941)
K. M. Munshi, *Indian Constitutional Documents Vol. I* (Bombay, 1967)
K. F. Nariman, *Whither Congress?* (Bombay, 1933)
J. Nehru, *A Bunch of Old Letters* (Bombay, 1958)
——, *The Unity of India* (London, 1941)
S. Orwell and I. Angus (eds), *The Collected Essays, Journalism and Letters of George Orwell: Vol. II: My Country Right or Left 1940–1943* (London, 1968)
N. D. Parikh, *Sardar Vallabhbhai Patel* (Ahmedabad, 1956)
U. Phadnis, *Towards the Integration of the Indian States* (London, 1968)
C. H. Philips and M. D. Wainwright (eds), *The Partition of India: Policies and Perspectives 1935–47* (London, 1970)
S. S. Pirzada, *Foundations of Pakistan: The All-India Muslim League Documents 1906–47; Vol. II 1924–47* (Karachi, 1970)
B. Prasad (ed), *Official History of Indian Armed Forces in the Second World War 1939–1945:* B. Prasad, *Defence of India – Policies and Plans* (Calcutta, 1963); N. Prasad, *Expansion of Armed Forces and Defence Organisations 1939–45* (Calcutta, 1956); N. C. Sinha and P. N. Khera, *The Indian War Economy* (Calcutta, 1962)
R. Prasad, *Autobiography* (London, 1967)
N. G. Ranga, *Peasants and Congress* (Madras, 1939)
——, *Kisans and Communists* (Bombay, 1949)
——, *Revolutionary Peasants* (Delhi, 1949)
Reading, Lord, *Rufus Isaacs 1914–1935* (London, 1945)
A. Redford, *Manchester Merchants and Foreign Trade Vol. II 1850–1939* (Manchester, 1956)
Reports of the Congress Select Committee on the Financial Obligations between Great Britain and India (Bombay, 1931)
Report of the United Provinces Zamindari Abolition Committee (Allahabad, 1948)
R. E. Robinson and J. A. Gallagher, *Africa and the Victorians* (London, 1961)
Sampurnanand, Dr, *Memories and Reflections* (London, 1962)
Swami Sahajanand Saraswati, *Kisan Sabha ka Sansmaren* (Allahabad, 1947)
——, *Mera Jivan Sangharsa* (Patna, 1952)
S. B. Saul, *Studies in British Overseas Trade 1870–1914* (Liverpool, 1960)
K. B. Sayeed, *Pakistan – The Formative Phase 1857–1948* (London, 1968)
A. Seal, *The Emergence of Indian Nationalism* (Cambridge, 1968)
L. P. Sinha, *The Left Wing in India* (Muzaffarpur, 1965)
S. L. N. Sinha, *History of the Reserve Bank of India 1935–51* (Bombay, 1970)
P. Sitaramayya, *A History of the Indian National Congress Vol. II* (Delhi, 1947)
R. Skidelsky, *Politicians and the Slump* (London, 1967)
S. Strange, *Sterling and British Policy* (London, 1972)
D. V. Tahmankar, *Sardar Patel* (London, 1970)
A. J. P. Taylor, *English History 1914–1945* (Oxford, 1965)
D. G. Tendulkar, *Mahatma – A Life of Mahatma Gandhi* revised ed. (Delhi, 1961–2)
C. N. Vakil and M. H. Patel, *Finance under Provincial Autonomy* (Calcutta, 1940)
S. D. Waley, *Edwin Montagu* (London, 1964)
M. Weiner, *Party Building in a New Nation* (Chicago, 1967)
——, *Party Politics in India – The Development of a Multi-Party System* (Princeton, 1957)
M. Weiner and R. Kothari (eds), *Indian Voting Behaviour* (Calcutta, 1965)
S. Wolpert, *Morley and India 1906–10* (Berkeley, 1967)
Zetland, Lord, *Essayez* (London, 1956)

Glossary

anna	one-sixteenth of a rupee
ashram	a religious retreat
bakasht	in Bihar, land from which the hereditary tenant had been evicted and which was let out to an occupancy tenant
bania	moneylender
begari	the right to extract forced labour
charka	hand-turned spinning wheel
crore	ten million
firka	a sub-taluka unit of revenue administration (also *mandal*)
gaddi	(lit.) throne
harijan	Gandhi's name for untouchables (lit., 'Children of God')
-ji	honourific suffix
khadi, khaddar	hand-woven cloth made from hand-spun yarn
khilafat	(adj.) of the anti-British Muslim agitation against the abolition of the Caliphate by the Treaty of Sèvres (1920)
kisan	peasant
lakh	one hundred thousand
mandal	see *firka*
muffosil	countryside
pandit	a learned man, used as honourific title
pie	one twelfth of an anna
raj	(lit.) rule; especially used of British rule in India and of large *zamindari* estates
ryotwari	(as adj.) land revenue system in which the cultivator pays revenue direct to government
sabha	organisation; committee; assembly
sanad	charter; grant of rights
satyagraha	Gandhi's name for his 'science' of passive resistance
satyagrahi	one who offers *satyagraha*
swadeshi	Indian-made
swaraj	independence
sir	in U.P., land cultivated by a landlord for his own, either directly or under tenants-at-will
taluka, taluq	a sub-division of a district (also *thana*)
taluqdar	owner of a certain class of large feudal estate in parts of the United Provinces
thana	see *taluka*
zamindar	landholder, usually hereditary, who pays a fixed revenue to government and collects rent from his tenants
zamindari	(as adj.) land revenue system under *zamindars*

Index